Three recent full-length scholarly biographies—Kate Clifford Larson's *Bound for the Promised Land: Harriet Tubman: Portrait of an American Hero*; Jean M. Humez's *Harriet Tubman: The Life and the Life Stories*; and Catherine Clinton's *Harriet Tubman: The Road to Freedom*—also have been invaluable in my efforts to solve the riddles of Tubman's life. Larson's prodigious research and Humez's sensitivity to spiritual matters in particular made my work much easier.

So many scholars have generously contributed their thoughts and findings that it would be impossible to name them all. I am grateful to the many academic historians, National Park Service personnel, librarians, and archivists who have been so helpful in suggesting material and tracking down information about Tubman and the antislavery movement. Many thanks to the librarians at the New-York Historical Society, the Library of Congress, the National Archives, Fenwick Library at George Mason University, and Gelman Library at George Washington University. For research assistance, I am especially indebted to Kevin Strait and David Kieran.

Friends and family endured many Tubman stories yet continued to express interest. My appreciation goes to James Oliver Horton, for his confidence through good times and bad, and to Christine Berry, Nancy Smith, Michael Horton, and Kelly Geer for their encouragement. I thank Dana Horton-Geer and Alex Horton-Geer, who bring such joy and who remind me that telling these stories is important. The steadfast friendship and intellectual companionship of Nancy Weiss Hanrahan and Dawn Jones have been immeasurable gifts throughout.

Finally, my gratitude goes to Bedford Series in History and Culture advisory editor David W. Blight, who is a remarkable scholar and good friend, for his faith in the possibility of this volume. For their thorough reading, challenging questions, and thoughtful suggestions, special thanks go to reviewers Adam Arenson, University of Texas at El Paso; Barbara Krauthamer, University of Massachusetts Amherst; Matthew Pinsker, Dickinson College; Trisha Posey, John Brown University; Jeff Forret, Lamar University; Earl Mulderink, Southern Utah University; Calvin Schermerhorn, Arizona State University; and one other reviewer who wishes to remai~ ~nonymous. My developmental editor, Debra Michals, had an ᵃ˙ ᵇility to attend to myriad details while remaining focused ˢ. This volume is much better for all their contriᵇ ᵉ to thank Mary Dougherty, William Lomᵇ⁻ ᵉr, Laura Kintz, and the rest of the staff at ᵦatience, encouragement, and assistance.

Lois E. Horton

and discrimination African Americans faced after the war. Tubman's many years of private philanthropy and the home she established for elderly freed people illustrate her efforts, and those of many other African Americans, to continue the black freedom struggle the government neglected during the post-Reconstruction period.

The primary source documents in Part Two bring this rich history to life, giving readers a deeper, more immediate understanding of the fight for African American freedom. They provide an opportunity for students to learn to draw conclusions from historical sources, to interpret historical information and place it in a larger context, and to work with historical evidence. Included here are fugitive slave laws, which demonstrate the power and interest of the federal government in maintaining slavery; correspondence between abolitionists, which offers a sense of the anti-slavery movement, its grassroots network, and Tubman's place in it; and newspaper accounts, which detail the drama of rescuing and protecting fugitives from slavery and chronicle Tubman's wartime exploits. Selections from government records show Tubman's decades-long pursuit of a military pension and provide descriptions of her life in her own words. These documents also convey the hardships faced by African Americans in post–Civil War America. Articles from the end of her life, as well as an obituary, recount her contributions to African American freedom and also demonstrate the nation's changing attitudes about race.

The appendixes provide additional support for classroom work. A chronology of Tubman's life and times sets important events in her life within the context of significant developments in the struggle for black freedom. Questions for consideration and a selected bibliography provide interesting and provocative starting points for class discussions and assignments and resources for further study.

ACKNOWLEDGMENTS

As with many such endeavors, work on this book took many years and the support of several key institutions and individuals. A Gilder Lehrman Scholarly Fellowship in 2001 made the original research both possible and pleasurable, and support from George Mason University aided my research and writing. The questions and enthusiasm of my students at George Mason University and the University of Hawaii were invaluable in shaping the book and its pedagogical materials. The final version is much better for the comments of Michelle Zacks, who not only read early drafts, but whose exceptional work as a graduate assistant gave me more time to write.

THE BEDFORD SERIES IN HISTORY AND CULTURE

Harriet Tubman and the Fight for Freedom

A Brief History with Documents

Lois E. Horton

George Mason University

BEDFORD / ST. MARTIN'S   Boston ◆ New York

For Bedford/St. Martin's

Publisher for History: Mary V. Dougherty
Senior Executive Editor for History: William J. Lombardo
Director of Development for History: Jane Knetzger
Senior Editor: Heidi L. Hood
Developmental Editor: Debra Michals
Production Supervisor: Victoria Sharoyan
Senior Marketing Manager, U.S. History: Amy Whitaker
Editorial Assistant: Laura Kintz
Project Management: Books By Design, Inc.
Cartography: Mapping Specialists, Ltd.
Permissions Manager: Kalina K. Ingham
Text Designer: Claire Seng-Niemoeller
Cover Designer: Marine Miller
Cover Photo: © Bettmann/Corbis
Composition: Achorn International, Inc.
Printing and Binding: RR Donnelley and Sons

President, Bedford/St. Martin's: Denise B. Wydra
Presidents, Macmillan Higher Education: Joan E. Feinberg and Tom Scotty
Director of Marketing: Karen R. Soeltz
Production Director: Susan W. Brown
Associate Production Director: Elise S. Kaiser
Manager, Publishing Services: Andrea Cava

Copyright © 2013 by Bedford/St. Martin's

Manufactured in the United States of America.

8   7   6   5   4   3
f   e   d   c   b   a

For information, write: Bedford/St. Martin's, 75 Arlington Street, Boston, MA 02116
   (617-399-4000)

ISBN 978-0-312-46451-6

Acknowledgments

foe. It was the country's most powerful institution, the very foundation of the nation's economy, and it had existed in North America for nearly 250 years. African Americans and a handful of whites carried on a complex and protracted campaign against this dehumanizing system, risking ostracism, financial loss, incarceration, and sometimes their lives. Tubman's dramatic story shows how the threat of sale into the Deep South, separation from family, and unjust punishment propelled many enslaved people onto the dangerous path toward freedom.

This volume gives students an opportunity to study both Tubman and her times in a condensed form appropriate for a week's work in college and advanced high school classes. It marries two often separate literatures: the iconic story of Harriet Tubman and scholarship on antislavery and antebellum reform. Part One provides a brief biography of Tubman that focuses on her life and legend but also situates her in the larger story of black communities and leaders, abolitionist activism, the Civil War as an antislavery endeavor, the relationship of antislavery to women's rights, and the post–Civil War struggle for black rights. Although Tubman's work with the Underground Railroad is a significant part of the introductory essay and subsequent documents, the book's main purpose is to use Tubman's biography as a lens onto broader issues in African American and U.S. history in the antebellum and postbellum years.

The introduction connects Tubman to many aspects of African American and women's history. It addresses interracial abolitionist networks and controversies through Tubman's relationships with such notable abolitionists as William Lloyd Garrison, Frederick Douglass, Thomas Garrett, and William Still. By exploring Tubman's relationship with John Brown and his raid on the federal arsenal at Harpers Ferry, Virginia, and her reverence for Brown's sacrifice of his life in pursuit of black freedom, the introduction examines the issue of violence and nonviolence in the antislavery movement. It also addresses how, in raising her voice for women's rights, Tubman helped attack the barriers she faced as a woman and became part of the powerful movement for women's suffrage that grew out of the abolition movement. Similarly, the opening essay explores Tubman's spirituality and ties to African culture through her family and the memories and traditions of those who surrounded her. Her life provides a window on the centrality of religion and spirituality in the black community and on the power of the quest for freedom and equality in African American culture.

Finally, Part One highlights Tubman's work as a Civil War nurse, spy, and scout who actually led soldiers into enemy territory and thus illuminates the role women and regiments of freed slaves played in the war. Her campaign for a Civil War pension sheds light on the poverty

Preface

A 2008 national survey named Harriet Tubman among the top ten most famous people in American history, excluding presidents and first ladies. Adults ranked her ninth, and high school students ranked her third, after Martin Luther King Jr. and Rosa Parks.[1] This is nothing new: For decades, Tubman has ranked among the best-known and most highly regarded historical figures. Tubman's fame is astounding for a poor, illiterate black woman who lived more than a century ago and who began her life in slavery. Most likely, her renown is due to stories of her work as a daring conductor on the Underground Railroad, which helped many enslaved people escape to freedom. These stories were told by Tubman herself, recorded in an early biography, and recounted in a host of contemporary children's books. But her other work, which relatively few people today know much about, makes her equally worthy of historical recognition and study. Tubman spent many of her ninety-one years actively involved in the antislavery movement, the Civil War, and the struggle for black equality and women's rights.

This volume situates Tubman within a full historical context that includes her work and her community. It moves beyond the legend of Tubman the Underground Railroad conductor, which often depicts her as a unique and solitary individual in the fight against slavery, to show that she entered an already-established network of courageous fugitives and their abolitionist allies. It shows her as part of an underground movement based in free black communities that included formal urban vigilance committees and informal networks of people acting on their belief that slavery was inhumane, contrary to God's will, and incompatible with the nation's founding principles. The threats of fugitive slave laws, slave patrols, and bounty-hunting gangs were doubly dangerous for Tubman, who was an escaped slave herself. Slavery was a formidable

---

[1] Sam Wineburg and Chauncey Monte-Sano, "Who Is a Famous American? Charting Historical Memory across the Generations," *Phi Delta Kappan* 89, no. 9 (May 2008): 643–48.

Foreword

The Bedford Series in History and Culture is designed so that readers can study the past as historians do.

The historian's first task is finding the evidence. Documents, letters, memoirs, interviews, pictures, movies, novels, or poems can provide facts and clues. Then the historian questions and compares the sources. There is more to do than in a courtroom, for hearsay evidence is welcome, and the historian is usually looking for answers beyond act and motive. Different views of an event may be as important as a single verdict. How a story is told may yield as much information as what it says.

Along the way the historian seeks help from other historians and perhaps from specialists in other disciplines. Finally, it is time to write, to decide on an interpretation and how to arrange the evidence for readers.

Each book in this series contains an important historical document or group of documents, each document a witness from the past and open to interpretation in different ways. The documents are combined with some element of historical narrative—an introduction or a biographical essay, for example—that provides students with an analysis of the primary source material and important background information about the world in which it was produced.

Each book in the series focuses on a specific topic within a specific historical period. Each provides a basis for lively thought and discussion about several aspects of the topic and the historian's role. Each is short enough (and inexpensive enough) to be a reasonable one-week assignment in a college course. Whether as classroom or personal reading, each book in the series provides firsthand experience of the challenge— and fun—of discovering, recreating, and interpreting the past.

Lynn Hunt
David W. Blight
Bonnie G. Smith
Natalie Zemon Davis

PART TWO
The Documents   101

1. U.S. Constitution, *Provision regarding Fugitive Slaves*, 1787   103

2. *Fugitive Slave Law*, 1793   104

3. *Fugitive Slave Law*, 1850   106

4. Austin Bearse, *Reminiscences of Fugitive-Slave Law Days in Boston*, 1818–1830   110

5. Solomon Northup, *Kidnapped into Slavery*, 1853   112

6. Eliza Ann Brodess, *Runaway Advertisement*, 1849   116

7. Liberator, *Slave-Hunters in Boston*, November 1, 1850   117

8. Thomas Garrett, *Sending Underground Railroad Passengers to Philadelphia*, 1854   119

9. William Still, *Moses Arrives with Six Passengers*, 1872   120

10. Boston Vigilance Committee, *Fugitive Slaves Aided by the Vigilance Committee since the Passage of the Fugitive Slave Bill 1850,* 1850–1858   122

11. John Brown, *Letter to John Brown Jr.*, April 8, 1858   124

12. Liberator, *Tubman Addresses Fourth of July Meeting*, July 8, 1859   126

13. Lewis Hayden, *Letter to John Brown*, September 16, 1859   127

14. Douglass' Monthly, *Charles Nalle Rescue*, June 1860   128

15. William Wells Brown, *Emancipation Eve*, December 31, 1862   130

16. Commonwealth, *Account of Combahee River Raid*, July 10, 1863   132

17. Commonwealth, *Solicitation of Aid for Harriet Tubman*, August 12, 1864   133

18. Freedmen's Record, *Moses*, March 1865   134

19. Thomas Garrett, *Memories of Harriet Tubman and the Underground Railroad*, June 1868   140

Contents

Foreword   iii

Preface   v

LIST OF MAP AND ILLUSTRATIONS   xii

PART ONE

Introduction: An Uncommon Woman and Her Times   1

Myth and Reality   1

Slavery in Maryland   3

The Multiracial Underground Railroad and
   Antislavery Movement   11

Radical Antislavery   14

Resistance to the Fugitive Slave Law of 1850   17

The Moses of Her People   20

Growing Sectional Tensions and Greater Militancy   33

Tubman and the Antislavery Network   37

John Brown's War   42

The Divisive Politics of 1860 and a Perilous Rescue   52

Fighting the War to End Slavery   56

Tubman's Postwar Life   74

Tubman's Life into the Twentieth Century   80

Harriet Tubman in History and Memory   85

20. Frederick Douglass and Wendell Phillips,
    Testimonials, June and August 1868 — 142

21. William Wells Brown, *Moses*, 1874 — 144

22. Sarah H. Bradford, *Harriet Tubman Biographies*,
    1869 and 1886 — 145

23. Harriet Tubman Davis, *Affidavit*, May 28, 1892 — 149

24. Harriet Tubman Davis, *Affidavit*, November 10, 1894 — 150

25. Wilbur H. Siebert, *Letter to Earl Conrad*, September 4,
    1940 — 152

26. U.S. Senate, *Committee on Pensions Report*, 1899 — 153

27. Syracuse Herald, *To End Days in Home She Founded*,
    June 4, 1911 — 156

28. New York Times, *Harriet Tubman Davis Obituary*,
    March 14, 1913 — 158

29. Auburn Citizen, *Harriet Tubman Memorialized*,
    June 11, 1914 — 159

APPENDIXES

A Chronology of the Life and Times of Harriet Tubman
(1822–1913) — 161

Questions for Consideration — 163

Selected Bibliography — 165

Index — **171**

Map and Illustrations

MAP

Harriet Tubman's Underground Routes to Freedom,
1849–1860   23

ILLUSTRATIONS

1. Thomas Garrett, Wilmington, Delaware, ca. 1850   16

2. William Still, ca. 1872   16

3. Frederick Douglass, probably late 1840s   41

4. John Brown, ca. 1857   41

5. Harriet Tubman as Civil War Scout   66

6. Harriet Tubman, late 1886   82

Introduction:
An Uncommon Woman and
Her Times

Harriet Tubman was an African American woman born into slavery in the first quarter of the nineteenth century. Although she remained illiterate throughout her ninety-one years, today she is one of the most famous people in American history. Tubman is best known for her daring slave rescues and escapes to freedom via the Underground Railroad, but most people know little about the rest of her life's work—her nursing, spying, and scouting for the Union during the Civil War; her contributions to black equality and women's rights; and her efforts to aid the elderly in the decades after the Civil War. Much of her historical significance has been obscured by the legend that grew up around the work she did with the Underground Railroad during her own lifetime and that has continued to grow throughout the twentieth and twenty-first centuries.

MYTH AND REALITY

The legend of Harriet Tubman, the Underground Railroad conductor, preserved in early histories and children's literature often depicts her as unique in the fight against slavery. Although Tubman's achievements were certainly remarkable, most of these accounts make it seem as if Tubman herself created the Underground Railroad and single-handedly led countless people out of bondage. In reality she entered an already established underground network of courageous fugitives and their abolitionist allies—a network based in free black communities, including formal urban committees (called vigilance committees) and informally organized groups—people who acted on their belief that slavery was inhumane, contrary to God's will, and incompatible with the nation's founding principles. Slavery was a formidable foe; it existed in British North America for nearly 250 years, was the foundation of the United States' economy, and was a politically powerful institution. Tubman joined other African Americans and a handful of whites who, risking ostracism, financial loss, incarceration, and sometimes their lives, carried on a complex and protracted campaign against this dehumanizing system that went far beyond their work with the Underground Railroad.

The fabled Tubman was a dauntless loner, yet much of her strength and accomplishments rested on her social networks. Under the yoke of slavery during childhood and early adulthood, she was part of a close family with a sense of their history. Indeed, her Underground Railroad activity was based on efforts to free members of her family. In freedom she received support for her daily needs and activism from both humble and elite members of black communities, as well as famous white abolitionists. The mythology of Tubman has often exaggerated the number of people she herself rescued from slavery. In fact, there were others who aided many more than she did. But in her lifetime her importance was less about those numbers and more about the antislavery fervor she inspired with tales of successful escapes and the courage with which she faced danger.

The Tubman myth also obscures her larger, far more important role in history by focusing on the Underground Railroad legend alone. In reality Tubman's accomplishments during her long life extended well beyond the Underground Railroad and her exploits during the Civil War. As this volume demonstrates, her story provides a window onto many of the important issues and historical events of the nineteenth century: slavery and the varied strains of antislavery activism, women's rights, the Civil War and Reconstruction, and the racism of the Jim Crow era. Along with the Underground Railroad, she was involved in a wide range of antislavery activities, faced both racial and gender discrimination, and spoke out for women's rights. John Brown enlisted her aid as he planned and recruited people for his ill-fated 1859 attack on the U.S. arsenal at Harpers Ferry, Virginia. (He planned to use the weapons seized there to arm local slaves as part of a planned rebellion.) Tubman was also concerned with the well-being of African Americans once they were free, and she took people into her home, contributed to black settlements in Canada, raised funds for freed people's education, and founded a home for elderly blacks. Understanding her life and how it has been retold and remembered can illuminate crucial aspects of America's racial and gender history. The Tubman myth is a heroic tale; the reality is a more complex story of a courageous woman who joined a centuries-old struggle against slavery, poverty, and discrimination to serve her people and advance African American freedom.

SLAVERY IN MARYLAND

Before her escape from slavery in 1849, Tubman had been a slave on the Eastern Shore of Maryland, the part of the state east of the Chesapeake Bay. As an institution, slavery was changing during the first half of the nineteenth century. Slaveowners still controlled Maryland politics, but slaveholding had declined there by the late 1840s, and by 1850 there were roughly equal numbers of slaves and free blacks on the Eastern Shore. The first enslaved Africans had been brought to the Chesapeake Bay area of Virginia in 1619. More than a century of tobacco cultivation around the Chesapeake had depleted the soil, and tobacco gradually gave way to wheat, a crop that required less labor—and therefore fewer slaves—in its cultivation. Additionally, slave revolts and the constant threat of violent rebellion, along with the avowed commitment to liberty during the era of the American Revolution, convinced many slaveholders that the gradual abolition of slavery was desirable and prudent. Indeed, a few slaveowners freed their slaves in the immediate aftermath of the Revolution. Two developments around the turn of the nineteenth century, however, dramatically changed the prospects for ending southern slavery. In 1793 Eli Whitney's invention of the cotton gin, a simple machine that made removing the seeds from cotton fibers easier and faster, made growing cotton much more profitable. In 1803 President Thomas Jefferson's Louisiana Purchase doubled the size of the country and opened a vast area of rich, fertile land for cotton cultivation.[1]

The explosive growth of the Cotton Kingdom in the lower South generated an internal slave trade (Document 4). Enslaved people were transported by ship or forced to walk the long distances from the less profitable plantations in Maryland and Virginia to the booming plantations of Georgia, Alabama, Mississippi, and Louisiana, where they could be sold for much higher prices. The labor-intensive cultivation of cotton and sugar in the lower South brought even more hardships to people transported there. Ripped from families and long-established communities in the upper South, they typically worked in gangs in the fields from sunup to sundown, were whipped to speed up the pace of their work, and were harshly punished if they didn't meet production quotas set by the overseers. Slaves who ran away, shirked work, stole, or broke other rules were commonly branded with a hot iron or whipped, or they had ears, fingers, or toes cut off. Between 1808, when the United States ended its legal transatlantic trade in enslaved Africans, and the Civil War of the 1860s, approximately one million Africans and African Americans were forcibly relocated to newly cultivated land in the lower and western areas of the South. This internal slave trade meant increased profits for slaveowners, but for the enslaved it produced a constant fear of being sold far beyond the reach of friends and family into the everyday brutality of slave life in the lower South.[2]

All slaves lived with uncertainty, their fate primarily dependent on what their owners found economically profitable. The surplus of slave labor in the upper South, with its mixed agricultural economy, fledgling manufacturing enterprises, and the loss of many slaves to the voracious cotton plantations, also created conditions favorable to renting out slaves for limited periods of time, a practice called hiring out. Renting slaves brought slave labor within the reach of many white nonslaveholders and provided a more flexible workforce. Although it occurred everywhere, hiring out became especially common in the upper South during the nineteenth century, and regularly changing masters added to the unpredictability of slave life.

Those fortunate enough to be hired out to people in cities could find a measure of freedom compared to life on the plantation. Some hired-out slaves managed to negotiate arrangements with their owners that allowed them to keep part of their wages, and occasionally they could save enough to buy their own freedom. Permitting people to buy themselves out of slavery provided owners with a quick profit and perhaps a better price, allowed them to avoid having to negotiate with slave traders, and saved the cost of even scant food and clothing. Formerly enslaved parents who bought their own children also saved the owner the upkeep of less productive or not yet productive workers.

During the early Republic, the Chesapeake Bay area had the highest number of slaves. But during the antebellum period, as a result of the internal slave trade, manumission (being freed by owners), and self-purchase, the number of slaves there dwindled. Whereas in 1820 only 27 percent of African Americans in Maryland had been granted, bought, or inherited their freedom, by 1850 45 percent of blacks living in the state were free.[3]

Running for Freedom

Harriet Tubman had lived in slavery a long time before she ran to freedom in 1849. Born in 1822, she was by that time a grown woman, married to a free black man named John Tubman and living on a plantation on Maryland's Eastern Shore (Document 24). Subject to her owner's whims and the vicissitudes of his fortunes, she lived in constant fear of being sold away from her family. She prayed fervently that God would soften the heart of her owner, Edward Brodess, but in March 1849 she gave up this hope and prayed for his death instead. Brodess died almost immediately. Faced with the increased threat of being sold, she soon began having a frightening recurring dream. The dream was reminiscent of the tales told by people captured in Africa and sold to slaveholders in America, or perhaps it recalled the earlier sale of her two older sisters to a slave trader in the Deep South. In her dream horsemen pursued Harriet, and she could hear the terrified screams of women and children. She ran toward a beautiful, sun-washed, flowering field, where lovely white ladies held out their arms to welcome her, but she always fell before she reached them.

When rumors circulated that members of her family were to be sold to slave traders, Harriet and two of her brothers decided to strike out for freedom. Her husband said she was being foolish, but she understood the seriousness of the situation. No one in the family had seen or heard any news of her sisters in the decade since they had been sold; the family did not know whether the women were alive or dead. Although leaving her husband and family was painful, Harriet was afraid that if she stayed and was sold farther south, she would never see them again.[4]

Harriet and her younger brothers Ben and Henry struck off for the North in the middle of September 1849. For two weeks they struggled to get away from Maryland, hiding in the woods and running through swamps. Frightened by an advertisement posted for their return, her brothers insisted they go back (Document 6). Just a few days after returning home, still fearful of being sold, Harriet ran away again—this time alone. Although it was risky, she took a white woman into her confidence, and the woman gave her directions to the first of two people who would help her escape. The ad Edward Brodess's widow, Eliza Ann, placed in the Cambridge, Maryland, newspaper described Harriet as "aged about 27 years . . . of a chestnut color, fine looking, and about 5 feet high." The reward for her capture was $50 if she was found in Maryland and $100 if she was found out of state.[5]

There was a Quaker settlement not far from where Harriet lived, and it was undoubtedly this network that aided her escape. Many Quaker congregations in Pennsylvania, Delaware, and Maryland had long opposed slavery and were active in the Underground Railroad. Harriet carefully made her way to the first contact, where the woman of the house told her to pose as a servant and sweep the yard. When the woman's husband came home that evening, he hid Harriet in a loaded wagon and took her to a second house outside the next town. With the help of this network, she made her way through Maryland and Delaware to Pennsylvania, a free state. In Philadelphia she found an established anti-slavery society and a precarious freedom. She had to be careful of slave catchers from the bordering slave states of Delaware, Maryland, and Virginia, who often ventured into Pennsylvania looking for runaways, as well as gangs that roamed the area looking for free African Americans to kidnap and sell into slavery (Document 5). For the next few years, Harriet resided in Philadelphia, found work as a domestic servant and cook, and saved money. It was dangerous there, but she was close enough to be able to stay in touch with her family in Maryland.[6]

Family and Early Life

Harriet Tubman's family had lived in Dorchester County on Maryland's Eastern Shore for four generations, moved from owner to owner by wills or sales. According to family stories, Harriet's grandmother Modesty had been captured in West Africa as a young girl, brought to Maryland sometime late in the first half of the eighteenth century, and sold to a man named Pattison. Her mother, Harriet (Rit or Rittia) Green, had been born to Modesty sometime in the late 1780s. Rit was about ten years old when her owner, Atthow Pattison, died and bequeathed her to his granddaughter Mary, stipulating that Rit be freed at age forty-five and that any children she might have also be freed upon reaching age forty-five. He left other Green family members to other relatives, most in the same geographic area. Pattison's heirs never honored their forebear's promise, a pledge Tubman confirmed some fifty years later when she hired a lawyer to investigate the story passed down in her family.[7]

Harriet Green, Mary Pattison Brodess's personal slave, accompanied her mistress when she married Anthony Thompson and moved to his estate. About 1808 Green, then owned by Mary's son Edward Brodess, married Benjamin Ross, a timber manager owned by Thompson. Though important to enslaved people, society did not recognize slave marriages, and they did not carry the legal status or protections afforded to the marriages of whites or free blacks. Some owners encouraged slave marriages, knowing that having a spouse made escape less likely, but they respected the marriages only when economically convenient.

By the 1830s Rit and Ben Ross reportedly had nine children: Linah, Mariah, Soph, Robert, Harriet (called by the common slave name Araminta or Minty), Benjamin, Rachel, Henry, and Moses.[8] There was an age difference of more than twenty years between the oldest and the youngest child. Rit and Ben lost at least two of their children, Linah and Soph, when the Brodesses sold them to a Georgia slave trader. Harriet also recalled hearing that two other siblings had been sold away from the family before she was born, so there may actually have been more than nine children. Some of the confusion was undoubtedly caused by the practice of repeating names in different generations and the fact that many people changed their names when they became free (as did at least three of Harriet's brothers). In addition, many enslaved children died in infancy, causing even more confusion. What is clear is that some of Harriet's siblings were sold to slaveowners farther south, and some were held by various local owners. When Rit found out that her master intended to sell her youngest child, Moses, she threatened to physically attack a local white slaveowner who came looking for him, and hid Moses in the woods for a month before Brodess abandoned the idea of selling him. Harriet vividly remembered the family's agony when her two older sisters were sold. The sale tore Linah away from her own two children, the youngest of whom was only two years old. Later Harriet reported that while she was in slavery, every time she saw a white man she was afraid of "being carried away in a chain-gang," tied together with others and marched off to slavery in the lower South, just like her sisters had been. Slavery, Harriet once told an interviewer, was "the next thing to hell." She continued, "I grew up like a neglected weed, ignorant of liberty, having no experience of it."[9]

Like virtually all enslaved people, Harriet was just five years old when her owner first put her to work. He hired her out, and she began doing domestic work in white people's homes, living away from her family. In her first job she took care of an infant during the night. If she couldn't keep the baby from crying, her mistress would whip her on the neck. From then until her early teens, she did a succession of jobs—housekeeping, weaving, and tending animal traps in a cold stream. Twice she became so ill that she had to be sent home: Once she suffered from heavy work and a lack of nourishment, and once she contracted the measles.

Working in white households subjected young enslaved girls to their mistresses' constant oversight and frequent punishment. In the patriarchal households of the nineteenth-century South, relatively powerless slave mistresses sometimes took out their frustrations on the slaves under their control. As girls grew into adolescence, they were also subject to sexual harassment and rape by their masters or other male family members.[10] Angry mistresses were likely to harshly punish slave women who received too much attention from their masters, which mistresses took as a sign of their spouses' sexual interest in them. Fortunately for Harriet, she was not a victim of such sexual violence. By the time she was twelve, her independent spirit made her owner consider her too quick tempered and undisciplined for domestic labor, and he sent her to work in the fields. He frequently hired her out as an extra hand for the harvest or for special farm jobs, which meant that she was often not under his observation and direct control. She was proud that she could do physically demanding work, and field labor meant that she could often work with her family members. Although she never grew more than five feet tall, the work she did made her physically strong.

When Harriet was about fifteen, she was helping with the harvest on a plantation near Bucktown, Maryland, not far from her home. When a male field hand left the plantation without permission, Harriet rushed to the store where she knew he was to tell him that the overseer was coming after him. At the store the furious overseer hurled a heavy weight at the offending slave, but Harriet was in its path. The lead weight fractured her skull and drove a piece of the shawl she was wearing into the bloody wound. Some men carried her to a house, where she lay for two days, slipping in and out of consciousness, before she was sent home to her family. It was months before they were sure she would live. During her long recovery she frequently fell into a deep sleep and had periods of intense sensory experience followed by crippling fatigue. Her owner tried to sell her during this time, but he could find no one willing to make such a risky investment.[11]

For the rest of her life Harriet felt the effects of her head injury, which today would likely be diagnosed as temporal lobe epilepsy. She endured headaches and often fell asleep for a few minutes at a time whenever she was still, even if she was in the middle of a conversation. When she awoke, she would pick up where she left off as if no time had passed (Document 25). She also experienced dreamlike trances, hearing music, rushing water, voices, screams, and loud noises and seeing bright lights and colorful auras. Less clearly connected to her injury were her vivid, often prophetic, dreams and visions. Noting that her father had the gift of foretelling, Harriet interpreted her dreams as messages from God and came to trust his guidance in both ordinary and dangerous circumstances.[12]

The injury's effects didn't pose a serious handicap for most activities, although Harriet wasn't able to work as hard as before. Her owner believed her to be intellectually impaired, and there were constant rumors that he would sell her, although he never did. When Brodess died a few years later, his plantation and slaves were put under the guardianship of Dr. Anthony Thompson, a minister and son of the Anthony Thompson who owned Harriet's father. During the following years Harriet, her father, and her brothers were hired out to John Stewart, said to be a less cruel slaveholder. Stewart owned a business shipping lumber to Baltimore and other towns along the Chesapeake. Harriet gained strength chopping wood and carting timber, and she soon earned enough money above the regular allowance she owed her owner to buy a pair of steers. Harriet's father, Ben, also did well working as Stewart's timber inspector. Thompson died in 1836 before carrying out his promise to free Ben at age forty-five, but four years later Dr. Anthony Thompson honored his father's wishes and emancipated Ben. As a free man, Ben took on more responsibility in Stewart's timber operation, and when Thompson bought a large tract of timberland in 1846, Ben became his foreman.[13]

In her early twenties Harriet fell in love with a free black man named John Tubman and married him in 1844. Their relationship was not surprising: The area's black community comprised both enslaved and free people, and many families contained both. Harriet and John apparently lived together on the Thompson plantation, near Harriet's mother and father as well as many other family members.

Escapes from the Eastern Shore

The close association between free blacks and slaves on Maryland's Eastern Shore undoubtedly made it more difficult for slaveowners to control the people they owned as property. They worried about the impact free blacks would have on slaves—that such visible freedom would inspire slave revolts and that free blacks, especially free black sailors, might help enslaved people escape. In fact, the conditions of slavery on the Eastern Shore and the proximity to free states meant that many people did manage to escape. Several of them, including Frederick Douglass, later became antislavery activists and allies and friends of Harriet Tubman. Douglass, the most famous runaway and the leading black abolitionist, escaped from Baltimore in 1838. Like Tubman, Douglass (then named Frederick Bailey) had been hired out from his Eastern Shore plantation. He worked in the shipyards of Baltimore and fell in love with a free black woman named Anna Murray, who helped him escape. He was also aided by a sailor friend, who lent him a seaman's protection certificate that identified him as being free.[14]

The fact that he was a man and had some money helped Douglass in his escape. A black man traveling alone was less likely to arouse suspicion than a black woman. Female slaves, and indeed women in general, did not commonly travel by themselves at that time. Douglass also was assisted by the unspoken acquiescence of other blacks and whites. Dressed as a sailor, he could take advantage of sailors' freedom to travel, as long as no one scrutinized his certificate too closely. According to Douglass, the train conductor merely glanced at the paper; several passengers with whom he was acquainted failed to recognize him; and a German blacksmith, who did seem to recognize him, did not sound the alarm.

Douglass traveled by train, ferryboat, and steamboat to Philadelphia and then by train to New York City, where another Baltimore fugitive warned him about the southerners and slave catchers who watched the docks and boardinghouses. After a night on the streets Douglass approached a sailor who took him into his home and introduced him to the black abolitionist David Ruggles, secretary of the city's vigilance committee. Douglass stayed with Ruggles until Anna Murray joined him, and the pair were married at Ruggles's home. Ruggles then sent them to New Bedford, Massachusetts, a busy seaport where they settled, became active in the African Methodist Episcopal (AME) Zion Church, and started a family. Other runaway slaves from the Eastern Shore who became well-known antislavery activists included Samuel Ringgold Ward, Henry Highland Garnet, and James W. C. Pennington.[15]

Maryland slaveholders' fears were reflected in two proposed but unsuccessful pieces of legislation. The first, proposed in 1832, would have required freed blacks to leave the state. It was unworkable because of Maryland's dependence on black labor. The second, introduced in 1850, would have prohibited manumissions entirely. One legislative committee in the late 1850s, arguing that the presence of free blacks created "discontent" among slaves, recommended sending all free blacks to Africa. This proposal also failed to pass. In fact, the networks of enslaved and free African Americans, and the family ties between them, did facilitate the covert passage to freedom in which Harriet Tubman became an important participant.[16]

THE MULTIRACIAL UNDERGROUND RAILROAD AND ANTISLAVERY MOVEMENT

By the time Tubman escaped from slavery in the fall of 1849, the Underground Railroad had already been in operation for well over fifty years. This secret, informal network of people, both black and white, willing to defy the law to help fugitives from slavery developed gradually in the United States, facilitated in some places by changing attitudes and laws concerning slavery. During and after the American Revolution, most northern states had abolished slavery, some immediately—as in most New England states—and others with gradual emancipation laws from 1784 to 1804. Under each gradual emancipation law, enslaved people born before the law took effect—even the day before—remained slaves for life. Children born to slaves after the law was in force were free, but not completely free. They were required to work as unpaid indentured servants until an age in early adulthood defined by the law. The age of majority for black indentured servants ranged from twenty-one in Rhode Island to twenty-eight in Pennsylvania, with New York and New Jersey freeing indentured women at age twenty-five and indentured men at age twenty-eight. Maintaining lifetime slavery for people born before the law reduced slaveholders' economic losses.[17]

As northern states abolished slavery, they acted as beacons of freedom for enslaved people in the South. Massachusetts's 1780 constitutional declaration of freedom for all men—and the 1783 state supreme court decision confirming it—made the state an important early destination for fugitives. Its bustling seaports connected Massachusetts to the South and the rest of the world, bringing the promise of freedom within reach for those who could take to the sea. By the early 1790s a small network of Quaker traders in New Bedford, Massachusetts, and Providence, Rhode Island, protected runaway slaves from owners and slave catchers. The Northwest Ordinance of 1787 had prohibited slavery in the western territory north of the Ohio River and in future states from that territory, eventually including Ohio, Michigan, Indiana, Illinois, and Wisconsin. A few large Virginia planters, touched by the principles of the Revolution, freed their slaves and settled them in the free territory of southern Ohio. There, free blacks became the hub of the developing western line of the Underground Railroad.[18]

There were other hopeful developments. Spain promised freedom for slaves who could escape to Florida, but after the United States purchased Florida in 1819, it established military control to protect the interests of slaveholders in nearby states. In 1821, however, Mexico's abolition of slavery provided an alternative southern Underground Railroad route to freedom. This was an important haven until Mexico's northern area became the independent Republic of Texas in the mid-1830s and eventually became the slaveholding state of Texas in 1845. To the far north another haven opened up in Canada when Britain abolished slavery in its empire in 1834. Canada's strong antislavery sentiment and its refusal to extradite runaways created a refuge that enslaved people celebrated in story and song as the Promised Land.

White allies provided important aid to those escaping slavery, but free black communities were the foundation of the Underground Railroad. As free communities formed in the late eighteenth and early nineteenth centuries, black organizations such as churches, mutual aid societies, and Prince Hall Masonic lodges dedicated themselves to fighting slavery. Organizations made public antislavery pronouncements, and members provided fugitives with shelter, food, clothing, and medical care and helped them find employment and legal aid. Most assistance was given in secret, since the federal fugitive slave law of 1793 made aiding fugitives illegal (Document 2). Secret communications within the network adopted a code derived from the latest technology—the railroad—calling operatives conductors and stationmasters and referring to people escaping from slavery as packages. In such perilous border areas as Pennsylvania and Ohio, aid often came complete with the secret hiding places that became legendary. Such precautions were generally deemed less necessary by abolitionists farther north.[19]

The sea continued to be a vital route to freedom during the nineteenth century. Black sailors averaged 14 percent of ships' crews, sometimes constituting as much as one-third and occasionally the entire crew. Some sailors, mainly African Americans, and blacks who worked around the docks helped slaves stow away on ships bound for northern or foreign ports. South Carolina slaveholders, fearing that black sailors would spread ideas about freedom and help slaves escape, passed a law in 1824 requiring African American sailors to be held in jail while their ships were in port. Runaways received assistance from white families, often Quakers, and from black families in rural areas, but they were most likely to find the anonymity that protected their freedom in northern urban black communities. Centers of abolition in Boston, New York, and Philadelphia attracted large numbers of fugitives from slavery, including Tubman and many of the people she assisted.[20]

In the late 1820s and 1830s the evangelical activity of the Second Great Awakening added many sympathizers to the antislavery cause, and a dynamic grassroots organization begun by the radical white Boston abolitionist William Lloyd Garrison after 1830 greatly increased the number of people who might aid runaways. Although some people — such as Tubman's later friends and allies William Still, the African American clerk at Philadelphia's antislavery office, and the white abolitionist Thomas Garrett in Delaware — devoted much of their time to helping fugitives, others participated only occasionally or spontaneously when confronted with someone needing assistance. Whites joined blacks on vigilance committees to coordinate legal aid and protection for fugitives (Document 10). Many committees and antislavery societies organized systems of safe houses and established routes run by trustworthy antislavery men and women, resources Tubman could use in rescue efforts.[21]

Running away was dangerous, and captured runaways were likely to be subjected to horrific punishments by masters and captors, including severe whippings, imprisonment, and the amputation of toes. They might also be forced to wear a collar outfitted with bells or be sold to slaveholders in the lower South. The best-known Underground Railroad stories are about conductors who defied the law by helping fugitives move from place to place, but runaways were generally on their own for the most dangerous parts of their escapes. Enslaved people decided how and when to escape, whether or not to trust someone else with their plans, where to go, whether to go alone or with others, how to avoid capture, and how to survive the journey. The vast majority who escaped were young men in their teens or twenties. Men generally had much more freedom of movement than women in the eighteenth and nineteenth centuries, and the work of some enslaved men on ships and riverboats, or as coachmen or body servants, allowed them to travel. Thus black men, alone or in small groups, were less likely than women to arouse suspicion on the road. Strong young men could better endure the hardships of traveling hundreds of miles on foot without adequate food than could children or old people. Though fewer in number than single young men, desperate pregnant women, as well as men and women with small children, did brave the odds and run away. Traveling quickly and quietly was much harder with children, but some were able to escape despite the dangers and hardships.[22]

Given the difficulties and risk of capture, most who ran away were truant only for a short time, hiding someplace near their plantations to seek respite from labor or to visit relatives, before ultimately returning to the plantation. Historian and folklorist John Vlach has called such "lying out" periods "trial runs for a future escape." Thousands of other runaways remained in the South, establishing settlements in the woods or swamps called maroon communities, a term derived from the Spanish *cimarrón*, referring to fugitives from slavery and their descendants who lived in the mountains of Latin America. From the colonial period into the nineteenth century, these runaways organized to protect their freedom, some in small groups and others in much larger settlements. They attracted official attention when they conducted raids on slave plantations, stealing supplies and bringing others to freedom. The most famous of these communities was in the Great Dismal Swamp, covering a thousand square miles along the border of Virginia and North Carolina. This settlement had as many as two thousand residents.[23]

RADICAL ANTISLAVERY

By the 1830s people escaping from slavery could find encouragement in the antislavery sentiment publicized by William Lloyd Garrison's newspaper, the *Liberator*. Slaveholders tried to convince their slaves that harsh conditions, discrimination, and the cold climate would make life much worse for them in the North, but reading or hearing about the Garrisonian abolitionists gave potential runaways hope of finding freedom and better lives. This radical abolitionism rejected colonization schemes to transport black people to Africa and opposed gradual emancipation, instead advocating the immediate elimination of slavery. Like the many Quakers among his followers, Garrison was a pacifist who shunned violence in favor of education and persuasion—what he called "moral suasion." He also believed that women should play an equal part in society and in antislavery organizations and promoted them as public speakers and organization officers, much to the consternation of more conservative abolitionists. Garrison disapproved of political parties, believed that slavery was a sin, and used the *Liberator* to expose the horrors of slavery and promote freedom. Garrisonian antislavery societies blossomed in villages and towns throughout New England, New York, Pennsylvania, Ohio, and Michigan. In 1828, before Garrison's American Anti-Slavery Society was founded, there were 120 antislavery groups with an estimated 7,000 members from New England to the upper

South. By the 1830s it had become more difficult and even dangerous to be openly antislavery in the South, except for those few individuals identified with the African colonization movement's efforts to move free blacks to Africa. The radicals, however, undertook massive grassroots organizing among whites and blacks in the North and by the early 1840s claimed 1,000 organizations with 500,000 members. Aiding runaways and rescuing captured fugitives sparked intense discussions among abolitionists about the morality and necessity of violence in defense of black freedom.[24]

During the 1830s and 1840s one remarkably courageous group of African Americans operated in and around Washington, D.C., a slave-holding district surrounded by slave states.[25] Many held jobs that allowed them to travel to surrounding plantations, providing opportunities for them to offer information, shelter, and financial assistance to enslaved people in Maryland and Virginia. A free black painter in Baltimore named Jacob R. Gibbs collected the certificates of freedom of blacks who had died and gave them to fugitives to aid their escape. Free blacks in the South were required to carry such papers to show that they were free people and not slaves. Two market women in Baltimore, one white and one black, reportedly also furnished free papers to slaves seeking freedom in the North, with the understanding that the papers would be mailed back to them to be used again by other fugitives.[26]

Harriet Tubman relied on this antislavery network when she made her successful run for freedom from Maryland's Eastern Shore in the fall of 1849. At least two of the people she encountered while heading north became lifelong friends and associates. One was Thomas Garrett, a white Quaker iron and hardware merchant in Wilmington, Delaware. The other was William Still, one of the best-known Underground Railroad stationmasters and the director of the Philadelphia Vigilance Committee. Still's family had experienced firsthand the difficulties of gaining freedom, even with the help of the Underground Railroad. In 1807 his father, Levin Steel, purchased his own freedom and moved to the North, while his mother, Sidney, a slave, escaped from the Eastern Shore with her four children, only to be caught by slave catchers in New Jersey and returned to Maryland. Months later, after her owner had relaxed his vigilance, Sidney tried again, bringing her two younger daughters and leaving her sons, six-year-old Peter and eight-year-old Levin, in slavery. This time she managed to join her husband. The Steels changed their names to Still, marking their new life in freedom and helping them avoid detection. Although William was born later in New Jersey, a free state, he was technically a slave, since his mother had escaped from slavery.[27]

Figure 1. *Thomas Garrett, Wilmington, Delaware, ca. 1850*
Harriet Tubman's Quaker friend and one of her primary contacts on the
Underground Railroad, Garrett reported helping two thousand people to
freedom.

Figure 2. *William Still, ca. 1872*
William Still was director of the Philadelphia Vigilance Committee, and his
Underground Railroad station was an important stop on Tubman's route north.
Still kept detailed records of the people he helped to freedom and published
their stories in *The Underground Rail Road* in 1872.

Peter and Levin were eventually sold to a slaveowner in Alabama, where Levin died and Peter married and had three children. Being hired out enabled Peter to save money to buy his freedom, and in 1850 he changed his name to Peter Freedman and went looking for his parents. At the Philadelphia Anti-Slavery Society office, William Still listened to Peter's story, soon learning that the man before him was his own brother. William helped Peter arrange his family's escape to Indiana, but they were captured there and sent back into bondage. It took Peter four years on the abolitionist circuit, telling his touching story and asking for donations, to raise the $5,000 the slaveowner demanded to purchase his family. Finally, in late 1854, Peter settled his family on a farm in New Jersey.[28]

Tubman, too, counted on the Underground Railroad to remain connected to the family she left behind. In freedom Tubman supported herself by working as a domestic servant and a cook in Philadelphia and in the resort town of Cape May, New Jersey. From these free areas, she could keep in touch with her family through messages carried by Underground Railroad conductors and stationmasters and African Americans who could travel—free people, sailors and riverboat men, traders, and slaves who accompanied their masters on business.

RESISTANCE TO THE FUGITIVE SLAVE LAW OF 1850

Barely a year after Tubman's escape, in the fall of 1850, a new federal fugitive slave law made black freedom in the North more precarious for her and other runaway slaves. The law also made life in northern border states more hazardous and efforts to aid fugitives more difficult (Document 3). The new federal law was a response to slaveholders' view that the earlier 1793 version of the law was not being vigorously enforced. Many northern states—including Pennsylvania, New York, Connecticut, and Massachusetts—had passed laws giving accused fugitives legal rights, such as the right to a jury trial, to have a lawyer, and to testify in their own defense, or forbidding state officials and facilities to be used in capturing fugitives, and this law was designed to nullify those state statutes. The Fugitive Slave Law of 1850 was one of five laws passed by Congress collectively called the Compromise of 1850, an attempt to balance the interests of slave and free states. California was admitted to the Union as a free state, and the embarrassing slave trade in the District of Columbia was ended, although slavery remained legal there. For slaveholders the stricter law attempted to ensure that fugitives would be returned to their owners by simplifying the process of claiming a runaway—making it an administrative process in the hands of commissioners, with no trial required—and requiring a $1,000 fine and six months in jail for anyone helping an escapee. It imposed the same penalties for bystanders who refused to aid authorities trying to capture a fugitive. This bystander provision effectively enlisted everyone in the slave-catching business. The law prohibited accused fugitives from speaking in their own defense—something abolitionists argued was unconstitutional—and paid federal officials $5 if the captive was found to be free and $10 if he or she was found to be a slave. Abolitionists believed the law to be so biased that it would encourage the kidnapping of free African Americans, exacerbating the problem presented by slave catchers who roamed border areas seeking to make quick money by capturing fugitives and kidnapping free blacks.[29]

The battle lines were drawn. Southern slaveholders were determined to have the law rigorously enforced, and northern abolitionists, especially black abolitionists, grew increasingly militant in their conviction that black freedom should be protected. Even northerners who were not abolitionists questioned many of the law's provisions. Senator William Henry Seward of New York noted the change in northern public sentiment: "The cause of political justice is stronger now than ever heretofore by just the extent to which the public conscience has been educated."[30] Northern sympathy notwithstanding, African Americans felt much more vulnerable, and hundreds of fugitives—some in the North for a generation or more—along with many free blacks fled to Canada.[31]

One of the most dramatic and celebrated cases was orchestrated by future Tubman ally Lewis Hayden shortly after the law took effect. William and Ellen Craft, who had escaped from slavery in Georgia, were threatened with arrest in Boston. Ellen, a light-skinned woman, had escaped by posing as a young, elegant white southern gentleman traveling north for medical treatment. Her face was wrapped so that her lack of a beard would not be apparent, and her arm was in a sling so that she wouldn't be called upon to sign hotel registers. William acted as the gentleman's faithful body servant, attending to all his needs. William Still received them when they reached Philadelphia and passed them on to relative safety in New England.[32]

For more than a year, the Crafts thrilled audiences at antislavery meetings in New England and Great Britain with the story of their lives in slavery and their daring escape. Their owner also followed their speaking career, and after passage of the Fugitive Slave Law, he sent two agents to recover them (Document 7). Boston abolitionists kept the slave catchers under surveillance and harassed them with arrests for slander and conspiracy to kidnap. At angry meetings, people vowed to protect the Crafts at all costs. Hayden, relatively new to Boston and himself a fugitive, stood near his front door between kegs of gunpowder and, with a lighted torch in his hand, threatened to blow everyone up rather than surrender William. The slave catchers left the city, and abolitionists spirited the Crafts to safety in England.[33]

Tubman also risked her own freedom to defy the new law. Early in the excitement over the law, she received word that her niece Kessiah was about to be sold farther south. Years before, Kessiah's mother, Tubman's sister Linah, had been sold away from her own children, and Tubman was determined that this would not happen to Kessiah and her children, James and Araminta. She enlisted the aid of Kessiah's free black husband, John Bowley, and her own brother-in-law Tom Tubman, who lived in Baltimore near the waterfront. At the slave auction Bowley successfully bid for his family and hid them while the auctioneer took a break for dinner. Later he failed to show up to pay the bill. After nightfall the Bowleys took a small boat to Baltimore, where Harriet and Tom waited. Harriet lodged the family with friends for a few days and then took them to Philadelphia and freedom. Three months later, in March 1851, she used her Baltimore and Delaware connections again, this time to aid the escape of her brother Moses and two other men. The men escaped on their own to Baltimore, and Harriet conducted them the rest of the way to free soil.[34]

Baltimore's extensive and highly organized free black population was an important resource for people escaping from slavery in Maryland and Virginia, especially after the passage of the Fugitive Slave Law of 1850. In the 1850s the more than 25,000 free African Americans (and nearly 3,000 slaves) there maintained two banks, thirty mutual aid societies, fifteen African Methodist Episcopal (AME) churches, and fifteen schools. Shipping in Baltimore's harbor connected the waterways of the South with the transportation network of the North. In Baltimore young Frederick Douglass had learned to read and become a ship caulker. During the time that Tubman was active in the area, at least one black shipowner, Captain Robert Henry, linked Baltimore with the Eastern Shore.[35]

Determined enforcement of the Fugitive Slave Law convinced abolitionists of the need to redouble their efforts. It also confirmed many abolitionists' belief that Garrisonian nonviolence was unworkable. Authorities arrested nearly twice as many fugitives in 1851 as in any other year of the law's existence, and of the eighty-seven fugitives arrested from the end of September 1850 until the end of December 1851, seventy-seven were returned to slavery. Once arrested, a fugitive's chances of escape or release were poor; nearly 90 percent of those arrested were reenslaved. It was even more important, then, for the Underground Railroad and its conductors to prevent an arrest in the first place.[36]

THE MOSES OF HER PEOPLE

By the fall of 1851 Harriet Tubman was settled in Philadelphia among friends and relatives. She had worked for two years, saved some money, and decided to risk a trip into Maryland to persuade her husband, John, to move to Philadelphia. In preparation Harriet bought him a suit so that he would fit in better in the North—and perhaps also to convince him that she was doing well in freedom. Fearing capture if she went to her old home, she hid with friends in the neighborhood and sent word to him. Harriet was shocked to learn that in her absence John had married a free black woman named Caroline and had no interest in going north with her. His refusal shattered her plans for their life together, and his faithlessness infuriated her. She considered the reckless satisfaction of confronting him, but instead, possibly emboldened by righteous anger, decided to hazard bringing more of her family members out of bondage. Later she reported that God had called her to embark on a career as an Underground Railroad conductor. At first she demurred, she said, but God assured her that he had chosen her for this work.[37]

In Philadelphia Tubman added her niece Kessiah and her family to the group, and by the time they arrived at Frederick Douglass's home in Rochester, New York, on their way to Canada, they numbered eleven including Tubman, the largest party Douglass had ever sheltered.

Douglass's participation in the Underground Railroad was particularly risky because he was one of the best-known and most identifiable abolitionists in the country. Since his escape from slavery in 1838, the self-educated Douglass had spent years on the American antislavery lecture circuit, traveled to Great Britain, published his *Narrative of the Life of Frederick Douglass* in 1845, obtained his freedom, edited the antislavery newspaper the *North Star* (later called *Frederick Douglass' Paper*), and been active in antislavery politics. Through the Underground Railroad, he also remained connected to networks in Maryland. In September 1851, 75 to 150 African Americans had confronted a small slave-hunting party in Christiana, Pennsylvania. A Maryland slaveholder named Edward Gorsuch was killed in the melee, and the leaders of the blacks, William Parker and two other men, fled before they could be arrested. Douglass had known Parker when they were both enslaved in Maryland, and he provided them with food and clothing in his Rochester home. In the evening he drove them to a boat landing on Lake Ontario, where the black man who worked there put them on a British boat bound for Canada.[38]

It was an exceptionally cold December when Harriet Tubman led her charges from Rochester to safety in St. Catharines, Canada, where she had established a home. The fugitives boarded with her there through the frigid Canadian winter of 1851–1852. In the spring she returned to Philadelphia, where she lived with John and Kessiah's son, James, and in the summer she took a job as a cook in Cape May, New Jersey. Thereafter Tubman established her pattern of living in Canada during the winter, working in the Philadelphia/New Jersey area during the spring and summer, and venturing into the South to bring out slaves once or twice a year.[39]

Joining the Antislavery Army

As an Underground Railroad conductor, Tubman tapped into and further developed an extensive support network that extended from Maryland through Delaware, Pennsylvania, and New York, then north to Canada. Her network grew as she became known among enslaved people and abolitionists for successfully helping slaves escape. Her most important early contacts outside her family and African American friends in Maryland were William Still and Thomas Garrett. By his own count Garrett helped 2,700 people escape from slavery. He spent most of his savings on fines for these efforts but always stood ready to help freedom seekers. Garrett and Still introduced Tubman to their contacts, and she made more connections, particularly among free blacks, as she traveled. Eventually, she depended on an extensive network of abolitionists, both black and white.

The local Underground Railroad network that Tubman stepped into when she crossed the Maryland border into Delaware was knit together through the bonds of family, religion, and antislavery zeal. The Chesapeake and Delaware Canal near Garrett's home ran from the Chesapeake Bay to just five miles from the Pennsylvania line. Garrett's wife Rachel's cousins Isaac and Dinah Mendenhall lived just inside the Pennsylvania border. The Mendenhalls and other Quaker families in the area sold farm produce in both Philadelphia and Wilmington, Delaware, perfectly positioning them for Underground Railroad activities. Not all Quakers, however, were antislavery activists. Many believed that they should not become embroiled in political controversies and that breaking laws protecting slaveholders' property rights was immoral. Disagreements over the appropriate way to achieve slavery's abolition led the radical group of Quakers committed to antislavery action to form their own progressive meeting, the Longwood Meeting of Kennett Township, in southeastern Pennsylvania's Chester County. Thomas Garrett; the Mendenhalls; the black abolitionist Robert Purvis and his wife, Harriet; and the white Philadelphian James Mott were among the founders of the Longwood Meeting, and the building they dedicated in 1855 became an important venue for antislavery speakers. They were closely tied to Boston abolitionists, and Minister Theodore Parker and William Lloyd Garrison both spoke at their meetinghouse.[40]

Robert Purvis was the principal recipient of the fugitives Garrett—and later his friend Tubman—sent north. Purvis had been born in 1810 in Charleston, South Carolina, to a wealthy English cotton broker and a freeborn African American woman. His maternal grandparents were an enslaved woman and a Jewish businessman. Purvis's father moved his wife and three sons to Philadelphia when Robert was nine years old and established a school for black children there. Robert received an exceptional education, attending his father's school, and two academies in Massachusetts. He then settled in Philadelphia and married Harriet Forten, daughter of businessman James Forten, thereby becoming a member of a wealthy, well-established black Philadelphia family. The following year Purvis was a founding member of the American Anti-Slavery Society, established in Philadelphia in 1833 under Garrison's leadership.[41]

Philadelphians James and Lucretia Coffin Mott connected Tubman to another important thread in the antislavery network and to some of the most important leaders in the early movement for women's rights. Lucretia Mott and her younger sister Martha, both original members of the American Anti-Slavery Society, came from a prominent New England Quaker family. When Martha was widowed in 1826 at age nineteen, she moved to Auburn, New York, to teach at a Quaker girls' school in order to support herself and her child. In Auburn Martha married lawyer David Wright, who became the law partner of William Seward, governor of New York from 1839 to 1842 and U.S. senator from 1849 to 1861. Seward's home in Auburn was a station on the Underground Railroad, and he became a stalwart supporter of Tubman.

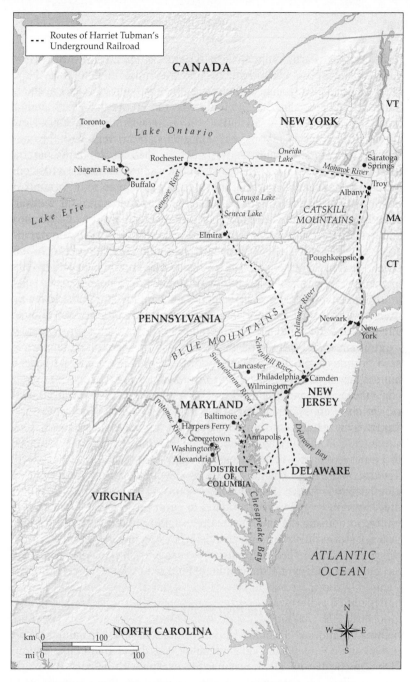

Map. *Harriet Tubman's Underground Routes to Freedom, 1849–1860*

Tubman began in the area around Cambridge, Maryland, and from Baltimore, Maryland, and Wilmington, Delaware, she generally followed the major routes of the Underground Railroad's eastern line to Canada.

Through Seward, Tubman also became acquainted with the New York philanthropist and abolitionist Gerrit Smith in Peterboro, New York. Smith, an advocate of voting rights for women, was Elizabeth Cady Stanton's cousin. Stanton had spent more than five years among the radical activists in Boston but now lived in nearby Seneca Falls, New York. She and her friend Susan B. Anthony were active in both the antislavery and women's rights movements. In 1848 Stanton and Lucretia Mott were among the organizers of America's first women's rights convention, at Seneca Falls, where they presented Stanton's Declaration of Sentiments demanding equal political and economic rights for women, including the right to vote. Thus, through her first contacts out of slavery, Tubman became connected to a widespread network of antislavery and women's rights activists in Delaware, Pennsylvania, New York, and Massachusetts. She soon expanded this network into black settlements in Canada. As she extended her contacts, she developed a way to test their dependability. She carried pictures of abolitionist friends, probably their visiting cards, and if a new acquaintance recognized the photos, she believed she could trust the person.[42]

Tubman relied on her extensive network for economic support of slave rescues and to help protect fugitives from slave catchers. Even so, her solitary trips into slave territory were exceedingly dangerous, especially since most captured escapees were arrested in border areas, particularly in Pennsylvania, where she operated, and in Ohio. Of the 330 fugitives arrested from the passage of the Fugitive Slave Law in 1850 through 1860, 96 were apprehended in Ohio and 86 in Pennsylvania. Of those arrested, only 11 were released, 22 were rescued, and 1 escaped. Tubman's personal risk increased as slaveholders reportedly posted rewards as high as $12,000 for her capture. The more trips she made and the more people she attempted to save, the greater the danger of her apprehension became. Nevertheless, her legend grew, and as she told her stories in parlors and at antislavery meetings—which she often did to raise money for the antislavery cause—she became renowned for never losing anyone she conducted out of bondage (Document 9).[43]

God's Guidance and Practical Strategy

Tubman met the perils of the Underground Railroad with calm determination and deep faith in God's guidance, but she also took precautions (Documents 18 and 19). It was hard to escape with babies, who might not be silent on command, so she always gave them something to keep them calm and quiet. Accounts differ, but she gave them either paregoric or the much stronger laudanum, both opium-based drugs generally used as cough suppressants at the time. Fearful escapees who decided to return to the plantation endangered the rest of the group and those who helped them, she said, and she did not hesitate to assert control. A runaway having second thoughts might face not only her resolve but also the revolver she carried (Documents 9 and 18). Tubman exercised clear authority over the groups she conducted out of slavery, an unusual position for a woman at the time. On one occasion a man suffering the physical hardships of escape could not be dissuaded from going back. Under her orders, other men in the group were fully prepared to kill the man. Convinced of her intentions, the man decided to continue his escape.[44]

According to the young white abolitionist and editor Franklin Sanborn, Tubman was "shrewd and practical" when it came to aiding runaway slaves yet "a firm believer in omens, dreams and warnings." Tubman's religion was a blending of Christian and African beliefs, common in nineteenth-century black communities, particularly in the slave South. At the heart of black Christianity was the Old Testament God who led Moses and the Israelites out of bondage in Egypt and promised justice for his people. African customs and beliefs prevailed well into the nineteenth century and were expressed in African American culture, including religion, music, art, crafts, and medical practices. African religions were characterized by a lack of separation between the spiritual and physical worlds. For example, in the ecstatic spiritual practice called the ring shout, dancers shuffled in a counterclockwise circle, engaging their whole bodies in a rhythmic symbolic integration of the physical and spiritual realms. Such beliefs touched the religious practices of nineteenth-century whites as well. The religious revivals of the Second Great Awakening beginning in the 1820s, in which African Americans were important participants, emphasized "ecstasy and spontaneity," and many white northern abolitionists engaged in mystical spiritualist gatherings. The God who Tubman said spoke to her was characteristic of what one scholar has called the "this-worldly mysticism" fundamental to black religion — "the God of ecstatic vision, of mystic communion, of the soul, God in the soul."[45]

Tubman's symbolic dreams and prophetic visions were part of a black oral tradition. Such dreams, visions, and audible inner voices were seen as evidence of the sanctification that gave religious authority to some black women in the mid-nineteenth century. Generally opposed by respectable male church authorities as practitioners of "heathenish" religion, these women formed "praying and singing bands" that were especially active in Baltimore and Philadelphia. Commonly, these groups were offshoots of more established churches, where women were not accepted in the pulpit. A few women, such as Jarena Lee and Rebecca Cox Jackson, became preachers, and Jackson founded the black Shakers, a group practicing a form of ecstatic Quakerism, in Philadelphia. Far from unusual, Tubman's mystical experience had its roots in African cultures and expressed African American traditions actively being practiced by other black women in America.[46]

One important reason that Tubman's charges put such trust in her was their perception that she had a strong supernatural source of power. In 1860 William Wells Brown, the black abolitionist and former fugitive slave from Kentucky, interviewed some of the people Tubman had led to Canada (Document 21). When asked whether he was afraid of being caught, one man replied, "O, no, Moses is got de charm." Whites couldn't catch her, the man insisted, because she was "born wid de charm." Blending Christianity's belief in the power of the Holy Spirit with traditional African beliefs in charms, or protective/sacred objects, he said, "De Lord has given Moses de power." Tubman, too, believed that the Lord had given her the power, and her daring close escapes certainly lent credence to the conviction that she had the charm.[47]

Practical factors also contributed to Tubman's success. Since she was no longer working outdoors in the sun all day, her complexion was lighter, and this undoubtedly made it less likely that the casual observer would identify her. Once, awaiting an opportunity to make a rescue, she lived near her old master for three months and even met him in broad daylight twice without his recognizing her. At first glance even her brother and sister did not recognize her. Additionally, her physical appearance didn't conform to people's expectations of how a daring slave rescuer should look. She remained strong from housework and her years of field work, but she was only five feet tall. Her labor apparently had taken its toll, however, because in 1854, when she was in her early thirties, Thomas Garrett estimated her age at fifty-five. Being able to pass for a much older person often allowed her to move about without arousing suspicion. Few would imagine that the feeble old woman they saw was the notorious Harriet Tubman, the one African Americans called Moses.[48]

Tubman combined such advantages with clever planning and an ability to think quickly in a crisis. Occasionally, when closely followed, she and her charges would take a train heading south, on the assumption that their pursuers would expect them to be moving north toward freedom. She conducted many of her rescues at the end of the year, when slave families separated by work for different masters might be reunited for the Christmas holiday. Winter nights were longer, providing additional cover of darkness, although this often meant risking the arduous passage in cold and stormy weather. On one cold night, she said that God had told her to leave the road to escape pursuers, so she and the men she was leading had to wade twice through deep, icy water and walk across the countryside in wet, freezing clothes before they reached a home where they could be sheltered. Unfortunately, such strategies took their toll. After this escape, Tubman developed a severe respiratory illness.[49]

Tubman generally did not go to the plantations where escaping slaves lived and worked. To reduce the danger of being caught, she instead arranged to meet them some distance away, sometimes miles away, and often communicated with them in coded messages. She sang hymns and slave songs to pass her message along or to communicate with her hidden charges during an escape. She sometimes spent months hiding, waiting for the right time to organize an escape. When directly threatened, she might break up a group of runaways and conceal them in different places—in homes, in a swamp, or in the woods—until she could return or send someone to help them.

It is difficult to know how many people Tubman helped to freedom. Some she conducted personally all the way to Canada, some she passed along to others in Pennsylvania and New York, some she brought into the free states and gave material aid, and some she simply gave instructions about escape routes and strategies. Popular writings have generally relied on Sarah Bradford's 1869 biography, *Scenes in the Life of Harriet Tubman*, for the number of Tubman's rescues. Making deductions from Tubman's recollections and the memories of others who knew her, Bradford estimated that Tubman made nineteen trips and rescued more than three hundred people. Tubman herself remembered about eleven trips from Canada, and Garrett believed that she rescued between sixty and eighty people. In her exhaustive study, historian Kate Larson put the number that Tubman personally rescued at about seventy, with about fifty more instructed.

It is safe to conclude that Tubman made at least a dozen dangerous trips into slave territory and personally brought sixty to eighty people out of bondage in her approximately twelve years of Underground Railroad activity. Including those she aided more indirectly, she probably rescued well over one hundred people. She brought out nearly all of her immediate family members, many neighbors, family members of fugitives who had escaped to the North earlier, and some strangers who sought her aid. Though a lone hero in legend, she relied on an extensive network of blacks, both slave and free, and some sympathetic whites to help people to freedom. Her fame as an Underground Railroad conductor was based less on the number of slaves she rescued and more on the daring exploits she recounted to antislavery supporters—often as part of her fund-raising efforts for future rescues and the support for runaways.[50]

Stationmaster Thomas Garrett also encountered the power of Tubman's certainty that God, acting through her friends and contacts, would provide what she needed. Garrett frequently corresponded with two Quaker sisters in Scotland, Eliza Wigham and Mary Edmundson, friends of American abolitionists and members of the Edinburgh Ladies' Emancipation Society. Garrett wrote to them about Tubman, and they sometimes sent him money for her. Astoundingly, Tubman always seemed to arrive when he had just received a donation for her, saying that God had told her to come. A year after he first gave her money from the Scottish society, she arrived at his house and declared that she knew he had a donation for her, though not as much as before. She was right—he had just received a smaller donation than the first. Once Tubman came after Garrett had not seen her for several weeks. Teasing her, he said that God may have deceived her about his having money for her, since fugitives had made great demands on his resources, and he had nothing to give. She would not be deterred, and he finally admitted that less than a week before, he had received a donation, enough for her planned rescue of a woman and three children in Maryland.[51]

Slaveholder Determination and Increased Danger

In March 1852 the publication of Harriet Beecher Stowe's *Uncle Tom's Cabin* enraged slaveholders and made rescues even more dangerous for Tubman and her Underground Railroad cohorts. Written to express her indignation over the Fugitive Slave Law of 1850, Stowe's book created a sensation in America and abroad and became an immediate bestseller. Selling ten thousand copies during the first week and three hundred thousand during the first year, it fueled antislavery sentiment both in the North and in Europe. Importantly, the sympathy the book aroused led Britain to keep Canada's borders open to fugitives from American slavery. Black communities just across the border from Michigan and New York, including Dawn, Wilberforce, and Chatham, continued to grow.[52]

That year Harriet Tubman's brothers Benjamin, Robert, and Henry made repeated attempts to purchase their freedom, but their mistress refused, and they failed in their escape attempts. Once, after six months in hiding, they became discouraged and returned to their owner. Their father tried to find someone to help them escape, but his efforts also failed. Finally, in the spring of 1854, they learned that their mistress planned to sell them. Tubman, sensing the young men's danger, went to Maryland to get them, but they refused to try another escape. Undoubtedly, the men were being closely watched, and perhaps they didn't believe they would actually be sold into the harsh slavery of the Deep South.[53]

In fact, slaveholders in the Chesapeake Bay area had reason to be confident that they could keep and recover their slaves. In May 1854 Anthony Burns, a fugitive from Virginia, was arrested in Boston, and his arrest and trial were widely publicized. An abolitionist mob, led by the black activist Lewis Hayden and the white abolitionist minister Thomas Wentworth Higginson, stormed the courthouse where Burns was being held and killed a U.S. marshal but failed to rescue Burns. The trial brought thousands of sympathizers to Boston; an estimated seven thousand to eight thousand people thronged the square in front of the courthouse. The city, state, and federal governments, however, were dedicated to enforcing the Fugitive Slave Law. Burns's guards included marshals and their enlisted deputies, local police, a hastily recruited volunteer militia, a city militia of more than fifteen hundred men, an artillery company, and a company of U.S. Marines. Burns's return to slavery was a great victory for proslavery forces, but the failure to save him made abolitionists even more determined. Watching the heavily guarded Burns march from the federal courthouse down State Street to the wharf for his return to slavery shocked the sensibilities of many Bostonians and gained antislavery converts. Thomas Garrett was among the throngs who had come to Boston to witness the city's shame, and when some in the crowd recognized him, they gave him three rousing cheers for his dedication to abolition.[54]

Tubman also visited Boston sometime in 1854, and the government's determination to capture and return fugitives may have reinforced the urgency she felt to free the rest of her family. By the end of the year Tubman was increasingly concerned about her brothers. She communicated with them through their free black neighbor Jacob Jackson, using misinformation she hoped he would understand and biblical language in a code she hoped the authorities could not decipher. The letter she dictated and sent to Jackson was signed with the name of his only son,

William Henry Jackson, also free and living in the North. It said, in part, "Read my letter to the old folks, and give my love to them, and tell my brothers to be always *watching unto prayer*, and when *the good old ship of Zion comes along, to be ready to step on board*." Authorities screened Jackson's correspondence, and they were suspicious but could not make sense of the letter. When they asked Jackson to explain its meaning, he read it carefully and committed it to memory. He then told them he was innocent of any conspiracy. The letter must be for someone else, he said, because his son had no brothers. He immediately informed Tubman's brothers to be alert because she was coming for them.[55]

As promised, Tubman arrived the day before Christmas, just two days before her brothers were to be sold. She sent word to them to meet her at her parents' home, some forty miles from where they were working. Tubman had not seen her parents in more than five years but was afraid to make herself known to her mother, lest her mother's emotional reaction draw unwanted attention. Rit was busy cooking for the Christmas holiday, hoping to have her children gather as usual. She stopped her work often to look for her boys.

Tubman's two younger brothers Benjamin and Henry, who were in their mid- to late twenties, came to their parents' home immediately upon receiving Tubman's message and hid themselves in the fodder shed. Benjamin brought along Jane Kane, a young girl he intended to marry. Two other enslaved men, John Chase and Peter Jackson, also joined the group. The strangers went to the house to tell Ben that they were there, and he brought out food for them. It was bad timing for Tubman's older brother, Robert. His wife went into labor with their third child on Christmas Eve, and he was loath to leave. Torn between the necessity of escape, lest he be sold and separated from his family forever, and his desire to be with his wife during childbirth, he waited, and the party left without him. Tubman left instructions for Robert, though, and he joined them a short time later without his family. Tubman's father donned a blindfold and accompanied the runaways down the road, turning around and removing his blindfold when he could no longer hear their footsteps, so that he might truthfully deny having seen them. Her mother never knew they were there.[56]

The group made its way to Thomas Garrett's house in Wilmington, Delaware. On December 28, Garrett forwarded them to Philadelphia, sending a letter to alert the antislavery office to their impending arrival (Document 8). They picked up two other escapees, George Ross and William Thompson, along the way, and on December 29 J. Miller McKim and William Still received the party of nine at the American Anti-Slavery

Society office. Still interviewed the runaways and carefully recorded their names, ages, information about their families, and the names they had chosen for their life in freedom. Tubman's brothers changed their names to Stewart, possibly marking their experience being hired out to lumber dealer John Stewart, reputedly a fair man. It had been John Stewart who had hired Harriet from her owner after her accident, allowing her to work with her father and save money.[57]

Such name changes were fairly common in African American society. There was a very practical reason for this: New names made it more difficult for slaveowners to track down fugitives. However, the practice also had cultural roots. Many Africans took new names to mark a new stage in their lives—the attainment of manhood or warrior status, for example. Black Americans who went to sea for long periods often took new names for seafaring. Similarly, people who escaped from slavery very often shed their slave names and chose new ones to mark their freedom. Those names might be ones by which they had been known to fellow African Americans or might just convey their new status. A runaway might also take the name of an owner who was less brutal or in some way fairer than others, or an owner known to be his or her father. "Freeman" or "Freedman" were common choices, as in the case of William Still's brother, who became Peter Freedman when he escaped in 1850. Still took a great risk by keeping detailed records of his illegal Underground Railroad activities, but his records enabled many people to find family members after they escaped to freedom.[58]

After meeting with Still, Tubman and her party left Philadelphia for New York. They followed a route she often used, through New York City to Albany and Troy, and then to either Syracuse or Rochester. From western New York, it was a short, though risky, trip across the Niagara River, Lake Erie, or Lake Ontario to Canada. Tubman accompanied the group to St. Catharines in Canada, where her family members took refuge in her home. The following year, James and Catherine, formerly Ben and Jane, moved west to a fugitive slave settlement in Chatham, across the river from Detroit, where they lived with his niece Kessiah and her husband, John Bowley. For a time Tubman's other two brothers took up farming on the outskirts of St. Catharines.[59]

Tubman was based in Canada until 1859, also spending time in Philadelphia, Boston, and New York State, where she earned money and raised funds to support her rescues. She made repeated trips to Maryland, hoping to rescue her sister Rachel and her children, Benjamin and Angerine, about twelve and fourteen years of age, respectively. The children had been hired away from their mother, however, and she wouldn't leave without them. Meanwhile, Tubman rescued many others, including her brother William Henry's wife and child; friends of the family; other Marylanders who had heard of her exploits; and her sister Rachel's sisters-in-law, Eliza and Mary Manokey, along with Mary's three children. That Tubman was so often willing to risk the increased danger of discovery by rescuing children testifies to her commitment to her family and her assurance that God would protect her.

Tubman made at least four forays into Maryland in 1856. In October she rescued Tilly, a lady's maid and dressmaker, whose fiancé, also a fugitive, had been waiting for her in Canada for seven years. Tubman agreed to conduct Tilly from Baltimore and arranged for passage, with no questions asked, south across the Chesapeake Bay to Delaware through a contact who knew a boat's clerk. Reaching the boat landing, they discovered that the expected boat had been replaced by another with which she had no connection. Standing in line, the two women aroused onlookers' suspicions, and they knew they would be asked for passes or freedom papers before they could get tickets. Tubman asked for tickets but was told brusquely to stand aside until other (less suspicious) passengers were accommodated. She led Tilly to a secluded spot at the bow of the boat, knelt on the seat, and, while Tilly waited in an agony of anxiety, repeatedly implored the Lord for assistance. Finally, the formerly antagonistic clerk approached, touched Tubman on the shoulder, and informed her that they could get their tickets.[60]

After arriving in Delaware the women spent a fretful night in a hotel. In the morning a slave dealer tried to arrest them but let them go when Tubman showed him a fraudulent certificate of freedom she had previously obtained from a sympathetic Philadelphia steamboat captain. With the help of other Underground Railroad workers, Tubman and Tilly traveled by train and carriage to Garrett's home in Wilmington. From there Tilly continued her journey to Canada, while Tubman returned to Maryland.[61]

Tubman told a similar story about rescuing a cook from Baltimore whose children had been sold away from her. They boarded a night steamer together, and Tubman told the woman to stay by the rail while she went to purchase tickets. Again she was told to wait. She returned to her charge, and when the woman asked quietly if she had the tickets, Tubman stared out at the dark water. Suddenly seeing the vision of a bright light over the river, she replied, "Yes, I have got them now, I am sure of it." The clerk then came to them with the tickets, saying, "Here, Aunty, are your tickets," and they made good their escape.[62]

Bringing out Eliza Manokey and three slave men in mid-November was especially difficult. One of the men, Josiah Bailey, was a readily identifiable, muscular man in his late twenties with a bald head and a scar under his eye. Although it meant leaving his wife and three children behind, Bailey had become determined to escape after his owner beat him. He knew Tubman's father and asked to be alerted the next time she came to Maryland. When she arrived, Bailey, his older brother William, twenty-five-year-old Peter Pennington, and Eliza Manokey were ready to go north. The men's three owners, however, posted ads offering high rewards all along their suspected route—$1,500 for Joe Bailey's capture and return, $300 for Bill Bailey, and $800 for Peter Pennington. Getting these men out of slave territory required all of Tubman's resources and ingenuity. She enlisted the aid of other guides, sometimes hid the fugitives separately, placed them with a number of black families, and used disguises. The normally three- or four-day trip out of Maryland and Delaware took nearly two weeks, with slave catchers in hot pursuit.[63]

As the group reached the bridge at Wilmington, they found it under heavy guard, so Tubman concealed her charges once again and went for Garrett's assistance. To cover their escape, Garrett assembled two wagonloads of bricklayers in Pennsylvania and sent them over the bridge. Pretending to picnic and drink all day, the rowdy bricklayers returned after nightfall and provided the perfect distraction for the unsuspecting police and slave catchers waiting on the other side. The guards didn't know that the runaways they sought were hidden in the bottom of the wagons. The fugitives arrived safely at the antislavery office in Philadelphia and then took the train to New York City. Even there, they found wanted posters for the men. Josiah Bailey was convinced that he would never avoid detection, and his anxiety made him mute during the trip through Albany, Syracuse, and Rochester. Tubman couldn't convince him to look at Niagara Falls as the train crossed the bridge into Canada or to sing with his traveling companions. Once they were safely on Canadian soil, though, and Bailey realized he was truly free, he was irrepressible and broke into joyful songs of praise.[64]

GROWING SECTIONAL TENSIONS AND GREATER MILITANCY

The following spring the U.S. Supreme Court's ruling in *Dred Scott v. Sandford* on March 6, 1857, seemed to seal the fate of enslaved people and raised questions for Tubman and all African Americans. Scott had been born in slavery in Virginia but sued for his freedom in Missouri on the basis of his having lived for many years with his owner in the free areas of Illinois and Wisconsin Territory. Others had won their freedom with such arguments, and Scott had prevailed in a lower court, but the Supreme Court decided he was not entitled to freedom. Furthermore, Chief Justice Roger B. Taney of Maryland issued an expansive opinion contending that no African Americans had rights that whites need respect and declaring that blacks were not, had never been, and could never be U.S. citizens.[65]

Taney's opinion threw free black communities and white abolitionists into an angry uproar. It seemed to continue the federal government's assault on black freedom begun with the 1850 Fugitive Slave Law and advanced by the Kansas-Nebraska Act of 1854. The Missouri Compromise of 1820 had admitted the state of Missouri as a slave state but divided future states created from the western territories into free states north of Missouri's southern border and slave states south of that border. The Kansas-Nebraska Act effectively nullified that arrangement. It allowed the people of Kansas and other future states in those territories to decide whether they would be slave or free, regardless of geography. These changes, along with the Supreme Court's *Dred Scott* decision, made black abolitionists more militant and increasingly willing to use violence to defend their own freedom and protect those escaping from slavery. They organized black militias to train for bringing slavery to an end by whatever means necessary. Many African Americans, especially former slaves, were even more convinced that their only true security lay in Canada.[66]

On Saturday, March 7, the day after the *Dred Scott* decision, eight people in Dorchester County on Maryland's Eastern Shore armed themselves with knives and pistols and ran away together. The two couples, James and Lavinia Woolfley and Bill and Emily Kiah, and four men, including Henry Predeaux, Thomas Elliott, and Denard Hughes, followed Tubman's directions, stopped for shelter at her parents' home, and then set out for Thomas Otwell's home outside Dover, Delaware. Otwell, an African American, was one of Tubman's Underground Railroad operatives. He had agreed to guide the group safely north of Dover in return for $1 each. Unfortunately, when confronted with eight fugitives, the reward for whom totaled nearly $3,000, Otwell's greed overcame his dedication to the cause. He conspired with a local white friend and the Dover sheriff to take the runaways to the Dover jail, where they would stay until recovered by their owners.[67]

Otwell assured the fugitives of the white men's good intentions, but when the sheriff escorted them to the second-floor cells, Predeaux became suspicious. The group refused to enter the cells, and the sheriff dashed downstairs to the apartment where his wife and children were sleeping to retrieve his pistol, with the runaways close on his heels. Perceiving the sheriff's intentions, Predeaux scooped hot coals from the fireplace and scattered them around the room to make it harder for the sheriff to seize the fugitives. He then broke the window and held the sheriff at bay with a hot poker while his fellows climbed out, dropped the twelve feet to the ground, and scaled the enclosure's wall. Predeaux was the last to leave and was saved from injury or death only by the fact that the sheriff's gun jammed as Predeaux went out the window and over the wall.

The three men's owners were waiting for them in Wilmington, but Predeaux managed to arrive safely at Thomas Garrett's house. Six of the runaways went back the way they had come and caught up with Otwell, who agreed, under great duress, to take them to the next Underground Railroad station. Some made it to Garrett's, while others took different routes to Philadelphia. William Still passed all but William and Emily Kiah along to Canada, including Lavinia Woolfley, who managed to get to Still's office some months after her husband had gone on to freedom. The group, called the Dover Eight, became widely known among abolitionists for their daring escape, and their experience remained a cautionary tale for other blacks about the dangers of trusting anyone on their quest for freedom. Generally, it was safe for runaway slaves to seek assistance in black communities, where they could assume other African Americans were sympathetic to their plight. Even there, however, some relatively few blacks, out of personal animosity or simple greed, would betray fugitives. On the plantation enslaved people seeking freedom might be betrayed by other slaves trying to gain favor with the master, and in the North a few African Americans preyed on escapees to claim the reward for their capture.

Successful escapes intensified Maryland slaveholders' concerns about the threat free blacks posed to the control of their enslaved people. In 1857 a Maryland House of Delegates committee investigating the possibility of removing free blacks from Charles County reported that the state's free black population was increasing more rapidly than the white population. Since free blacks were prohibited from returning to Maryland if they left the state for a protracted period, legislation had "walled them in," it observed, "as though we were preserving them to breed from." As "actual, present, living representations" of freedom, free African Americans were bound to "produce discontent." The committee agreed with Chief Justice Taney's opinion in *Dred Scott* that Congress had no constitutional right to control slavery anywhere in the country except to protect slaveowners' property rights, and that blacks had no citizenship rights since they "had no part in the formation of our Government." The committee's proposal for free blacks was "to sell them out," putting them up for hire and confiscating their wages, until they made enough money to pay for their own removal and transportation to Africa.[68]

Those close to Tubman were affected by the heightened tensions that followed the spectacular escape of the Dover Eight. Incensed Maryland slaveholders suspected two free black men, Tubman's friend, the Reverend Samuel Green, and Tubman's father, Benjamin Ross, of aiding their escape. Green's son had run away from slavery three years before, and Green had recently visited him in Canada. During the month following the Dover Eight escape, the local sheriff searched Green's Eastern Shore home and found a map of Canada; railroad schedules to the North; some letters from runaways, including Green's son; and a copy of Harriet Beecher Stowe's *Uncle Tom's Cabin*. He arrested Green, who was then convicted of possessing material that could "stir up insurrection" (Stowe's novel) and sentenced to ten years in the state penitentiary.[69]

Concerned for her father's safety, Tubman headed for Maryland, determined to bring her elderly parents north. Her father was aware of the danger. Rumor was that the authorities were about to arrest him, and his former owner, with whom he had always been on good terms, advised him to leave the area. Tubman couldn't expect her parents, both in their seventies, to walk a long distance, and the authorities were watching public transportation. To carry them out, she built a makeshift carriage by attaching a seating board to an axle and two wheels and tying on another board as a footrest. They boldly traveled on this horse-drawn contraption and arrived at Garrett's house without incident. From there they proceeded through Philadelphia, New York, and Rochester to St. Catharines in Canada.

As soon as her parents were safe, Tubman returned to Maryland to try once again to rescue Rachel and her children. She stayed for months into the fall but was unable find a way to bring them together and get them out. Her stay, however, was important for others' freedom. Tubman advised between forty and sixty people who escaped from Dorchester County that fall, giving them directions, cautioning them about dangers, and telling them how to connect with the Underground Railroad. Incredibly, some even fled in two large groups of fifteen and twenty-eight. With this torrent of escapees from Maryland, slaveholders met again to consider ways to establish greater control and raised the possibility of enslaving all free blacks. People continued to escape despite the slaveholders' heightened scrutiny, but in the late fall more diligent slave patrols made it more dangerous for Tubman to remain. Unable to rescue Rachel and her children, she returned to Canada.[70]

TUBMAN AND THE ANTISLAVERY NETWORK

Harriet Tubman's contacts with antislavery organizations and activists facilitated the next phase of her work. Having brought most of her family and many other people out of slavery to settle in Canada, she felt responsible for their welfare. Much of her time in the late 1850s was devoted to raising funds for Canadian refugee communities, as well as for her continuing rescues. She solicited donations from prominent abolitionists, from antislavery organizations, and from attendees at antislavery fairs and conventions. William Wells Brown described Tubman's presence at antislavery gatherings: "For eight or ten years previous to the breaking out of the Rebellion, all who frequented anti-slavery conventions, lectures, picnics, and fairs, could not fail to have seen a black woman of medium size, upper front teeth gone, smiling countenance, attired in coarse, but neat apparel, with an old-fashioned reticule, or bag, suspended by her side, and who, on taking her seat, would at once drop off into a sound sleep. This woman was Harriet Tubman, better known as 'Moses'"[71] (Document 21).

In the mid-1850s Tubman became well acquainted with many of Boston's black community leaders, such as Lewis Hayden and John Stewart Rock, staying with Rock and others when she was in town. Hayden and his family had escaped from slavery in Kentucky in 1846, when he was thirty-five years old. Before settling in Boston, Hayden had lived in Detroit, and like Tubman he had made trips into the South, where he was implicated in a Louisiana slave uprising. He was a member of the Boston Vigilance Committee, and his Beacon Hill home was an important Underground Railroad station. He had sheltered William and Ellen Craft and led the charge on the courthouse where Anthony Burns was incarcerated. Hayden's used-clothing business brought him into contact with many of the city's black sailors and laborers. As a result he provided a link between middle-class black leaders and lower-class blacks, whom he could mobilize for such rescue operations.[72]

Tubman's friend Rock was extraordinarily accomplished. He had been born in New Jersey, was active in antislavery work in Philadelphia,

and spoke before the 1849 Annual Meeting of the Pennsylvania Anti-
Slavery Society. He practiced dentistry, opened a night school for African Americans, and graduated from the American Medical College in
1852. Rock moved to Boston in 1853 and belonged to the Twelfth Baptist Church, also known as the fugitive slave church, near his home on
Beacon Hill. Rock preached black pride and economic self-sufficiency
and provided medical care for people escaping slavery. He studied law,
was admitted to the Massachusetts Bar Association in 1861, and opened
a law office on Tremont Street in Boston. In 1865 he became the first
black man admitted to practice law before the U.S. Supreme Court. That
Harriet Tubman, an unlettered escaped slave, had such a close relationship with this impressive man speaks volumes about the high regard in
which she was held by the black community.[73]

Tubman also met many prominent white Massachusetts abolitionists, including William Lloyd Garrison, Samuel Gridley Howe, and John
A. Andrew. In Concord, home of many of the progressive social critics
and philosophers called transcendentalists, she regaled eminent intel-
lectuals with stories of her heroic exploits, thrilling them by acting out
her daring rescues and singing the songs she used to communicate with
her charges. She stayed at the Concord homes of philosopher Ralph
Waldo Emerson, intellectual and teacher Bronson Alcott, and educa-
tional reformer Horace Mann, and they and their wealthy friends gave
her money to support her work.[74]

Tubman sometimes stopped at antislavery society offices when she
needed funds and once applied not-so-subtle pressure to an antislavery
official to get what she needed. Facing the difficulty of moving her parents in 1857, she asked God where she could find the money required
and settled on Oliver Johnson's office at the New York Anti-Slavery Society. Johnson told her that he did not have $20 to give her, regardless
of the Lord's guidance, but she would not be denied. Determined to
get the money, Tubman sat in the office all day, dozing periodically and
obdurately refusing food and drink. By the end of the day visitors to the
office, moved by her story and impressed by her determination, had left
her a total of $60, much more than her original request.[75]

On Tubman's frequent travels to Massachusetts, she sometimes
recounted her breathtaking adventures at large public antislavery gatherings, inspiring people to renew their antislavery commitment and raising money to continue her work. At smaller meetings and in activist
women's parlors, she acted out the dangers of rescuing slaves, occasionally telling of her anger and dashed hopes when her perfidious husband

refused to accompany her to the North. It was still unusual for women to speak in public in the mid-nineteenth century; they often faced strong disapproval and sometimes were physically attacked. This was a period of great social and economic change. As northern urban areas grew, the household economy of the farm began to decline, and more men worked outside the home. White women in the emerging middle class were expected to devote their efforts to running the household, maintaining traditional morals, and providing emotional support to their husbands. As part of women's moral duty, it was acceptable for them to be active in church and reform movements but generally not acceptable for them to take leadership roles, and certainly not to speak to audiences that included men and women.

Women did much of the day-to-day work of the abolition movement, including harboring and aiding fugitives, raising funds, and gathering signatures on petitions, but they rarely chaired meetings, and relatively few addressed antislavery gatherings. Doing antislavery work led many women to question the restrictions society placed on them, and abolitionism became a natural avenue into the women's rights movement. In black society women had done heavy labor alongside men in slavery, and they traditionally met somewhat less disapproval than white women when they took public roles. Indeed, the woman credited with being the first woman to address a public gathering of men and women was a black woman named Maria Stewart, who spoke in Boston in 1832 and 1833. When Tubman, who had escaped from slavery, and New York's Sojourner Truth, who had been legally freed, told their stories, or when other women promoted the antislavery cause by speaking in public, they were breaking new ground for American women. Truth was a generation older than Tubman, but both were active on the antislavery platform, and both were outspoken advocates of black rights and women's rights.[76]

In 1859 Tubman spoke at the Massachusetts Anti-Slavery Society's outdoor Fourth of July commemoration in Framingham, presided over by Thomas Wentworth Higginson, the Unitarian minister who had been in the forefront of the attempt to rescue Anthony Burns in Boston (Document 12). The *Liberator* reported that Higginson, the Reverend M. B. Bird of Haiti, and the wealthy white Boston abolitionist Wendell Phillips addressed a crowd of thousands in the morning. In the afternoon, after the white abolitionist Edmund Quincy and the black abolitionist William Wells Brown spoke, Higginson introduced Tubman simply as "a conductor on the Underground Railroad" known as Moses in the South.

According to the newspaper, her short speech told "the story of her sufferings as a slave, her escape, and her achievements on the Underground Railroad, in a style of quaint simplicity, which excited the most profound interest in her hearers." In the perspective of the time, her "quaint simplicity" attested to the authenticity of her slave past, since uneducated slaves could not be expected to speak with proper grammar. Indeed, when Frederick Douglass developed his own talents and became an eloquent speaker, an antislavery colleague angered him with the advice that to be believable as a former slave, he should retain "a *little* of the plantation" in his speech. With an observation sure to increase Tubman's popularity as a speaker, the *Liberator* continued: "The mere words could not do justice to the speaker, and therefore we do not undertake to give them; but we advise all our readers to take the earliest opportunity to see and hear her." An appeal for funds netted $37 (about $885 today) to help with the expenses of housing and supporting her parents.[77]

Tubman spent time in New England that summer, speaking, raising funds, and visiting some of the people she had helped move from slavery to Massachusetts towns. In early August she spoke to a meeting of the New England Convention of Colored Citizens at Boston's Tremont Temple, where she was introduced as Harriet Garrison (borrowing that famous abolitionist's name) to conceal her true identity from authorities. Tubman and other black abolitionists stayed in Boston after the convention for a two-week celebration of the twenty-fifth anniversary of the abolition of slavery in the British Empire.[78]

By 1858 Tubman was well established in northeastern antislavery circles, especially in New York and Massachusetts. Philosophical differences, particularly those between political abolitionists centered in New York and others headed by William Lloyd Garrison in Boston, had split the abolitionist movement in the 1840s and 1850s. Garrison shunned political affiliation and argued that the U.S. Constitution was a slaveholders' document, while Frederick Douglass and Gerrit Smith, among others, believed that political organizations could use the nation's founding documents to support the cause of freedom. In 1847 Douglass had split with Garrison, his former mentor, colleague, and friend, and moved his family from Massachusetts to Rochester, New York, where he published his antislavery newspaper, the *North Star*. Another disagreement among abolitionists was over the role of women in antislavery organizations, with Garrison arguing that women should be in leadership roles. Pragmatically, Tubman maintained friends in both the political and nonpolitical camps.[79]

Figure 3. *Frederick Douglass, probably late 1840s*
Douglass escaped from slavery in Maryland and became a famous antislavery orator and newspaper publisher. His home in Rochester, New York, was a stop on Tubman's Underground Railroad route.

Figure 4. *John Brown, ca. 1857*
Brown was an antislavery crusader who led a militia in the struggle over the future of Kansas and attacked the federal arsenal at Harpers Ferry, Virginia, in 1859. He met Harriet Tubman in 1858, enlisted her help in recruiting followers, and hoped she would join his Harpers Ferry raid.

JOHN BROWN'S WAR

Another divisive factor in black and white antislavery circles in the late 1850s was John Brown and his planned use of violence to bring an end to slavery. Tubman first met Brown, a friend of Frederick Douglass and the abolitionist most identified with antislavery violence, in 1858, and she greatly admired him. Brown also came to believe that she would play a vital role in his antislavery raid on the federal arsenal at Harpers Ferry, Virginia. Brown was a militant abolitionist who believed in and practiced racial equality. He had close ties to northeastern abolitionists and had hosted Douglass in his Massachusetts home while Douglass was on speaking tours ten years before. Brown had bought land from Gerrit Smith in the black settlement called Timbucto in the Adirondack Mountains, where he settled his family in 1849, surveyed land for the residents, and operated an Underground Railroad station.[80]

Brown stayed with Douglass for three weeks beginning on January 28, 1858, while he drafted a scheme to establish a free state in the wilderness of western Virginia as a base for a military campaign to free slaves. Increasing violence and antislavery militancy in the 1850s made armed attacks on slavery seem more feasible, and a popular referendum provision in the Kansas-Nebraska Act of 1854 sparked a rush to Kansas by proslavery and antislavery forces, each attempting to dominate the popular vote and determine the future of slavery or freedom in the state. The resulting conflict between settlers from New York and New England and those from Missouri and the South became a virtual civil war, earning the territory the nickname Bleeding Kansas. Abolitionists gave Brown money and sent rifles to the informal band of "free state" volunteer militiamen he established there.

Warfare in Kansas and periodic violence in Congress convinced Tubman that there would soon be a war over slavery in the United States. Massachusetts senator Charles Sumner's impassioned speech on Kansas, including derogatory remarks about Senator Andrew P. Butler of South Carolina, was answered with a savage beating by Butler's nephew, South Carolina congressman Preston S. Brooks, on the floor of the Senate on May 22, 1856. An attack on abolitionists in Lawrence, Kansas, and news of the incapacitating attack on Sumner enraged Brown. Two days later he conducted a retaliatory raid, dragging five proslavery men out of their cabins on Pottawatomie Creek and murdering them.[81]

By the end of the year Brown, a wanted man, headed east to raise money. In Boston he contacted Franklin Sanborn, the young Harvard graduate, Concord schoolmaster, fledgling revolutionary, and manager of the Boston office of the Massachusetts State Kansas Committee, whom he had met through Gerrit Smith. Sanborn introduced Brown to other financial backers, including physician Samuel Gridley Howe, merchant George Stearns, and minister Theodore Parker. When a serious depression in 1857 hampered fund-raising and abolitionist hopes of triumphing through the ballot box quieted the turmoil in Kansas, Brown spent time in Iowa, adding recruits and readying his men to foment a slave rebellion in Virginia.[82]

In early 1858 Brown began to finalize his plans; received pledges of material support from Douglass, Stearns, Howe, Parker, Thomas Wentworth Higginson, and Gerrit Smith; and met with three prominent African Americans — Philadelphia lumber dealer Stephen Smith, William Still, and New York's Henry Highland Garnet. At a meeting with the fugitive slave and militant abolitionist minister Jermain W. Loguen in Syracuse, New York, Douglass, Gerrit Smith, and Loguen advised Brown that if he was intent on carrying out his risky plan, Harriet Tubman was the one person who might be able to bring Virginia slaves to his cause.[83]

Tubman had a disturbing recurrent dream that spring. In it she stood among rocks and bushes in a barren landscape. A large snake raised its head from the rocks, and the head transformed into that of an old man with a long white beard. He seemed about to speak to her when two other snakes arose on either side of the first, these with younger men's faces. In her dream, before she could find out what the man wanted, a mob rushed in and beat down first the younger men's heads and then the old man's. When Loguen brought Brown to St. Catharines to meet Tubman in April 1858, she recognized Brown immediately as the old man in her dream.[84]

Brown made his intentions toward Harriet clear by addressing her three times as "General Tubman." He told her about his plans and implored her to help recruit men to his cause. He had much in common with Tubman, having told friends that he devised his plan in response to a message from God and saw himself as an agent of God's justice. She related some of her experiences conducting southern slaves to freedom, told him of her contacts in the Canadian settlements, and promised to help. In an eccentric expression of admiration for her courage and daring, generally considered masculine traits, and in recognition of her commanding presence, he wrote to his son, "He *Hariet* [sic] is the most of a *man* naturally; that *I ever* met with" (Document 11).[85]

On May 8, 1858, Brown addressed a meeting at the black settlement in Chatham, Canada West. He and his band of twelve men met with thirty-four blacks, discussed the proposed operation, and approved the "provisional constitution" he had drafted for his new free government in

Virginia. Neither Douglass, Loguen, Tubman, nor any of the men from St. Catharines attended the meeting. Brown's plans were disrupted when Hugh Forbes, a Scotsman who served as his drillmaster, threatened Brown's financial supporters with exposure and disclosed Brown's intentions to a few members of Congress. Pressured by his backers, Brown postponed his invasion.[86]

Meanwhile, Tubman continued to raise funds for black refugees in Canada and began to consider moving back to the United States. Her elderly parents suffered from Canada's cold, harsh climate, and her mother in particular complained bitterly that having endured the winter of 1857–1858, she didn't look forward to another. Over the next year Tubman spent a great deal of time in Boston, staying with Lewis Hayden or John Rock and also boarding at the home of a black laborer named Burrell Smith on Cambridge Street. During the next few years Tubman entertained many visitors in Boston and became acquainted with Ednah Dow Cheney and other white female abolitionists active in the women's rights movement (Document 18).[87]

Tubman's travels took her through Massachusetts and New York and into Canada. Sometime in the summer or fall of 1858 she became friends with Franklin Sanborn, who shared her interest in John Brown's plans. She stayed with Frederick Douglass in Rochester at the end of that year, and they, too, discussed Brown's upcoming campaign. After that visit Douglass wrote to the Ladies' Irish Anti-Slavery Association in Dublin about Tubman and seemed to anticipate her being involved in Brown's raid, as he intimated future action that could be even more consequential than the many rescues she had accomplished. "She possesses great courage and shrewdness," he said, "and may yet render even more important service to the Cause."[88]

After a year fighting guerrilla skirmishes with proslavery forces along the Kansas-Missouri border, Brown gave his men a final test. Just before Christmas 1858, a Missouri slave named Jim Daniels approached one of Brown's men scouting along the border. Daniels said that he, his wife, and their two children were about to be sold, and he was seeking antislavery men who might help his family and some friends escape. Brown immediately formed two companies and led them ten miles into Missouri. Brown's company freed ten slaves from two plantations by force of arms, took two white men hostage, and escaped back to Kansas. The other company rescued an enslaved woman from a different plantation, killing her owner in the process.[89]

After nearly a month in hiding and the birth of a baby, the closely pursued fugitives, guarded by fifteen armed abolitionists, undertook a torturous journey across frigid, windswept plains from Kansas to Iowa. They traveled at night by oxcart, stopped often to hide, and were confronted by slave hunters twice near Topeka. When a U.S. marshal with a posse of seventy-five surrounded them, Brown and his men stood their ground and took two members of the posse hostage for a day. The party reached eastern Iowa in February, and local abolitionists sent them to Chicago by boxcar in early March. There detective Allan Pinkerton hid them, raised more than $500 for them, and put them on another boxcar to Detroit. During three months of nearly constant danger, Brown and his men had successfully crossed into the South, confronted slaveowners, rescued people from slavery, and escorted them to freedom in Canada. That spring they moved to Chambersburg, Pennsylvania, within striking distance of Virginia, in preparation for a much more ambitious raid.[90]

Tubman also relocated that spring. She purchased a small six-acre farm with a house, a barn, and other outbuildings in Auburn, New York, from her friend Senator William H. Seward and settled herself, her parents, and her brother John there. She continued traveling and fundraising, using the money to support antislavery work, the Canadian settlement, and Brown, as well as to make the quarterly mortgage payments on the Auburn property. She also saw Brown as he met periodically with his New England supporters.[91]

The Raid on Harpers Ferry

Tubman had suggested Independence Day, ironically a traditional day for large southern slave sales, as the appropriate day for Brown's raid into Virginia. Brown and a few of his men arrived in Harpers Ferry on July 3 and consulted with a spy placed there the year before, but preparations dragged on through the summer. Gradually, Brown's men drifted into their rented farmhouse in Maryland, across the river from the town. On August 19 Brown, with a white follower named John Kagi, went to a quarry outside Chambersburg to pick up arms his son had sent from Ohio. There they met clandestinely with Frederick Douglass and Shields Green, a fugitive then working at Douglass's home. Douglass gave Brown money collected for him, and Brown made a last-ditch effort to convince Douglass to join the raid. Brown apparently had given up the idea of establishing small settlements of fugitives in the mountains for raiding plantations and protecting Underground Railroad routes. Instead of such guerrilla actions, he planned a full-scale attack on the federal arsenal at Harpers Ferry. Douglass argued that such a mission was suicidal. Although Brown conceded that he could be trapped in the arsenal, he thought that taking hostages would protect him. Douglass disputed Brown's reasoning and asserted that "Virginia would blow him and his hostages sky-high, rather than he should hold Harpers Ferry an hour." The four men debated the plan's feasibility for two days, but Brown would not be deterred. Douglass refused to take part, but Green stayed with Brown.[92]

By September Brown was feeling pressure to move before his Maryland neighbors became suspicious. He continued to hope that more recruits would come, but the danger of discovery grew with the slow increase of his band and their restlessness under the strain of waiting. With Douglass's refusal to participate, Tubman became even more important to Brown. Not knowing where she was, he left messages with friends in hopes that she would arrive in time. Franklin Sanborn speculated that Tubman might have become ill in New Bedford, Massachusetts. Lewis Hayden sent a letter urging her to return to Boston so that he could send her along to Virginia (Document 13). There were rumors that she might have returned to the South on another rescue mission or that she was somewhere in New York City. The historical record is silent on her whereabouts and feelings, but whatever the case Brown proceeded without her.

On the dark, damp Sunday evening of October 16, 1859, Brown led thirteen white men and five black men in an attack on the federal arsenal and armory and a rifle factory in Harpers Ferry, Virginia. Three men stayed at the farm to guard their store of weapons and receive any slaves who rallied to the cause. Brown and his men took possession of the buildings and the bridge over the river without firing a shot, taking about ten people hostage for protection and bargaining power. The raiding party they sent to the countryside returned with ten liberated slaves, whom they armed, and two captive slaveholders, including Colonel L. W. Washington, great-grandnephew of the first U.S. president.[93]

The following morning Tubman awoke in New York City, where she was visiting with friends, with a sense of foreboding. Puzzling over the reason for her disquietude, she informed her hostess that Brown must be in danger. The following day's newspapers' reporting on the raid confirmed her premonition. Brown's party had an estimated forty hostages and, ironically, had mistakenly killed Hayward Shepard, a free black railroad baggage master.

Rumors of a massive slave uprising swept the Harpers Ferry area and set off frenzied sniping from the local heights. Enraged citizens and a hastily organized militia surrounded Brown, his men, and eleven remaining hostages in the engine house and rifle factory. Brown's attempts to negotiate were rebuffed or ignored, and gunmen shot his two emissaries when they emerged under a flag of truce. Tuesday morning federal troops commanded by Colonel Robert E. Lee confronted the battered remnants of Brown's band and demanded their surrender. When Brown refused, marines battered down the engine house door, and by noon the fighting was over. Ten of Brown's men had been killed, including two of his sons. Brown, severely wounded, and six others were captured. Five men escaped.[94]

With Brown's capture, anyone who had befriended or supported him, including Tubman, was in great jeopardy. The authorities combed letters and papers found on the men and at the Maryland farm for clues to the names of co-conspirators. On the strength of a brief note Douglass had written two years before inviting Brown to dinner, the Virginia governor urged President James Buchanan to arrest Douglass for inciting a slave rebellion. Douglass was lecturing in Virginia and Pennsylvania and knew that before long more incriminating evidence of his relationship with Brown would be uncovered. A telegram ordering Douglass's arrest arrived in Philadelphia, but instead of delivering it, the telegraph operator rushed to the house where Douglass was staying and warned him. He then waited three hours before delivering the telegram. Fearing capture, Douglass took a steamboat instead of a train to New York City, then a ferry to Hoboken, New Jersey, where he stayed the night with a friend. The next morning they took a carriage to Paterson, New Jersey, where Douglass boarded a train for Rochester. In Rochester he received a warning letter from William Still and took a boat for Canada, just one day ahead of the U.S. marshal. Douglass then embarked for England and Scotland for a previously planned lecture tour. He stayed in Britain until just after his youngest daughter, Annie, died unexpectedly in the spring of 1860. By then the government, hoping to maintain peace in the face of growing concerns about civil war, did not pursue the charges against him.[95]

Tubman and Brown's other less well-known African American supporters and associates simply dropped out of sight, protected within black communities in Canada and the United States. The citizens of Peterboro, New York, vowed to prevent Gerrit Smith's arrest, but the guilt and prospect of legal action were too much for him. He had a mental breakdown, and his family committed him to the state insane asylum in Utica, where he remained from November to year's end. Virginia governor Henry Wise took Smith's breakdown as a sign of his innocence, essential good character, and purity of motive and did not press for his indictment.[96]

Franklin Sanborn, Samuel Gridley Howe, and George Stearns all took up short residences in Canada, but Thomas Wentworth Higginson's immediate reaction was to plan to rescue Brown. One letter to Brown from "A Native of the Old Dominion" asserted that an armed black military unit from Cincinnati, along with five hundred abolitionists, was making plans to rescue him and his men. Surprisingly, even the staunch pacifist and proponent of nonviolence William Lloyd Garrison wrote to Brown. Garrison addressed him as "My brave but unfortunate friend"; reiterated the rescue plans by advising, "Protract, to the utmost, your trial, your *delivery is at hand*"; and signed the letter simply "W. L. G." Brown was at best ambivalent about being rescued, and a guard of some fifteen hundred federal troops made it unlikely in any case.[97]

During the month and a half John Brown awaited trial, he took upon himself the mantle of martyr. With a great outpouring of letters from his Virginia jail cell to family, friends, supporters, and newspapers, he asserted the righteousness of his actions and the antislavery cause. Brown was convicted of "treason, and conspiring and advising with slaves and others to rebel" and of "murder in the first degree" for the seven people, including the town's mayor, whom he and his men had killed. In his last written note he declared presciently: "I, John Brown, am quite certain that the crimes of this guilty land will never be purged away but with blood. I had, as I now think vainly, flattered myself that without very much bloodshed it might be done."[98]

Brown's hanging on the morning of December 2, 1859, marked his transformation among abolitionists from a charismatic, rash, and some-times ill-advised activist to a Christ-like martyr. On the day of his death Harriet Tubman told her Boston friend Ednah Dow Cheney that consid-ering how Brown gave up his life for black people, "and how he never flinched, but was so brave to the end," it was clear that "it wasn't mortal man, it was God in him" (Document 18). Others agreed. Ralph Waldo Emerson observed that Brown was motivated by love for his fellow man and characterized him as a "new saint awaiting his martyrdom . . . who, if he shall suffer, will make the gallows glorious like the cross." Henry David Thoreau, another Concord transcendentalist, declared, "He is not Old Brown any longer; he is an angel of light."[99]

Anticipating War

Tubman believed that Brown's martyrdom heralded a war over slav-ery and told Sanborn, "They may say 'Peace, Peace!' as much as they like; I know there's going to be war!" Sure that war was coming, she was also convinced of its outcome. She told Cheney, "When I think of all the groans and tears and prayers I've heard on the plantations, and remember that God is a prayer-hearing God, I feel that his time is drawing near." A few months later, in early 1860, Tubman was staying in New York City with Henry Highland Garnet, a black minister and fiery abolitionist whose family had escaped from slavery on Maryland's Eastern Shore in the 1820s, when he was a child. Garnet was startled one morning as Tubman descended the stairs in the throes of ecstasy, singing, "My people are free! My people are free!" Garnet admonished her for tormenting the family with her joyous display, declaring that his grandchildren might see the end of slavery but that he and she never would. A dream had convinced her, though, that freedom for all blacks was imminent, and she continued the day in high euphoria.[100]

Abolitionists believed that Brown's raid would inspire southern slaves to rebellion, create a change in northern opinion, and spark an invasion of the South to end slavery. It was the beginning, they thought, of a second American Revolution that at long last would fulfill the promise of the first. Wendell Phillips proclaimed Harpers Ferry the latter-day Lexington, and poet Henry Wadsworth Longfellow declared that the death of John Brown would be marked as "the date of a new Revolution,—quite as needed as the old one." African Americans had long linked their struggle against slavery to the principles of the American Revolution, and Brown's raid reinforced their certainty that a war to extend liberty to blacks was fast approaching. The previous year, in the wake of the Supreme Court's *Dred Scott* decision, black Bostonians had held their first annual Crispus Attucks Day celebration, named after the black sailor and fugitive from slavery who became the first martyr of the American Revolution when he was killed in the Boston Massacre. The black abolitionist John Rock predicted, "The black man's service will be needed: 150,000 freemen capable of bearing arms, and not all cowards and fools, and three quarters of a million slaves, wild with the enthusiasm caused by the dawn of the glorious opportunity of being able to strike a genuine blow for freedom will be a power which white men will be 'bound to respect.'" African Americans were barred from nineteenth-century state militias, but beginning in the 1840s and accelerating in the 1850s after the passage of the Fugitive Slave Law, northern blacks formed their own informal militias to drill and train for the anticipated confrontation. Units in Ohio and New York named themselves after Crispus Attucks.[101]

The Charles Nalle Rescue

After Brown's death Tubman redoubled her efforts and was even more convinced that a war against slavery was imminent. In April 1860 she was involved in a slave rescue in New York State that demonstrated the growing conflict between abolitionists and slaveholders. She was staying with a cousin in Troy, on her way to an antislavery meeting in Boston, when authorities apprehended a fugitive named Charles Nalle (Document 14). Nalle, a light-skinned man in his late twenties who had escaped from slavery in Culpepper, Virginia, had been in New York State for about a year and was working as a coachman. He wanted to reunite his family and asked a local lawyer to write a letter for him, but the man betrayed him and informed his owner. A U.S. deputy marshal arrested Nalle about noon on April 27 at a local bakery and took him to be examined in the federal commissioner's second-story office.[102]

By 2:00 p.m. the hearing was over, and the commissioner had the papers drawn up to send Nalle back to slavery. The small group of mainly blacks who had gathered on the street in front of the building saw Nalle back up to the second-floor window with his hands chained behind his back, raise the window, and attempt to throw himself out. His jailors seized him, however, and drew him back into the building. While the abolitionist lawyer Martin Townsend went to obtain a writ of habeas corpus, Tubman, in her guise as a decrepit old woman, worked her way up the congested stairway to the commissioner's office. Meanwhile, a fire bell alerted the rest of the town, and soon the assembly grew to nearly one thousand. Townsend returned, and the deputy sheriff served the writ declaring that Nalle must appear before the judge.

As Nalle descended the stairs, Tubman, no longer seeming frail, took command. She yelled out the window to tell the crowd he was coming, rushed down the stairs, seized the prisoner's shackled wrists, and clung to him even as policemen beat her with clubs. Others in the crowd formed a line behind the prisoner and pushed him along, while the rest surrounded the contending forces. Running at full tilt, the rescuers finally wrested Nalle from the officials. With Tubman hanging on and shouting orders, they rushed Nalle to the river and put him in a rowboat. Fearing that he faced arrest on the other side, four hundred people crowded onto the steam ferry to follow his boat across the river.

Police, alerted by telegraph, arrested Nalle almost as soon as he disembarked, whereupon three officers, the postmaster, and a few other men barricaded themselves and the prisoner in the second-story chambers of Judge Steward, close to the ferry landing. The crowd, armed with stones and clubs, stormed the office but were momentarily repelled when the officers fired shots over their heads. On their third assault an enormous black man named Martin broke into the office and was knocked unconscious by a blow to the head from the butt of a hatchet head. His body landed in the doorway, preventing the defenders from closing the door. Tubman and several black women climbed over Martin, seized Nalle, and rushed him down the stairs, as bullets whistled over their heads.

On the street the rescuers commandeered a farmer's horse and wagon, but it quickly broke down. The party continued a short distance on foot until two black men with fast horses overtook them and carried Nalle away. Tubman, cut, bruised, and once more appearing to be a harmless old woman, melted back into the safety of the black community. Nalle was hidden in the countryside, but to throw off his pursuers, newspapers—including *Douglass' Monthly*—reported his safe arrival in St. Catharines, Canada. Local antislavery supporters soon raised $1,000 to purchase Nalle's freedom, and he returned triumphantly to Troy.

Facing intensified abolitionist activities and what seemed to be an upsurge in escape attempts, southern slaveholders again tried to limit the number of free blacks within their borders. On June 8, 1860, for example, the Southern Rights Convention in Baltimore adopted a resolution urging the Maryland legislature to pass a law driving free blacks out of the state. Such action raised African Americans' fears of revived calls to enslave free blacks and to sell farther south any enslaved people suspected of Underground Railroad connections. Ironically, such fears only increased the determination of many enslaved people to escape to freedom.[103]

Finally arriving in Boston for the antislavery meeting, Tubman also attended and spoke at a women's rights meeting. The theme of the large assembly at Melodeon Hall was "Education, Vocation, and Civil Position." The first speaker, a white woman named Caroline Dall, lamented the devaluation of kitchen work by many women in the movement, but the other speakers' main themes were that women were capable, as the Reverend Samuel J. May asserted, of doing anything that men could, and they should be given equal political rights. Tubman, introduced as Moses, delighted the gathering with her charisma and tales of daring. As William Lloyd Garrison reported from the meeting, Tubman, "herself a fugitive, [who] has eight times returned to the slave states for the purpose of rescuing others from bondage, and who has met with extraordinary success . . . told the story of her adventures in a modest but quaint and amusing style, which won much applause." Like Sojourner Truth, who declared the power of her womanhood at many antislavery and women's rights meetings, Tubman embodied the capabilities the movement asserted for women. Both reminded northern women of the oppression black women suffered in slavery and of their power to endure and overcome.[104]

THE DIVISIVE POLITICS OF 1860 AND A PERILOUS RESCUE

The issue of slavery occupied a primary place in contentious political debates during the summer of 1860. Senator William H. Seward, Harriet Tubman's patron, was the leading candidate for the presidential nomination by the Republican party, which he had helped organize. In the end the Chicago nominating convention chose the moderate lawyer and party organizer from Illinois, Abraham Lincoln, to be its standard-bearer, instead of the outspoken abolitionist Seward. Lincoln's position on slavery did not encourage African Americans and other radical abolitionists, but many supported him as the best feasible candidate. He was opposed to slavery's spread, he declared, but willing to maintain and protect slavery where it existed. With the country badly split over the issue, the Democrats fractured into a northern party and a strongly proslavery southern party. Men dedicated to preserving the Union and without an explicit stand on slavery except for observing the law, formed the Constitutional Union party. Consequently, four different parties vied for the presidency, and this split allowed Lincoln to win the election with less than 40 percent of the popular vote.[105]

Late that fall, in the tumultuous aftermath of Lincoln's election, Tubman made another journey to Maryland. She was determined to rescue her sister Rachel and Rachel's two children, the last members of her family still owned by the Brodesses. When she reached their neighborhood on the Eastern Shore, she was heartbroken to discover that her sister had died a short time before. Time and again Rachel had refused to leave without her children, and now Tubman was forced to devise an escape plan for Angerine and Ben without their mother. She arranged to meet them in the woods and waited in a heavy blizzard for them to arrive, but they never came. Whether this was because of the storm, the watchfulness of their owner, or frequent slave patrols, she did not know.[106]

Tubman was unable to rescue her niece and nephew, but she did guide Stephen Ennals; his wife, Maria; their three children, including a small baby; and a man named John to freedom. Taking such a group out of slavery posed many hazards, especially with greater surveillance of the roads and more active slave hunters. Tubman frequently hid the fugitives in swamps or the woods while she foraged for food. Along the way the group approached a black friend's house Tubman had used before as an Underground Railroad station. She rapped on the door using a special signal, expecting the door to be opened quickly and the group ushered in. When there was no response, she continued knocking until a brusque white man flung open a window on the upper floor. When Tubman asked after the home's former resident, the man informed her that he had been caught sheltering runaways and no longer lived there.[107]

Dawn was breaking, and with the man in the house alerted, the fugitives huddled in the pouring rain in the middle of the street were in great danger. Acting quickly, Tubman remembered a nearby swamp and led the group through the chilly water to an island where they could hide. She had them lie in the tall grass and settled down with them to pray for aid. They spent the entire day there without food or shelter until finally at dusk they saw a stranger, a Quaker, walking along the edge of the swamp. He seemed to be talking to himself about a wagon in the barnyard and a horse in the stable at the next farm. Tubman went to the farm and found a horse and a well-supplied wagon to carry them to the next town. This was the help she had been sure would come in answer to her prayers.

The group continued stealthily on their way, stopping often to hide from slave catchers. When Tubman left them to forage for food, she alerted them upon her return with prearranged signals in whistles or songs. Following her usual practice, she warned them of danger with one verse of "Go Down Moses":

> Moses go down in Egypt,
> Till ole Pharo' let me go;
> Hadn't been for Adam's fall,
> Shouldn't hab to died at all.[108]

To signal her charges that it was safe to show themselves, Tubman might sing through the many verses of "Go Down Moses," ending with,

> You may hinder me here, but you can't up dere,
> Let my people go,
> He sits in de Hebben and answers prayer,
> Let my people go!
> Oh go down, Moses,
> Way down into Egypt's land,
> Tell old Pharaoh,
> Let my people go.[109]

Another of Tubman's favorite songs to signal her charges whether it was safe expressed the promise of a life in freedom. Such slave songs, later known as Negro spirituals, were especially appropriate for Tubman's purposes. They expressed the slaves' longing for freedom, but in a coded way that made them sound simply like religious songs, unthreatening to the slaveowners. The Christianity of the slaves tended to emphasize the Old Testament, particularly the story of Moses leading the Israelites out of bondage. Identifying with the enslaved Israelites, African Americans placed their hope and faith in God's promise of freedom and in Tubman, the "Moses" who led them. She would sing with the passion and style of the slave quarters:

> Hail, oh hail, ye happy spirits,
> Death no more shall make you fear,
> Grief nor sorrow, pain nor anguish,
> Shall no more distress you dere.
> . . .
> Dark and thorny is de pathway,
> Where de pilgrim makes his ways;
> But beyond dis vale of sorrow;
> Lie de fields of endless days.[110]

On November 30 Tubman finally arrived at Thomas Garrett's door in Wilmington, Delaware. She had left the two men in a town about five miles down the river and the rest of the party, including a pregnant woman who had joined them in Baltimore, in hiding some thirty miles farther south. Garrett gave Tubman $10 to pay a man with a carriage to take them into Pennsylvania, where they made their way to William Still's antislavery society office. Still provided them with food, clothing, and money and warned them that travel had grown especially difficult, even in the North, during the year since John Brown's raid. Antiabolitionist feelings were running high in the country, and Still had hidden his journal in a cemetery building for fear of discovery, thereafter recording only brief information on scraps of paper. Despite the increased danger, people continued to stream out of Maryland and Virginia and through his office on their way to Canada.[111]

Tubman's friends farther north also faced intensified anti-abolitionist anger. Many Americans were increasingly fearful that tensions over the slavery issue would erupt into open warfare, and antislavery meetings became targets of their attacks. Nevertheless, Boston abolitionists defiantly commemorated the first anniversary of Brown's death. A distinguished committee of white and black abolitionists called a meeting at Tremont Temple for December 3, 1860, the day following the anniversary, to discuss the question "How Can Slavery Be Abolished?" and "to continue [Brown's] life by striving to accomplish what he left us to finish." When the meeting began, a group of well-heeled Constitutional Union party men and their rowdy followers invaded the hall and elected their own representative to the chair. Franklin Sanborn and the black minister John Sella Martin tried unsuccessfully to reestablish control of the boisterous meeting. Eventually, Frederick Douglass shouldered his way to the platform and was recognized by the chair. Ignoring the warning that he should be brief, as well as the chair's frequent interruptions to call "time," Douglass spoke louder and louder as he tried to drown out the threats and insults of the raucous Unionist crowd. A volley of insults resulted in a general melee on and near the stage, during which Douglass reportedly fought like "a trained pugilist." After more than an hour of argument, confrontation, and periodic fisticuffs, the police roughly cleared the abolitionists from the hall. The mob continued to threaten them outside, and forty volunteers provided a protective escort for Wendell Phillips on his way home.[112]

Antislavery forces reconvened that evening at the African Meeting House on Joy Street. Police held a mob at bay outside the church while speeches memorializing Brown by Martin, Phillips, Douglass, and John Brown Jr. proceeded inside without interruption. That evening Douglass spoke with full-throated belligerence. He advocated reaching "the slaveholder's conscience through his fear of personal danger. We must make him feel," he roared, "that there is death in the air around him, that there is death in the pot before him, that there is death all around him. . . . The only way to make the Fugitive Slave Law a dead letter," he continued, "is to make a few dead slave catchers." He called on his listeners to engage in "all methods of proceeding against slavery," including "war."[113]

The country had been in turmoil since the election, and serious federal efforts were under way to placate the South before Lincoln took office in early March 1861. To the great consternation of radical abolitionists, William Seward sought to keep the Union together, proving perhaps his qualifications for secretary of state, the position he would hold in Lincoln's administration. The futility of such efforts was forecast on December 20, 1860, when South Carolina declared its withdrawal from the United States. While white politicians labored to maintain the Union, many African Americans saw great hope in South Carolina's action, believing it would begin the war to end slavery that Tubman had foreseen. The black abolitionist and former Virginia slave H. Ford Douglas expressed their conviction that there could be "no union between freedom and slavery."[114]

Meanwhile, Tubman struggled to get her group of freedom seekers from Maryland to safety. By Christmas they had reached the relative security of Auburn. Tubman stayed for a week or more with Gerrit Smith while she recovered from the arduous journey, but by early

February 1861 the increased danger to runaways became clear. Emboldened slaveholders and their agents moved into New York State, and the rumor was that they had set their sights on Auburn. Smith feared that Seward had had a change of heart and might sacrifice his abolitionist principles for the preservation of the Union. If so, Tubman's connection with him might not save her, and thus Smith, Tubman, and the others quickly made their way to Canada. Tubman asked her white abolitionist friends to look after the family members she left behind in Auburn.[115]

FIGHTING THE WAR TO END SLAVERY

By February 1861 Tubman learned that six other states—Mississippi, Florida, Alabama, Georgia, Louisiana, and Texas—had joined South Carolina to form the Confederate States of America. Immediately after Lincoln's inauguration Confederates threatened federal forts in the Charleston, South Carolina, harbor, and on April 12 they began the Civil War by firing on Fort Sumter as the government tried to resupply it. Just three days later President Lincoln called for 75,000 short-term volunteers to fight the insurrection. Long anticipating a war to end slavery, African American men celebrated and immediately volunteered. Frederick Douglass declared that slaveholders, by waging war on the federal government, had "exposed the throat of slavery to the keen knife of liberty, and [had] given a chance to all the righteous forces of the nation to deal a death-blow to the monster evil." Individuals and black militia units sent letters and petitions to the War Department, but anticipating a short war and not wanting to alienate slaveholding border states, the federal government refused to let blacks become soldiers. Later that spring Virginia, Arkansas, Tennessee, and North Carolina joined the Confederacy.[116]

In October 1861 Tubman, again in Boston, discussed with her abolitionist friends the progress of the war, the situation in the South, and the prospects for freeing the slaves. Knowing she was eager to be involved in the struggle, George and Mary Stearns and Ednah Dow Cheney took her to meet the new abolitionist governor of Massachusetts, John A. Andrew. A lawyer and former Massachusetts state representative, Andrew had been a delegate to the Republican National Convention in 1860 and had become governor in early 1861. He was also a friend of Lewis Hayden and was familiar with Tubman's Underground Railroad exploits. Tubman and Andrew discussed her potential contributions to the war effort, particularly how her talent and experience would equip her to act as a scout and spy. In wartime women generally were hired as nurses, cooks, laundresses, or drawing-room spies, but Tubman's unique capabilities and departure from traditional women's roles fit her for life on the field of battle.[117]

The perfect opportunity presented itself in December when U.S. troops occupied the Sea Islands of South Carolina, Georgia, and Florida. The planters fled, leaving ten thousand former slaves in severe poverty but eager for education and their new life in freedom. The Army requested aid from northern abolitionists, who were quick to answer the call. In Boston they organized the New England Freedmen's Aid Society to raise funds, distribute charity, and recruit and train teachers. In March 1862 they sent the first group to Beaufort, on Port Royal Island, for what became known as the Port Royal Experiment, a concerted effort to prepare former slaves for independence.[118]

Probably sometime late that winter, Tubman made one last surreptitious trip to Maryland and brought out a young girl named Margaret, a child probably born around the time of Tubman's own escape to freedom. Family stories conceal more than they disclose. Margaret was said to be the daughter of Tubman's free black brother, but she had no brother who was legally free. Years later, Margaret's daughter maintained that Tubman kidnapped Margaret from her family, which she said included Margaret's twin brother. The difficulty of conceiving of Tubman kidnapping a child, since she spent so much of her life reuniting her family at such great personal risk, has led recent biographers to wonder whether Margaret may actually have been her own child. Indeed, if Margaret had been living with Tubman's ex-husband's free brother in Baltimore, it could explain the story of her being with Tubman's free brother (actually her brother-in-law).[119]

The available historical evidence leaves the question of Margaret's mother unanswered, but much of the evidence seems to point to Tubman. Whatever her parentage, she and Tubman had a very close relationship for the rest of Tubman's life. Tubman made very special arrangements for Margaret Stewart, also called Margaret Tubman, and identified the girl as her niece. In Auburn Margaret did not live in the crowded family household. Instead Tubman placed her in the care of William Seward's wife, Frances, and her widowed sister, Lazette Worden, who lived with the Sewards much of the time. Margaret was not treated as a servant in this wealthy household, but as a member of the family. Whenever Tubman was in town, they took Margaret to visit her. As Margaret's daughter Alice later recalled the story, in the Seward home Margaret learned "to speak properly, to read, write, sew, do housework and act as a lady." Growing up with the Sewards gave Margaret the promise of a much better life than she would have had growing up in Tubman's poverty-stricken home.[120]

During the first year of the war, the federal government attempted to reunite the country without attacking slavery. Hundreds of enslaved people, however, took matters into their own hands and sought government protection for their freedom by flocking to U.S. Army lines. Arguing that the Constitution protected property in slaves and mindful of the need to retain border state loyalty, President Lincoln instructed his officers to return fugitives. Some U.S. officers vehemently objected to returning slaves to their owners because it would effectively make the officers slave catchers. In May 1861 in Virginia, General Benjamin F. Butler devised a different tactic and declared three slaves who came into his lines "contraband of war" (items useful to the war effort—in this case human "property"—taken from the enemy), on the understanding that giving them refuge deprived the rebels of their labor. Three days after this declaration, $60,000 worth of "contraband" people had seized the opportunity for freedom with Butler's army. Finally, in early August 1861, Congress passed the First Confiscation Act, which stated that only those slaves used by the Confederate military would not be returned. Even that halfway measure was unevenly enforced, and many commanders continued to return enslaved people who ran to U.S.-controlled territory. When General John C. Frémont declared martial law in Missouri in late August, he went beyond the law and proclaimed all slaves of rebels to be free, but Lincoln reprimanded him and modified the order. In July of the following year Congress came closer to Frémont's position, passing the Second Confiscation Act, which freed slaves held by traitors and supporters of the rebellion. Regardless of the president's hesitancy to attack slavery, Tubman was confident that the war would end the institution. In December 1861 the white Massachusetts abolitionist and author Lydia Maria Child related her conversation with Tubman, "[t]hat remarkable fugitive slave, whom we call 'Moses,' by reason of the multitude she has brought out of bondage." "Nebber mind!" Tubman had declared. "God's ahead of massa Linkum. God'll make massa Linkum do de right ting; fur he nebber will let him *beat* till he do de right ting."[121]

Tubman as Civil War Spy

Harriet Tubman was prepared to do her part. In May 1862, when she was forty years old, Governor Andrew arranged for the Army to send her to work as a spy and military scout behind enemy lines. He instructed her to go to New York City to meet a military officer, who would accompany her south. Since African Americans were working for the Army only as laborers, cooks, and servants, she was to travel as the officer's servant. This was especially dangerous for her, a fugitive who could be betrayed and reenslaved at any time. She met her prospective escort in the parlor of his Broadway hotel, but his arrogant, condescending manner put her off immediately. He ordered her to go to the quartermaster and arrange their transportation, but not trusting him she decided not to comply. She set out for Beaufort, South Carolina, on her own.[122]

Tubman felt more confident traveling alone. Trusting her instincts and God's guidance had kept her free for many years. Along the way, she managed to get word to General David Hunter, who arranged her transportation on a ship from Baltimore to Beaufort. Federal forces had established their headquarters in the riverside resort town, using the planters' deserted summer homes as officers' residences, offices, and hospitals. They also created nearby contraband camps, where escaped slaves were housed in barracks, hired for support work, and protected from their former owners. Hunter, whose strong antislavery views were prized by northern abolitionists working with the freedmen at Port Royal, had taken over command of the Department of the South from General T. W. Sherman a few months before. By year's end soldiers and aid workers housed, fed, hired, supervised, and educated about ten thousand freedmen in contraband camps and on plantations on the Sea Islands.[123]

Hunter, a career officer from New Jersey, had lived in Illinois, was an acquaintance of President Lincoln, and had served under Frémont in the West in 1861. Following Frémont's example, he declared Georgia, South Carolina, and Florida under martial law and ordered the slaves freed. Lincoln rescinded this order as he had Frémont's, but the logic of the war was running against him. Mounting U.S. casualties argued for seizing any military advantage, including offering freedom to enslaved people and depriving the Confederates of their labor. Casualties in early April 1862 at Shiloh, Tennessee, had greatly increased the numbers of U.S. dead and wounded. The number of dead grew from about 1,400 in the first six months of fighting to more than 3,000 after Shiloh, and the number of wounded from just under 5,000 to more than 13,000.[124]

On his arrival in the Department of the South early in 1862, Hunter began recruiting former slaves to guard the captured Sea Island cotton plantations. Lincoln's disapproval made the recruits' status unclear, and they were unpaid. Unsurprisingly, Hunter had trouble recruiting African Americans at no pay, and so he drafted some, creating great resentment. His efforts were also impeded by rumors that he was conscripting blacks to sell in Cuba. Facing black anger and fear, as well as official opposition, Hunter eventually retained only one company of black trainees, for guard duty on St. Simons Island. That summer, however, with the war going badly and the government having greater difficulty enlisting white soldiers, Congress formally approved the recruitment of black troops.[125]

As the United States lost more battles and more men, Lincoln concluded that announcing freedom for people enslaved in areas under Confederate control would encourage them to flee the plantations and thereby serve the U.S. cause. Importantly, it would also garner support from Britain and France, where antislavery sentiment was strong, or at least prevent Britain from overtly aiding the cotton-producing South. More casualties that summer drove the point home, as stunning losses at major battles in Virginia raised the number of U.S. dead to more than 9,800 and the number of wounded to almost 44,000. In September Lincoln announced that on January 1, 1863, he intended to issue the Emancipation Proclamation, freeing all slaves still under rebel control. It would also reiterate the government's acceptance of African American troops.[126]

Black troops, however, were paid less than white troops. The government enlisted them through the Quartermaster's Department. Technically, they were laborers able to defend themselves, thus maintaining the fiction that blacks were used only in support of the white war effort. This tactic was designed to mollify the many northerners and border state residents who strongly objected to African American soldiers. It also meant they were paid as laborers, at roughly half what white soldiers received. The unequal pay, contrary to Secretary of War Edwin M. Stanton's previous promises, greatly angered blacks and persisted for more than two years. In late November the white Massachusetts radical abolitionist, adventurer, and friend of Tubman, Thomas Wentworth Higginson, took command of the First South Carolina Regiment, composed of former slaves that Tubman had helped recruit. Just a few weeks after his arrival, Tubman drove from Beaufort to the army camp to pay him a surprise visit.[127]

When she had arrived in coastal South Carolina that summer, she had found freedmen and soldiers in desperate need and set to work immediately at the most urgent tasks. Malarial swamps, contaminated food and water, and poor sanitation took their toll, filling military hospitals and afflicting contrabands. Tubman acted as a nurse, often using her own herbal remedies to treat the fevers, malaria, and smallpox that killed or made invalids of many soldiers during the war. Generations of African and African American lore came to her aid, and she became especially renowned for her ability to treat dysentery using plants that grew near the waters that had caused the illness. On one occasion the military sent her farther south to Fernandina, Florida, to help quell an outbreak of dysentery.[128]

Tubman knew that as a spy she must gain the trust of local blacks, people who spoke Gullah, a creole language so different from her own that at first she could barely understand them. In the beginning her special status with the military created difficulty. Her pass to travel by military transport caused no trouble, but some jealous freedmen resented her access to government rations. After about three weeks she gave up this privilege, bringing her status closer to that of the local people, but she then had to earn money to purchase food. With typical energy and determination, after finishing her nursing duties, Tubman worked making pies, gingerbread, and root beer in enormous quantities with supplies purchased from the military commissary. She hired freedmen to peddle this food while she worked in the hospital the following day. She also joined other women doing sewing and laundry for the troops and used her own money to build a washhouse where the freedwomen could earn money doing laundry.[129]

The Emancipation Proclamation

On December 31, 1862, after months of apprehension, abolitionists gathered in halls and churches throughout the North to await the president's proclamation. The traditional evangelical watch night celebration was imbued with new meaning, as people sang and prayed for the end of American slavery. Many of Harriet Tubman's antislavery and women's rights friends were among the three thousand who packed Tremont Temple in one of two great meetings in Boston. They listened to speeches, sang hymns, and waited for hours, their hope touched with the trepidation that Lincoln might not be true to his word. When a runner from the telegraph office finally brought news of the Emancipation Proclamation, the crowd burst into shouts and joyful tears, and Frederick Douglass struck up the hymn "Blow Ye the Trumpet, Blow," proclaiming the day of jubilee. When their rental of the hall expired, many of the jubilant abolitionists adjourned to the Twelfth Baptist Church, where they celebrated until dawn.[130]

Farther south, William Wells Brown found an emancipation eve gathering in a contraband camp especially poignant and deeply moving (Document 15). Brown had escaped from slavery in Kentucky when he was twenty years old, but his mother had been captured and sold into the Deep South, and he never heard from her again. Listening to the prayers, poems, and songs of the escaped slaves, Brown noted the singers' identification with the biblical Israelites in their repetition of the many verses of "Go Down Moses." A great many of these fugitives awaiting the federal government's confirmation of their freedom were from Virginia, a state still in rebellion. Just after midnight, the superintendent of the camp announced the proclamation, and the singers improvised a final verse appropriate for the occasion:

> Go down, Abraham, away down in Dixie's land,
> Tell Jeff. Davis to let my people go.[131]

Near Harriet Tubman's base of operations in Beaufort, a huge crowd assembled on New Year's Day at Camp Saxton to hear Lincoln's proclamation read. People came on foot and by horse, carriage, and steamboat to attend the formal celebration. After an opening prayer Dr. W. H. Brisbane, a local South Carolinian who had previously freed his slaves, read the proclamation. A chaplain then presented a flag donated by New Yorkers to the First South Carolina Regiment. The regiment's commander, Colonel Higginson, accepted and waved the flag, but before he could respond, an elderly black man near the platform began to sing "America" in a strong voice. He was joined by two women and then by all of the African Americans, who sang all the verses. The white abolitionists present were especially thrilled when the former slaves sang "sweet land of liberty . . . land where my fathers died . . . from every mountainside let freedom ring." Later Higginson remarked that it was "the first day they had ever had a country, the first flag they had ever seen which promised anything to their people." Speeches followed, including remarks by Higginson and Sergeant Prince Rivers and Corporal Robert Sutton, two African Americans from the regiment. After another musical selection the regiment closed the service with a rendition of "John Brown's Body."[132]

Since the Emancipation Proclamation applied only to areas under rebel control, where the federal government had no power, it freed no one directly. It remained for slaves in Confederate-controlled areas to free themselves. Nevertheless, the proclamation had great symbolic significance, placing the government squarely on the side of black freedom. As Tubman had urged, the war had become a war to end slavery. Attesting to the proclamation's symbolic significance, although it was not technically true, Tubman later remembered that day as the day the government granted her freedom.

Tubman as Military Scout

Tubman had helped recruit soldiers for the First South Carolina Regiment, and with the enlistment of black troops her wartime role expanded. As the head of a band of ten local scouts and river pilots, she was the only woman to lead men into combat during the war. With their knowledge of the terrain and their contacts among local blacks, her scouts could glean a great deal of useful information as they moved about the area. They were also familiar with local conditions and knew when rivers were likely to be navigable and when and where they became muddy marshes. Black soldiers from the area often had invaluable information about Confederate defenses, since during their days in slavery many had built those very defenses. Despite the danger and importance of Tubman's expeditions into the interior, she received only one payment of $200 in expense money from the secret service to support her work as a spy.[133]

Colonel James Montgomery arrived at Camp Saxton in late February 1863 to take charge of the Second South Carolina Regiment. In General Hunter, Tubman had a sponsor by way of Governor Andrew; in Colonel Higginson she had a radical antislavery ally; but in Montgomery she had a comrade in arms. Montgomery had been a friend and ally of John Brown in Kansas, where he commanded a unit of the renegade militia called the Jayhawkers, conducting raids into Missouri and fighting skirmishes with proslavery forces along the Kansas-Missouri border. Like Brown, whom Tubman revered, he was a militantly religious abolitionist. According to the disapproving Robert Gould Shaw, commander of the black Fifty-Fourth Massachusetts Regiment, Montgomery believed that "praying, shooting, hanging and burning [were] the true means to put down the Rebellion." Montgomery knew about Tubman through Brown and greatly respected her.[134]

Perhaps Tubman's best-known military action was a raid through the rice fields up the alligator-infested Combahee River, in which Confederate forces had placed explosives (Document 16). Slaveholders had moved their slaves from the area around Charleston as U.S. forces occupied the coast, and the troops could reach working plantations only after a long trip up the muddy, winding river. This operation clearly showed how much Tubman diverged from contemporary gender expectations and demonstrated that the generals, like Brown, trusted her experience and expertise and accepted her as an adviser and compatriot. She helped Generals Hunter and Montgomery plan the expedition, and she led a flotilla of three gunboats carrying Montgomery's Second South

Carolina Regiment and a contingent from the Third Rhode Island Battery. They set out on the tortuous twenty-five-mile trip on the night of June 1, 1863, with a full moon to light their way and pull the flood tide into the shallow waters, aiming to reach Confederate settlements just before dawn. Tubman and one of her men were in the lead boat to spot submerged torpedoes and clear the way for the other boats. As they traveled up the river, they destroyed bridges and railroad tracks to cut off Confederate supplies.[135]

The slaves were finishing their breakfast and heading to the rice fields for the day's work as Tubman, her men, and a company of soldiers disembarked at the first plantation. In the pale dawn they could see the boats but were unsure whose troops they carried. Montgomery ordered the boats to blow their whistles, and when the people realized they were U.S. boats, they began to stream to the shore. Ignoring the slave driver's threats and whip, people scooped up their belongings and ran for the protection of the U.S. Army. Hundreds of men and women with children on their shoulders and in their arms, with large bundles on their heads, bags of pigs on their backs, chickens tied by the feet in their hands, and carrying pots of steaming rice, came running from the fields and cabins.[136]

Higginson later interviewed an eighty-year-old man who escaped to freedom that day and recorded his description of the scene. The man said that everyone working in the fields when the gunboats arrived dropped their hoes and ran for the boats. The master hid in the woods, he related, and called, "'Run to de wood for hide! Yankee come, sell you to Cuba! Run for hide!' Ebry man he run, and, my God! Run all toder way!" This man was greatly impressed by the bearing of the black soldiers, who were "so presumptious, dey come right ashore, hold up dere head. Fus' ting I know, dere was a barn, ten tousand bushel rough rice, all in a blaze, den mas'r's great house, all cracklin' up de roof. Did n't I keer for see 'em blaze? Lor, Mas'r did n't care notin' at all, *I was gwine to de boat.*"[137]

The captain realized that the small boats carrying passengers to the gunboats were in danger of being swamped by the multitudes clinging to their sides and asked Tubman to reason with the desperately determined slaves. Doing so, he called her "Moses Garrison," the military pseudonym that combined her Underground Railroad code name and the alias, Harriet Garrison, by which she had addressed public antislavery meetings. At first Tubman was at a loss to know what to say to calm the people, but after a few minutes she improvised a song, lifting her voice to carry over the cacophony of people shouting and praying, children crying, pigs squealing, and chickens squawking.

Come from the East.
Come from the West.
'Mong all the glorious nations
This glorious one's the best.
Come along; come along;
Don't be alarmed,
For Uncle Sam is rich enough
To give you all a farm.

At the end of each verse the people on the shore threw up their hands rejoicing and shouting "Glory!" At that moment the rowboats could push off with their load of escapees.

U.S. gunboats carried from seven hundred to eight hundred people out of slavery that day. Montgomery's army also laid waste to the rice plantations, confiscating farm animals and crops and burning houses, barns, and other outbuildings. Tubman reported that her skirt had been torn to pieces while she hurriedly helped evacuate the slaves and concluded that her traditional women's clothing was unsuitable for military work. She wrote to Franklin Sanborn asking for a bloomer dress—ankle-length pants that fit under a knee-length skirt—to replace her long skirts. Popular with the most radical of her women's rights friends, the bloomer dress was much more practical for quick marches and crawling around behind enemy lines.[138]

Back in camp at Beaufort, Montgomery gave a celebratory address to the freed people, and they responded by lifting their voices in a rousing rendition of the hymn "There Is a White Robe for Thee." Tubman then spoke to them about their new freedom and the practicalities of camp life. Her work for them was not finished, however. As she had done with her charges on the Underground Railroad, after freedom she assumed responsibility for their continuing survival, soliciting aid from friends and authorities to make sure they had food, clothing, and medical care. She also tried to find employment for those who could work, hoping to help them achieve pride and dignity in earning their own living for the first time in their lives.[139]

Tubman's sense of responsibility to the freed people led her to testify in the court-martial of the superintendent of the contraband camp at Beaufort in early June 1863. She and fellow scout Walter Plowden had gone to General Rufus Saxton with their suspicions about Superintendent John E. Webster of the Forty-Seventh Pennsylvania Regiment, and their testimony helped convict him of profiting from the sale of food supplies intended for freed people. Tubman had bought sugar from Webster, and she and Plowden were among six black and four white witnesses in the case. At a time when black testimony against whites

Figure 5. *Harriet Tubman as Civil War Scout*

This woodcut by J. C. Darby of Auburn, New York, appeared in Sarah H. Bradford's *Scenes in the Life of Harriet Tubman* (1869).

was prohibited in the South and rare in the North, the acceptance of African American witnesses testified to the revolutionary change taking place in the U.S. forces and showed the Army's respect for Tubman and her men.[140]

All that Harriet Tubman did for the war effort and the freed people was essentially without remuneration. She supported herself through her own efforts and used the little money she received from the government for her intelligence activities. She was convinced that she was carrying out God's purpose for her, but she also felt responsible for her elderly parents in the North. Early in 1863 Tubman told Charlotte Forten, a young black woman from the prominent Philadelphia abolitionist family who was teaching at Port Royal, how worried she was about her parents. Tubman's friends had assured her they would look after them while she was away, and she sent them what money she could, but she was still deeply concerned.[141]

The Charleston Campaign

About six weeks after the Combahee River raid, Harriet Tubman was among the nurses and cooks who accompanied the troops forty miles up the coast, where they were organizing a campaign to capture Charleston. On July 16 three companies of the black Fifty-Fourth Massachusetts Regiment guarding marshy island crossings in Charleston harbor were overrun by much larger Confederate forces. The fierce fighting that ensued starkly confirmed Confederate policies toward black troops and their white commanders. Violating generally accepted rules of warfare, the Confederates killed blacks rather than let them surrender, insisting that they should be treated as escaped slaves rather than soldiers. U.S. troops later learned that the few who had been taken prisoner were then killed by bayonet or bound and shot. In that engagement the black troops managed to hold off the Confederate attack long enough for reinforcements to arrive, and the rebels were driven back.[142]

Fort Wagner, a log and sand fort at the mouth of the harbor, was crucial to the Charleston campaign. After a difficult night march, a ferry ride across a channel, another day of marching, and a second ferry ride, the Fifty-Fourth reached the area just a few hours before the evening assault on July 18. Tubman served the officers and men their supper before the battle. The regiment contained many men she knew from Boston, New York, and Pennsylvania, including two of Frederick Douglass's sons and their commander, the young white Boston abolitionist Robert Gould Shaw. Colonel Shaw was eager to prove that his black troops were brave fighters and volunteered to lead the three brigades in the attack. Under heavy shelling, the men of the Fifty-Fourth charged three-quarters of a mile up the cratered sandy beach. A hundred yards from the battery they broke into a run as the defenders of the fort began to fire. Many men fell, but others made it to the walls and into close combat with the Confederates. Colonel Shaw was killed as he led his men up the parapet. Six other regiments followed the Fifty-Fourth in the attack, but all were eventually driven back. Finally, another brigade threw themselves into the fight, but to no avail. After three hours of fierce combat General Quincy Gillmore ordered an almost equally dangerous retreat.[143]

The Fifty-Fourth Massachusetts Regiment suffered heavy losses at Fort Wagner. Of the regiment's 600 men, 116 were killed, including their commander, with another 156 wounded or missing. The total casualties suffered by northern units were 1,515, of whom 246 were killed, while the Confederates suffered 174 casualties, with 36 killed. For his bravery carrying the colors in battle, Sergeant William H. Carney became the first African American awarded the Medal of Honor. The Confederates buried Colonel Shaw in a mass grave along with his fallen men, an action intended as an insult but instead carried as a badge of honor by Shaw's family and abolitionist friends.[144]

Harriet Tubman was about a mile away, caring for the sick and wounded, and could hear the roar of guns as they battered the attacking soldiers. With great eloquence she later described the sound of the battle and its aftermath:

> And then we saw the lightning,
> and that was the guns;
> and then we heard the thunder,
> and that was the big guns;
> and then we heard the rain falling,
> and that was the drops of blood falling;
> and when we came to get in the crops,
> it was the dead that we reaped.[145]

After the slaughter Tubman helped bury the dead. During the next six weeks, casualties from the fighting around Charleston overwhelmed field medical facilities and the hospital in Beaufort. The Army enlisted teachers, nurses, officers' wives, and other women on the islands to help care for the wounded. Tubman worked long, exhausting days at the hospital, somehow continuing while many others were incapacitated by the heat and disease. In the late fall she took a leave and traveled north, spending a few weeks with her growing family in Auburn and going on to Canada to see her brother's family and check on the freed people there. She returned to the Charleston area after this short respite and probably accompanied black troops on forays to Florida. Medical resources were overtaxed again by the Battle of Olustee, Florida, in February 1864. The newly arrived, inexperienced, and poorly equipped Eighth U.S. Colored Troops from Pennsylvania bore the brunt of that battle, unexpectedly facing heavy fire, losing their commander, and suffering casualties amounting to more than half of the men before reinforcements arrived. Even with a great many additional troops, U.S. forces were forced to withdraw under heavy fire, leaving hundreds of dead and wounded comrades on the battlefield.[146]

Finally, in late May or June, with the reluctant consent of the military command, Tubman again took leave and headed north. In New York City she sought out Wendell Garrison to tell him that she had seen his brother George, an officer in the Fifty-Fifth Massachusetts Regiment, in Beaufort and that he was well. In Auburn she was relieved to find that local churches and abolitionists had been watching over her family. Her parents were nearly eighty years old and had been living on the townspeople's charity, what other family members could contribute, and the little she could send. She became ill while on furlough and remained home for about nine months, during which time she could contribute little to the household.[147]

Unequal Pay

Tubman's was not the only black family suffering from poverty while breadwinners served in the war. Despite earlier assurances, African American soldiers were still paid only half what white soldiers received. Black soldiers had written to President Lincoln asking the government to fulfill its promise, and Tubman followed the pay controversy avidly. The Fifty-Fourth Massachusetts Regiment had left Boston in the spring of 1863 amid great fanfare, fully committed to freedom. Still proud a year later, soldiers in the Fifty-Fourth had refused to accept any pay rather than receive the lesser amount. Others also protested, and the military executed Sergeant William Walker of the Twenty-First U.S. Colored Troops on March 1, 1864, for leading his company in a refusal to report to duty. Massachusetts governor John A. Andrew observed the bitter irony: "The Government which found no law to *pay* him except as a *nondescript or a contraband*, nevertheless found law enough to *shoot* him as a *soldier*."[148]

Like Tubman, black soldiers worried about their families at home. Local authorities refused to give assistance to a great many black households, and soldiers' families had to rely on the generosity of poor communities and what mothers, wives, and children could earn. Governor Andrew and other abolitionists provided some aid to the families, and Andrew engaged Mary Livermore, an abolitionist, journalist, and volunteer worker in Chicago for the U.S. Sanitary Commission, a private wartime charity, to help families of the Fifty-Fourth. One family Livermore helped had been enslaved in Beaufort when the war began. The soldier's wife and her sick child had been put out of her house in the cold Chicago rain because she owed $5 in rent. The child died of scarlet fever, and Livermore helped pay for the baby's burial.[149]

Finally, in mid-June 1864, Congress equalized the pay for African American soldiers who had been free on April 19, 1861, when the war began, retroactive to the time of their enlistment in 1862 or 1863. However, the men the war had freed continued to receive lower pay. Thomas Wentworth Higginson, whose First South Carolina Regiment was composed of freed slaves, forcefully decried the injustice in a letter to the editor of the *New York Tribune*. Echoing the Supreme Court's infamous *Dred Scott* decision, he charged the government with not respecting its contract with these soldiers. Thus, Higginson observed, apparently "a freedman . . . has no rights which a white man is bound to respect. . . . He is virtually a slave, and nothing else, to the end of time." The commander of the Fifty-Fourth Massachusetts Regiment skirted the injustice by having his men declare an oath saying they had owed no man any unpaid labor before April 19, 1861. Congress did not remove the inequity until the fall of 1865, after the end of the war.[150]

The unequal pay outraged Tubman. She visited Elizabeth Keckley, an organizer of freedmen's aid in the nation's capital, at the White House on wartime trips through Washington, and she sometimes saw First Lady Mary Todd Lincoln, for whom Keckley worked as a personal servant and seamstress. Sojourner Truth also visited, and Keckley arranged a meeting for her with President Lincoln, whom Truth greatly admired for his role in emancipation and for whom she campaigned in 1864. Tubman, however, angry that he had not stood firmly for black soldiers' rights, refused on principle to meet him.[151]

The pay equalization for black soldiers who were free before the war spurred Tubman to new efforts on her own behalf, but her position was anomalous. She had entered active duty as a spy in the South before the government put black troops into the field. She had accepted government transport some of the time, but probably not in her initial deployment. She had refused government rations in compensation for her scouting, instead earning money for her own support, and had worked as a volunteer nurse without pay. She also had overstayed her leave in the North when she became ill and refused government transport back to South Carolina. Perhaps most important, although she had recruited and led black troops, she was a woman.

Tubman believed that she was entitled to compensation for her war-time service. Not only did she deserve payment for scouting and nursing, but she also thought the government owed her a bounty for the many slaves she had recruited for the Army. She began to solicit testimonials from such prominent friends as Gerrit Smith to support her claims and, in the meantime, again tapped the antislavery network for money to support her and her family. Her Boston friends did what they could. She stayed with John Rock in Boston that summer, and Franklin Sanborn printed an appeal for funds for her in his *Commonwealth* magazine (Document 17).[152]

Ending Slavery and the War

Tubman was still in the North when a constitutional amendment abolishing slavery in the entire United States passed the Senate in April 1864. Even without representatives from seceded states, however, it failed to pass the House. President Lincoln warned Frederick Douglass that if he lost the November election, his Democratic opponent, George B. McClellan, likely would negotiate a peace with the Confederacy that would perpetuate slavery. Lincoln insisted that his party platform include support for the proposed amendment, and his victory gave new life to the issue. The House of Representatives passed the Thirteenth Amendment on January 31, 1865. Joyous celebrations throughout the North hailed slavery's abolition. Assuming ratification, a U.S. victory would mean no more African American enslavement, forced separation of families, or desperate fugitives. The great national sin of slavery would be expunged—but first the Confederacy had to be defeated.

Under the pressures of the war, even Confederate leaders reconsidered their unyielding commitment to slavery. In fact, as early as December 1863 they had contentious discussions about enlisting slaves in their army in exchange for a freedom resembling serfdom or peonage. Under this proposal former slaves would have certain rights—including the right to marry, learn to read, attend church, and own property—but would have no political rights and would work for subsistence, with working conditions controlled by white landowners. After losing Atlanta to General William Tecumseh Sherman's forces in the fall of 1864, the Confederacy had high desertion rates and was running out of white men to enlist. In desperation, in early March 1865 the Confederate Congress authorized the recruitment of 300,000 slaves. The Confederates recruited very few black soldiers, however, and none received even the qualified freedom they were promised. According to historian Bruce Levine, no black Confederate troops ever saw action. "A small company or two of black hospital workers was attached to a unit of home-guard irregulars. The regular army managed to raise another forty to sixty men who were drilled, fed, and housed at military prison facilities in Richmond."[153]

Abraham Lincoln had a plan to counter the albeit unlikely threat of the Confederacy's enlisting thousands of blacks in the war. In December 1863, nearly a year after the Emancipation Proclamation, black leader Martin R. Delany had written to Secretary of War Edwin Stanton asking to be sent behind enemy lines in the South to recruit enslaved blacks for the U.S. Army. Tubman, Montgomery, and others were already recruiting, but Delany believed that together he and Tubman could mount a more concerted effort. Delany was an impressive man with wide-ranging experience. He had been born in Charles Town, Virginia, in 1812 and had worked as a barber, a physician's assistant, and a newspaper editor in Pittsburgh. He was active in the Underground Railroad, traveled to Louisiana and Texas, and wrote a fictionalized account of African culture and slavery in the South. White students' objections forced his expulsion from Harvard Medical School in 1850. In 1856 he moved his family to Canada, where he convened the 1858 Chatham meeting with John Brown. In late February 1865 Lincoln agreed to send Delany to the South, and Stanton commissioned him a major, the first black field officer in the U.S. Army. Tubman was in Washington, D.C., that March, and Major Delany asked her to accompany him on this mission. She agreed to meet him in South Carolina, but it must have been a bittersweet assignment for her. Delany, after all, was given a military commission to undertake the work that she, a woman, had been doing for the Army in the South with no rank and no pay.[154]

Tubman had long seen her mission as following God's guidance in the fight against slavery and must have been thrilled on March 4 when President Lincoln's second inaugural address put him squarely on the side of God's justice for the enslaved. Lincoln saw God's purpose in the costly war, with his terrible justice visited on both North and South. God's righteousness may require, Lincoln declared, that "all the wealth piled by the bond-man's two hundred and fifty years of unrequited toil shall be sunk, and . . . every drop of blood drawn with the lash, shall be paid by another drawn with the sword."[155]

Even with the prospect of a new assignment, Tubman's financial situation was unchanged, and friends continued to help with her support. Ednah Dow Cheney included another appeal for her in a biography published in the *Freedmen's Record* in March 1865 (Document 18), and the New England Freedmen's Aid Society hired the illiterate Tubman at $10 a month to assist freed people in the South with their "practical education." On April 1 she addressed new black recruits at Camp William Penn near Philadelphia, telling them about her war experience. The African American *Christian Recorder* reported that Tubman's well-received talk was "a very entertaining homespun lecture . . . interspersed with several gems of music" and was followed by "a liberal collection for the lecturer."[156]

Two days after Tubman's speech Lee's army evacuated Petersburg, Virginia, the crucial supply hub for the Confederate capital, Richmond, twenty miles to the north. This U.S. victory was the culmination of a ten-month siege of Petersburg and a costly battle. The following day the military at Camp William Penn received word that Richmond had fallen. The war's end seemed imminent, the major battles of the war in the East had moved from the Carolinas to Virginia, and friends in Philadelphia convinced Tubman that the greatest need for her services was at the hospitals along the James River in Virginia, where conditions were very poor.

Thus Tubman was in Virginia when General Robert E. Lee's surrender of his Confederate Army of Northern Virginia on Sunday, April 9, 1865, heralded the war's end. Thousands of singing and shouting blacks left their homes and the unlocked slave pens and crowded the streets in joyous demonstrations to greet President Lincoln and the victorious U.S. Army. Among the African American troops in the vanguard of the liberators was Garland H. White, whose story epitomized the success of the Underground Railroad. White, born in Virginia and sold away from his family as a child, had escaped from slavery in Washington, D.C., where he was Georgia senator Robert Toombs's body servant. During the war he returned from his new home in Canada, recruited black troops, and became chaplain of a black Indiana regiment. An elderly woman approached White after he addressed the jubilant crowd in Richmond. She identified herself as his mother and was elated to see him, saying that she had "spent twenty years of grief about her son."[157]

The federal government organized a great celebration for the following Friday at Fort Sumter, where the war began, on the fourth anniversary of the fort's surrender. Military men and prominent northern abolitionists, including Martin Delany and William Lloyd Garrison, gathered to mark the occasion, raising the same flag that had been struck in 1861. The celebration was cut short that evening when word arrived that John Wilkes Booth had shot the president and another conspirator had stabbed Secretary of State William H. Seward. When Lincoln died the next morning, African Americans faced a more uncertain future. Elizabeth Keckley expressed the emotional turmoil of the time: "A nation suddenly paused in the midst of festivity, and stood paralyzed with horror—transfixed with awe."[158]

Tubman left her work at the Fortress Monroe hospital for black soldiers in Virginia in mid-July to visit Seward in Washington and began an excruciatingly long bid for a veteran's pension. Seward was still recovering from his injuries, and his wife had died just three weeks before. Nevertheless, he supported Tubman's claim for back pay and wrote a glowing assessment of her character: "I have known her long as a noble high spirit, as true as seldom dwells in the human form" (Document 26).

TUBMAN'S POSTWAR LIFE

Harriet Tubman's journey home in 1865 did not bode well for her life as a Civil War veteran. She left Virginia that October and stopped to visit friends near Philadelphia. Now that slavery had been abolished, their conversation, like discussions all over the country, centered on the prospects for black rights. Would the former slaves' freedom bring them citizenship and voting rights? What were their prospects, and those of formerly free blacks, for economic progress, or even survival? Would the federal government stand behind them, and what were the loyalties of the new president, Andrew Johnson? Were antislavery societies still needed, or had their work been accomplished? There were great hopes and fears in black communities.

Black troops were war heroes in the North, but antiblack sentiment was still high, exacerbated by white fears that newly freed blacks would stream north and compete for jobs. Tubman was traveling on government orders entitling her to half-price transportation when she boarded the train from Philadelphia to New York. The train conductor took exception to the presence of a "colored" woman and ordered her to the smoking car. Strong, defiant, and fearless, she refused to obey him and insisted proudly that he refer to her by the then more radical terms "black" or "Negro." The conductor twisted her finger and her arm trying to remove her from the car but was unable to do so. He then enlisted two other men, and as other passengers shouted encouragement, the three of them wrenched her out of her seat and threw her into the smoking car, breaking her arm in the process.[159] The war for black freedom may have been won, but traditional racial segregation remained.

Not all the passengers were unsympathetic. When Tubman disembarked in New York City, a young white man approached her, gave her his card, encouraged her to sue the railroad, and said he would be her witness. After a brief rest in the city Tubman made her way to Auburn, where friends urged her to pursue her case against the railroad. Unfortunately, the potential witness had given her only a carte de visite with no information about how to contact him. When he didn't respond to an advertisement in the paper, they decided that her testimony, along with that of her doctor, would be enough to bring suit. Tubman was disabled and could not work that winter, but there is no record that she ever sued the railroad. Perhaps in the end she believed that her testimony would not suffice.[160]

After the war Tubman had a great many responsibilities and very few resources. She supported and cared for her elderly parents, took in needy freed people creating new lives in the North, and cared for many children whose parents were working or looking for work. She also raised chickens, sold eggs, and took in boarders to help make ends meet and occasionally solicited charity for her family during the harsh New York winters. She raised hundreds of dollars for freedmen's relief by organizing fairs at the Central Presbyterian Church in Auburn during 1867 and 1868, supported freedmen's aid projects in the South, and collected funds for teachers and students at two freedmen's schools. She also spoke out for women's suffrage in the campaign for the vote that grew out of the prewar movement for women's rights. She tried to stay out of factional disputes that divided the movement after the war—heated arguments over whether the vote for black men should have priority or activists should hold out for women's suffrage as well. She didn't join with her old antislavery friends and comrades Susan B. Anthony and Elizabeth Cady Stanton when they insisted that any expansion of suffrage must include women.[161]

For twenty years after the war, Tubman's friends in Massachusetts and New York assisted her efforts to obtain back pay and a military pension for her years in the service, but it was not possible under the existing pension law, which provided aid only to veterans with war-related disabilities or their widows and children. Meanwhile, her friends found her another source of income. They enlisted Sarah H. Bradford, an author of sentimental moralistic fiction, to write down the oft-told stories of her Underground Railroad and wartime adventures. Bradford was a logical choice: Her father, Samuel Miles Hopkins Sr., had been a judge, New York congressman, and friend of William H. Seward, and her brother, Samuel Miles Hopkins Jr., was a professor at the Auburn Theological Seminary. She recorded Tubman's stories at her home in nearby Geneva, New York, and solicited corroboration and testimonials from Tubman's colleagues (Document 20). She hastily produced a slim volume in the summer of 1868 before she embarked on a European cruise. Bradford's pocket-size *Scenes in the Life of Harriet Tubman* was published early in 1869 and sold for $1. All proceeds went to Tubman, and with the $1,200 in sales she paid off some of her debts. Tubman's biography joined a long list of biographies and autobiographies designed to raise funds for their authors and promote the cause of black freedom. The nearly 150 slave narratives—including Frederick Douglass's *Narrative*, Solomon Northup's *Twelve Years a Slave*, Harriet Jacobs's *Incidents in the Life of a Slave Girl*, and Sojourner Truth's *Narrative*—had been extremely effective in bringing converts to the antislavery cause. Tubman's friends hoped that her story would help support a hero of the movement.[162]

Though primarily designed to raise money for Tubman's support, Bradford's biography also established the heroic mythology that became the Tubman legend, stories repeated in popular literature for more than a century. Bradford's biography gave this dramatic summary of Tubman's Underground Railroad career:

> There was one reward of $12,000 offered for the head of the woman who was constantly appearing and enticing away parties of slaves from their master. She had traveled in the cars when these posters were put up over her head, and she heard them read by those about her—for she could not read herself. Fearlessly she went on, trusting in the Lord. She said, "I started with this idea in my head, 'Dere's *two* things I've got a *right* to, and dese are, Death or Liberty—one or tother I mean to have. No one will take me back alive; I shall fight for my liberty, and when de time has come for me to go, de Lord will let dem kill me.'" And acting upon this simple creed, and firm in this trusting faith, she went back and forth *nineteen times*, according to the reckoning of her friends. She remembers that she went eleven times from Canada, but of the other journeys she kept no reckoning.[163]

Marriage

On March 18, 1869, just a few months after the publication of her biography, Tubman married Nelson Davis, a tall, young veteran also called Nelson Charles (Document 23). Davis was born in slavery in 1844 into a family owned by Fred Charles in Elizabeth City, North Carolina, near the Great Dismal Swamp and the Virginia border. He took his father Milford Davis's name when he escaped to the North in about 1861. He did farm labor in Oneida County, New York, and was drafted into the Army in September 1863. He signed up in Philadelphia with the Eighth U.S. Colored Troops under the name Nelson G. Charles. His regiment served in Florida, where they fought in the Battle of Olustee, and in Virginia. After the fall of Richmond the regiment was sent to Brownsville, Texas, where Davis/Charles was mustered out in November 1865. The twenty-one-year-old returned to New York, boarded with Tubman and her family, and worked as a farm laborer and brickmaker. Tubman met Davis when he became her boarder.[164]

Davis was married under the name Charles Nelson Davis, preserving all of his names, though in an unusual order. Throughout his life Davis was known both as Nelson Charles and as Nelson Davis. Tubman was forty-seven and Davis was twenty-four or twenty-five when they married, but they had much in common. They both had escaped southern slavery, had lived in New York before the war, were veterans who had seen combat in the South, and saw themselves as freed by Lincoln's Emancipation Proclamation.[165]

Many of Auburn's prominent citizens attended the service performed by the Reverend Henry Fowler in the basement chapel where the Central Presbyterian Church met. Tubman would have had a particular affinity for Fowler and his church. In 1862 the Second Presbyterian Church in Auburn had forced Fowler out because of his fiery antislavery preaching. Reportedly, the controversy came to a head when Fowler publicly prayed for the soul of the martyred John Brown. Sixty-six antislavery members followed their minister and formed the Central Presbyterian Church.[166]

Tubman's marriage to Davis was one more example of the ways she departed from traditional roles for nineteenth-century women. It was not uncommon for men to marry women twenty or more years younger, but it was very rare for a woman to marry a much younger man. Tubman, however, was an unusual woman. Enslaved women laboring in the fields did the same work as men, but free women, black and white, were told that their place was in the home, protected and directed by men. (Poor women, of course, generally found it impossible to live up to this ideal.) Tubman had often acted with daring and physical courage and was independent and strong-minded, even obstinate, in her decisions. She spoke at large antislavery meetings, something only a few radical abolitionist women did, and she took up the gun to fight in the war against slavery. In much of her life she violated contemporary gender expectations, and her union with Davis was no different.

Hardships

Tubman's marriage and the publication of her biography somewhat improved her economic situation, although the death of William Seward, her friend and benefactor, in 1872 added an element of uncertainty to her future. Her husband suffered from tuberculosis, which undoubtedly limited the labor he could contribute to the household. Tubman did domestic work, and the couple operated a brickyard on their property and raised chickens and hogs. Tubman continued to raise money for southern freedmen and helped the many people who came to her for aid, and Davis became a trustee of the new St. Mark's African Methodist Episcopal (AME) Church in Auburn. Fortunately, in early summer 1873, just months before a national financial panic, they paid off the mortgage held by Seward's son Frederick. Tubman's father, Ben, had died two years before, and she hoped to establish a home and hospital for the elderly, where her mother, then in her late eighties, could receive care.[167]

By the 1870s conditions for freedmen in the South were increasingly dire. Constitutional amendments had abolished slavery, guaranteed citizenship for African Americans, and granted black men the right to vote, but a concerted campaign of racist terror killed many freedmen and denied recently gained political power to most. Making matters worse, ten years of Supreme Court cases beginning in 1873 declared hard-won federal protections for black civil rights unconstitutional. Political rapprochement ended federal military protection for southern blacks in 1877. Consequently, arrests for vagrancy and contrived infractions placed thousands into leased convict labor systems, and many sharecroppers, who worked for the promise of a share of the crops they raised instead of wages, were under the control of their former masters. Northern philanthropists continued to provide aid, particularly education, for freed people, but a severe national depression, beginning with the failure of Jay Cooke's New York investment bank in September 1873, greatly curtailed aid societies' resources.[168]

Less than two weeks after the panic of 1873, two black men approached Tubman's brother John with a proposition promising a handsome profit. They said they had a chest filled with $5,000 in gold, but since it was southern contraband hidden during the war, they were afraid the government would seize it if they tried to exchange it for paper money. They were willing, they said, to exchange the chest for $2,000. John went to Harriet and Nelson Davis with the proposal. Both knew that many Confederates had hidden valuables during the war, so a trunk full of southern gold didn't seem out of the question. The men stayed with Tubman for some time, and to convince her of their reliability, they told her that they knew her nephew James Alfred Bowley, a member of the postwar South Carolina legislature. Always in dire need of funds, Tubman placed her trust in the scheme. Most people Tubman approached were suspicious of the pair's motives, but Anthony Schimer, a wealthy white businessman from her church, was willing to put up the $2,000. Schimer, his banker, Tubman, and her brother set off together to meet the two men and get the trunk filled with gold.[169]

When they arrived at the meeting place, only one man was there, and there was no trunk. He explained that the other man was suspicious of white people and refused to come out of hiding. Committed that far, the group conferred and decided that Tubman alone would accompany the man to where the other was hiding. The two men then led Tubman across a field to the woods and the partly buried trunk. Her suspicions had been aroused, however, and she refused to give them the money until she saw the gold. The men said they had forgotten the key and left her there with the trunk and the money. As darkness fell, she examined the trunk and found it had no keyhole. Planning to walk back to her friends, Tubman started to cross the field but frightened a herd of cows and so retreated to the woods to avoid the galloping animals. Back at the trunk, the men came up behind her, knocked her unconscious, and stole the money. She awoke bound and gagged and struggled through the field in the dark, laboriously climbing over fences, to meet her shocked brother and friends. Later they found that the trunk contained rocks. There were many such frauds and get-rich-quick schemes during and after the Civil War. The desperate economic conditions during the depression of the 1870s made Tubman, like many Americans, vulnerable to these two unscrupulous swindlers.[170]

Family Life

During the 1870s and 1880s Harriet Tubman Davis settled into life in Auburn. Her growing extended family was settled in the neighborhood, and she and Nelson experienced the normal cycles of family life. The year after Tubman's father died, Margaret Stewart married Henry Lucas and moved into a nearby house. The Lucases' son was born in 1874 and was followed by another child in each of the next two decades. Tubman had a number of grandnephews and grandnieces, and Margaret's son was not the only baby in the family in 1874. That year Harriet and Nelson adopted a baby girl named Gertie. Their household at the time also included Tubman's mother, an elderly blind woman, and other needy children and adults as they presented themselves. Tubman's mother, Rit, died in 1880, having lived nearly one hundred years.[171]

Many people depended on the Davises' ability to bring in money, and Tubman attempted again during the 1880s to secure a government pension. Her friends sent a petition with fifty-four signatures to New York representative Sereno E. Payne, but their efforts were fruitless. Sometimes the family's needs were especially great. In the early 1880s their wood-frame house burned down; her nephew John Henry Stewart died, leaving a wife and three children to be cared for; and at least forty of their hogs died, probably from rat poison in the garbage Tubman collected from Auburn households for their feed.[172] The townspeople were generous when they knew Tubman was in need, but she was proud and seldom asked for help.

During these years Tubman was active in the church, continued to support freedmen's aid, and occasionally engaged in women's rights activities. Her charismatic personality, strong singing voice, and spiritual convictions made her a leader in the AME Zion Church. Though still illiterate, she could quote scripture and give convincing testimony about God's guidance in her life. Friends complained that she would give anything she had away to the needy, but she lived in complete confidence that God would provide for her and those in her charge. She continued to have prophetic dreams and to receive divine assurances on both large and small matters. After the war, for example, a vivid dream informed her of the death of William Seward's daughter Frances before the news reached Auburn. In late 1869, when her crops failed and she desperately needed money, she arrived at Martha Coffin Wright's home without being summoned because she knew that a supporter had sent money for her. According to her biographer Sarah Bradford, Tubman also had visions of world events—a deadly South American earthquake and a disaster at sea. Her strong sense of God's guidance remained with her for the rest of her life.[173]

TUBMAN'S LIFE INTO THE TWENTIETH CENTURY

Harriet Tubman lost many friends during the 1870s and 1880s, as the old guard of the antislavery movement passed away. The funerals of prominent abolitionists periodically reminded the public of their triumph over slavery. They also provided opportunities for survivors to heal old divisions, renew friendships, reminisce about antislavery work, and discuss the state of the nation and black rights. In New York the Reverend Samuel J. May, William Seward, Jermain Loguen, and Gerrit Smith died in the early 1870s; in Massachusetts William Lloyd Garrison died in 1879 at age seventy-three.

The remaining antislavery elite gathered in Boston for Wendell Phillips's funeral in 1884. After a simple service black Civil War veterans and soldiers accompanied the casket through the wintry streets to Faneuil Hall, where for three hours an estimated fifteen thousand people filed by his body. The illustrious attendees included both white abolitionists—Theodore Dwight Weld, Julia Ward Howe, Thomas Wentworth Higginson, and Susan B. Anthony—and black abolitionists—George T. Downing and Frederick Douglass—as well as members of the next activist generation, including Lucy Stone and Garrison's sons. Douglass gave a eulogy at a memorial service in Phillips's honor a few days later. Tubman was said to be at one of these gatherings, but she was apparently not well-known enough for the newspapers to mention her.[174]

Nelson Davis succumbed to tuberculosis in the autumn of 1888, after nearly twenty years of marriage. He was only forty-four years old but, like many veterans, had been unhealthy since the war. Tubman, still vigorous in her mid-sixties, then presided over a family and household of frail elderly people and two younger generations. The following year Tubman's nephew John and his Indian wife, Helena, had a daughter. Shortly thereafter Helena, on her deathbed, asked Tubman to care for the child. Thus, at age sixty-seven, the widowed Tubman became mother to the infant Katie Stewart, in addition to Gertie, now fifteen. In June 1890 the federal government passed an act extending pensions to honorably discharged veterans, regardless of the cause of their disability, and to their widows and children. Tubman applied almost immediately.[175]

Unfortunately, the changes in Davis's name after slavery created problems, and nearly two years after her application pension officials returned her claim, asking for more documentation. Since Davis had enlisted as Nelson Charles, Tubman had to prove that Nelson Charles was her husband, the man known as Nelson Davis. Ironically, she also had to prove that she had not been married to John Tubman when she married Davis, which was easy enough, since John was dead before she married Davis. Of course, her first marriage wasn't legally recognized because she had been enslaved at the time, but the government still required proof that she was not a bigamist and that her second marriage was legal. After petitions, depositions, and many affidavits from family, friends, and neighbors, the federal government finally issued Tubman

Figure 6. *Harriet Tubman, late 1886*

A rare look at Tubman later in her life. She sat for this studio photograph in Boston when she was sixty-four years old.

a widow's pension of $8 a month in October 1895 (still an easier case to make than her claim for a pension for her own military service). Later that month she received the enormous sum of $500 retroactively to cover the period between her application and its approval.[176]

In her seventies Tubman attended women's rights meetings, supported women's suffrage, and visited family and friends in Washington, Boston, and New York. With the help of Gertie, she continued to take in needy African Americans while raising little Katie. Now one of a handful of venerable survivors of antislavery days, Tubman was honored at gatherings of the women's suffrage movement, inspiring younger women with tales of her Underground Railroad and Civil War exploits and introducing a new generation to the Tubman legend.

In 1896 Tubman was the oldest person at the inaugural meeting of the National Association of Colored Women in Washington, D.C. Rosetta Douglass Sprague, whose father, Frederick Douglass, had died the previous year, spoke on the first morning, placing Tubman in a pantheon with Phillis Wheatley, Margaret Garner, and Sojourner Truth. That evening at the Nineteenth Street Baptist Church, Tubman received a long standing ovation, to which she responded with a short war story and a song. The following day Tubman acceded to requests for another musical performance and on the third day urged the gathering to support homes for the aged in black communities. Later that year she spoke at a Rochester, New York, meeting of the National Woman Suffrage Association chaired by Susan B. Anthony, where she gave a much longer rendition of her adventures escaping from slavery, rescuing others, and caring for wounded soldiers in the war. In 1897, the year Tubman was seventy-five, Boston suffragists held a benefit for her to celebrate a new edition of the Bradford biography. She was honored with a number of receptions in Boston, spoke at the Old South Meetinghouse, and received a silver version of Queen Victoria's Diamond Jubilee medal and a letter from the queen, who had been impressed by her biography.[177]

While in Boston late in the 1890s, Tubman decided to see if something could be done about the constant pain in her head and the buzzing in her ears that made it difficult for her to sleep. She walked into Massachusetts General Hospital and asked a doctor if he could operate to relieve the pressure in her skull. The doctor operated that same day. Tubman refused any anesthetic, endured the surgery stoically, and when it was finished got off the operating table and put on her hat, intending to walk back to her lodgings. When her legs gave out, the hospital provided an ambulance to take her home. She reported that the surgery did relieve her symptoms.[178]

Continued efforts by Tubman and her friends to have the government acknowledge her wartime service finally paid off in February 1899, when her monthly pension was increased to $20 a month (Documents 26). The House of Representatives report, which recommended an increase to $25 a month, mentioned her role as a scout and spy but emphasized her nursing service. The Senate committee, fearing that other nurses would claim this higher than usual amount, reduced it to $20. This extra income was sorely needed for Tubman's family responsibilities and expanded charitable work.[179]

A few years before, in 1896, she purchased at auction twenty-five acres adjacent to her property in Auburn, complete with two houses, barns, and outbuildings, hoping to establish a small home for the elderly. This was the beginning of what she called John Brown Hall, known by most as the Harriet Tubman Home for Aged and Infirm Negroes, although for some years she continued to take people into her own home. In 1903 the AME Zion Church assumed the mortgage and began to raise funds. The church officially opened the renovated home in 1908 and employed a couple to act as chaplain and matron. Today the Harriet Tubman Home for the Aged is a national historic site administered by the National Park Service and may be visited by the public.[180]

Though elderly and increasingly frail, Tubman maintained her interest in social reform and women's and African American affairs. In Auburn in late 1902, she made a surprise appearance at an informal suffragist gathering of some of the descendants and survivors of the antislavery struggle. Susan B. Anthony later expressed her excitement at seeing Tubman: "This most wonderful woman—*Harriet Tubman*—is still alive.... [A]ll of us were visiting at Mrs. [Eliza Wright] Osbornes—a real love feast of the few that are left—and here came *Harriet Tubman!*" Tubman traveled to Boston in 1905 for the dedication of the Harriet Tubman Christian Temperance Union at Parker Memorial Hall. In 1911, at age eighty-nine, she finally joined the Geneva, New York, suffrage club, "Miss Susan B. Anthony's association." When a skeptical white woman asked if she actually believed that women should vote, she responded, "I suffered enough to believe it."[181]

Also in 1911 Tubman contracted a pulmonary infection, was confined to a wheelchair, and moved into the home she had founded (Document 27). The chaplain there was an old friend and comrade in arms, the Reverend Charles A. Smith. A retired minister, Smith had served in the Fifty-Fourth Massachusetts Regiment during the Civil War, and Tubman had cared for him after he was wounded at the Battle of Fort Wagner. In February 1913 Mary B. Talbert, chair of the executive committee of the

National Association of Colored Women, visited from Buffalo. Tubman's voice was weak as she told Talbert that she was well cared for, God had reassured her, and she was "at peace with God and with all mankind." On Monday afternoon, March 10, Tubman's death seemed imminent as she called for her family and friends. Her two grandnieces Alice and Eva Stewart were still in Washington for President Woodrow Wilson's inauguration, but the small group gathered at her bedside included Reverend Smith; the Reverend E. U. A. Brooks, minister of the local AME Zion Church; and her grandnephews Charles and Clarence Stewart. Tubman directed and participated in a final service of prayer, song, and Holy Communion. Shortly afterward, expressing her message of love for "all the churches" and repeating Christ's promise that she was going to prepare a place for them, she lost consciousness. Harriet Tubman Davis died of pneumonia a few hours later at the age of ninety-one, after, according to a local newspaper, "a life of exalted self-sacrifice."[182]

HARRIET TUBMAN IN HISTORY AND MEMORY

The transformation of Harriet Tubman's memory actually began during her lifetime, in 1886, when Sarah Bradford put out a revised and much expanded version of Tubman's biography. The previous version, published in 1869, had been titled *Scenes in the Life of Harriet Tubman*. Bradford had had more time to work on this version, and its new title, *Harriet: The Moses of Her People*, expressed its more romantic tone. The new work also reflected the changing mood of a nation then concerned with putting the struggle over slavery in the past, healing the wounds of war, and reconciling North and South. This rendition reflected increasingly acceptable forms of white racism: Black stereotypes were stronger, comic stories provided entertainment, slavery was portrayed as a somewhat more benign institution, and Tubman's words were presented in dialect more often than in the original biography. Whereas, for example, the original began with a straightforward statement that Tubman had spent many years in slavery and become a daring Underground Railroad conductor, the second version started out with a description of "a group of merry little darkies . . . rolling and tumbling in the sand" in front of a plantation mansion (Document 22).[183]

On March 11, 1913, the *New York Times* published a small article, dated the previous day and announcing her approaching death, with the subhead "Negro Woman Who Aided Hundreds of Fleeing Slaves is 95 Years Old." The newspaper mentioned her Underground Railroad activity and said that she had known Abraham Lincoln and William H. Seward and "was associated with John Brown in anti-slavery work." Her obituary in the *Times* on Friday, March 14, noted that she was reportedly ninety-eight years old, celebrated her Underground Railroad activity, mentioned her service in the Union army during the Civil War, and contained a long list of the important men who had held her in great "esteem," creating a sense of her importance to white society and contributing to the construction of her legend (Document 28). Reflecting America's fading memory of the antislavery crusade and African Americans' part in it, the newspaper identified Frederick Douglass, the only black man on the list, as "Ferderick Douglas."[184]

The attendance at the services for Tubman in Auburn, New York, on March 13, 1913, however, demonstrated her standing in the community and the continuing power of her legend. The family, residents, and hundreds of African Americans gathered that morning at the home for a prayer service in which Reverend Brooks delivered a eulogy for "Aunt Harriet" and the youth choir of the AME Zion Church sang. More than a thousand people attended the funeral service that afternoon at the black church, although only five hundred could fit inside the building. A cadre of AME Zion ministers conducted the service, following Tubman's directions. The funeral was an integrated affair, with a white quartet from the Presbyterian church, and the many speakers included the mayor of Auburn and the president of the city council. In a final tribute the Charles E. Stewart Relief Corps and the Women's Auxiliary of the Charles E. Stewart Post of the Grand Army of the Republic gathered around the flag-draped casket for a quasi-military ceremony. Late in the chilly, overcast afternoon, Harriet Tubman Davis was buried in the Fort Hill Cemetery, the final resting place of Auburn notables.[185]

Society's changing memory and ambivalent attitude toward antislavery radicalism were apparent in June 1914, when the town of Auburn held a gala celebration of Tubman's life and unveiled a memorial tablet to be installed on the Cayuga County Court House. The bronze tablet praised her daring Underground Railroad rescues, calling her the Moses of her people, and celebrated her service as a Civil War nurse and spy. With a notice in the *Auburn Citizen* on June 11, the mayor declared that flags would be flown the next day from all public buildings and urged citizens to display the American flag on their homes and businesses, as "a further mark of respect and as a token of appreciation for [Tubman's] loyal and patriotic service to our country and flag" and "to honor the memory of this faithful old slave who was willing to die for her race" (Document 29). Both blacks and whites crowded the auditorium on the evening of June 12 to hear speakers extol Tubman's character, her patriotism, and her role as a bridge between the races. Keynote speaker Booker T. Washington—former slave, prominent black leader, founder and principal of Tuskegee Institute, preacher of black self-help, and darling of American business—went further. In the face of increasing violence against black people, Washington argued that African Americans should cultivate respectable behavior and accept their position as workers at the bottom of the economic ladder. Since the war, southern blacks had been attacked and even killed for trying to exercise the rights freedom had brought them, or simply for being too successful, and Washington tried to assure his powerful backers that African Americans were no threat to the established racial order. Ironically, he urged that Tubman, who had stolen so many people from the clutches of slavery, be remembered as a symbol of the "law abiding Negro."[186]

These earliest remembrances of Tubman reflected the racial ambivalence of American society. The saga of post–Civil War reconciliation, uniting North and South in patriotic commemoration of the soldiers' valor and in forgetfulness of the war's roots in racial slavery, was in full flower by the mid-1910s. A period of wild speculation and economic growth had led the country into another devastating economic depression in the 1890s. Falling cotton prices had further ravaged the struggling postwar southern economy, and many white Americans blamed the destruction of slavery, and the freed people themselves, for the economic troubles. Northern white veterans in segregated organizations shared southerners' nostalgic memories of the supposed chivalrous virtues of the Old South. Despite overwhelming contrary evidence, this influential interpretation of the war argued that the Confederacy had not fought to preserve slavery but to patriotically preserve its citizens' rights. In this view slavery not only had been an immensely profitable system for the nation but also had protected the enslaved, who were incapable of caring for themselves, and the Confederacy's defeat in the Civil War had been a tragedy. The faithful slave became a touchstone of this mythology, what historian David W. Blight has called the tale of the Confederacy's "noble catastrophe."[187]

The developing film industry participated fully in rewriting the war's history and memorializing the South's "Lost Cause." A documentary film recorded President William Howard Taft's address to a joint encampment of northern and southern war veterans at Petersburg, Virginia, in 1909, and various short films depicted the stock characters of the war's transformed memory: the avaricious northerner, the loyal slave, the dangerous freedman, and the genteel southern lady and gentleman. In 1913 the government sponsored a reunion at Gettysburg, Pennsylvania, attended by more than 55,000 veterans from both the Union and the Confederacy. By then the African American soldier had virtually disappeared from the scene, and black veterans were not invited to participate. Virginian Woodrow Wilson, elected president the previous fall, was the first southerner and the first Democratic president since the war. The summer after Tubman's death, Wilson instituted racial segregation in federal agencies. In 1915, when director D. W. Griffith released his technically stunning, groundbreaking epic (and racist) movie, *The Birth of a Nation*, celebrating southern heroism and lauding the role of the Ku Klux Klan in the postwar South, Wilson endorsed it. The president, a historian and former president of Princeton University, screened the film at the White House and declared it "like writing history with lightning." His "only regret," he said, was that it was "all so terribly true."[188] During this era the Tubman legend was crafted to depict her in the acceptable and nonthreatening image of the heroic former slave.

Reviving the Radical Tubman

The Great Depression of the 1930s, a generation after Tubman's death, sparked another period of remembrance. American Communists and other leftists revived black history scholarship as part of their critique of American society and campaign for gender and racial equality. Their outpouring of publications reignited interest in black history generally, and the antislavery, feminist Harriet Tubman they rediscovered reflected their identification with the struggles of African Americans and women. In the late 1930s Earl Conrad, a white former Teamsters union organizer in Harlem and a correspondent for the black *Chicago Defender* newspaper, attempted to recover Harriet Tubman's story by interviewing people who had known her. He was unsuccessful getting his manuscript published by mainstream publishers, but finally, in 1943, the Associated Publishers, headed by Carter G. Woodson, the African American founder of the Association for the Study of Negro Life and History and the father of black history week, published Conrad's *General Harriet Tubman*. In 1940 a twenty-three-year-old artist named Jacob Lawrence celebrated Tubman's life at the Museum of Modern Art in New York City with a thirty-one-panel series depicting scenes from her life. In 1944, during World War II, the federal government honored Tubman by launching a Liberty ship named the SS *Harriet Tubman*.[189]

Another period of civil rights activity brought Tubman to Americans' attention in the mid-twentieth century. The fight against racial segregation prompted the study of previous fights for racial equality, and young people found inspiration in being part of the long history of the struggle for racial justice. Dorothy Sterling, a noted historian who recovered black women's stories, published *Freedom Train: The Story of Harriet Tubman* in 1954, and Ann Petry published *Harriet Tubman: Conductor on the Underground Railroad* in 1955, both to inspire young adults. Tubman's Underground Railroad activity led to a plethora of books for children and young people, most based on Sarah Bradford's biographies and thereby perpetuating the myth of Tubman as a heroic former slave. One comic book–style *Golden Legacy* magazine was published in 1967 by a collection of writers and artists, with the respected black historian Benjamin Quarles as consultant. Titled *The Saga of Harriet Tubman: The "Moses of Her People,"* it brought the story of Tubman the abolitionist to a large audience of schoolchildren and adults. The modern women's movement, built on the civil rights movement, revived and emphasized the memory of Tubman as a daring rescuer and warrior—a model of strength and the courage of conviction for young women. According to historian Catherine Clinton, one novel and more than forty juvenile biographies on Tubman were published during this period.[190]

Imaginative and beautifully illustrated children's books on Tubman continue to acquaint young readers with her adventures and, often, her myth. Many, such as *Minty: A Story of Young Harriet Tubman* by Alan Schroeder and Jerry Pinkney, on her childhood in slavery, and *Journey to Freedom: A Story of the Underground Railroad*, written by Courtni C. Wright and illustrated by Gershom Griffith, on Tubman the Underground Railroad conductor, are fictionalized accounts from a child's perspective. The inventive *Aunt Harriet's Underground Railroad in the Sky* by Faith Ringgold draws on the Tubman saga and African mythology to educate readers about the Underground Railroad. Unfortunately, a great many modern children's books repeat the discredited legend of quilts used as common signals on the road to freedom, something for which there is no historical evidence. Many others perpetuate the romantic myth, first fostered by Bradford, that Tubman was a lone hero who, through courage and native wit, rescued many hundreds of people from slavery. The outpouring of inspirational juvenile literature undoubtedly helped account for the fact that in 2008 high school students named Harriet Tubman the third most famous American in history, excluding presidents and first ladies.[191]

From Myth to Reality

By the 1990s the burgeoning study of women's history prompted scholars who had grown up inspired by Tubman's Underground Railroad successes to take a closer look at her story. Social historical methods and a large body of work on slavery and abolition held promise for a more

complete study of her life, moving beyond the prototypically American
rugged individualist to show her place in nineteenth-century reform.
Three full-length biographies of Tubman came out in quick succession
in 2003 and 2004: Jean M. Humez's *Harriet Tubman: The Life and the Life
Stories*, exploring the creation of the Tubman myth through storytelling;
Kate Clifford Larson's exhaustive, prodigiously researched *Bound for
the Promised Land: Harriet Tubman: Portrait of an American Hero*; and
Catherine Clinton's engaging *Harriet Tubman: The Road to Freedom*.
With these works and with Milton C. Sernett's weighing of the evidence
in *Harriet Tubman: Myth, Memory, and History* in 2007, we have a much
more complete picture of Tubman's life and can better distinguish the
historical actor from the woman of American mythology. Our greater
understanding helps explain Tubman's long-standing appeal: She was a
woman of wit, compassion, and extraordinary courage, whose exploits
crossed the barriers of traditional gender expectations. She was deeply
imbedded in a network of dedicated social activists, inspired the confidence of others, risked her life for her family's and her people's freedom, dedicated herself to African American advancement, and always
believed in God's guidance and freedom's promise.

NOTES

[1] By 1850 there were 24,770 free blacks and 25,997 slaves on the Eastern Shore.
Barbara Jeanne Fields, *Slavery and Freedom on the Middle Ground: Maryland during the
Nineteenth Century* (New Haven, Conn.: Yale University Press, 1985), 70.

[2] Walter Johnson, *Soul by Soul: Life inside the Antebellum Slave Market* (Cambridge,
Mass.: Harvard University Press, 1999), 5.

[3] Ira Berlin, *Slaves without Masters: The Free Negro in the Antebellum South* (New
York: Random House, 1974), 136–37. See also T. Stephen Whitman, *The Price of Freedom:
Slavery and Manumission in Baltimore and Early National Maryland* (Lexington: Univer-
sity Press of Kentucky, 1997).

[4] Jean M. Humez, *Harriet Tubman: The Life and the Life Stories* (Madison: University of Wisconsin Press, 2003), 182; Kate Clifford Larson, *Bound for the Promised Land:
Harriet Tubman: Portrait of an American Hero* (New York: Ballantine, 2004), 72–73.
Enslaved Africans brought to the Americas often described being captured in raids on
their native villages. Anta Majigeen Ndiaye Kingsley, for example, told the vivid story
of warrior slaves on horseback who raided her village in Senegal, West Africa, in 1806;
killed most of the men; and carried her, along with the rest of the women and children,
into slavery. See James Oliver Horton and Lois E. Horton, *Slavery and the Making of
America* (New York: Oxford University Press, 2005), 13, and Antoinette T. Jackson,
"The Kingsley Plantation Community in Jacksonville, Florida: Memory and Place in a
Southern American City," *CRM: The Journal of Heritage Stewardship* 6, no. 1 (Winter
2009): 23–33.

[5] Catherine Clinton, *Harriet Tubman: The Road to Freedom* (New York: Little, Brown,
2004), 34; Larson, *Bound for the Promised Land*, 80.

[6] Larson, *Bound for the Promised Land*, 79–80; Earl Conrad, *General Harriet Tubman*
(1943; repr., Washington, D.C.: Associated Publishers, 1990), 35; Horton and Horton,
Slavery and the Making of America, 147. The 1943 edition of Conrad's book was titled
simply *Harriet Tubman*.

[7] Larson, *Bound for the Promised Land*, 5–8; Clinton, *Harriet Tubman*, 28–29.

[8] Larson, *Bound for the Promised Land*, 296–99.

[9] Benjamin Drew, *The Refugee, or the Narratives of Fugitive Slaves in Canada* (Boston: John P. Jewett, 1856), 30.

[10] Harriet Jacobs, *Incidents in the Life of a Slave Girl, Written by Herself, with Related Documents*, ed. Jennifer Fleischner (Boston: Bedford/St. Martin's, 2010). Jacobs's narrative and Fleischner's essay provide a portrait of the victimization of slave women by both white masters and their jealous wives.

[11] Clinton, *Harriet Tubman*, 22; Conrad, *General Harriet Tubman*, 14–16.

[12] Larson, *Bound for the Promised Land*, 42–47; Conrad, *General Harriet Tubman*, 16–19.

[13] Conrad, *General Harriet Tubman*, 21–22; Clinton, *Harriet Tubman*, 113.

[14] Ira Berlin, *Generations of Captivity: A History of African-American Slaves* (Cambridge, Mass.: Belknap Press of Harvard University Press, 2003), 220–24; Frederick Douglass, *Life and Times of Frederick Douglass* (London: Collier, 1962), 198–99.

[15] Douglass, *Life and Times*, 200–205; Frederick Douglass, *Narrative of the Life of Frederick Douglass, An American Slave, Written by Himself*, ed. David W. Blight (Boston: St. Martin's Press, 1997), 174.

[16] Clinton, *Harriet Tubman*, 25; Robert S. Reeder, *Reports, Speeches, and Fragmentary Reflections on the Colored Population of Maryland and Slavery* (Washington, D.C.: Polkinhorn's Steam Job Office, 1857), 39.

[17] Horton and Horton, *Slavery and the Making of America*, 66–67. Vermont's constitution abolished slavery in 1777, Massachusetts's constitutional ban was confirmed in 1783, and New Hampshire's Declaration of Rights was passed in 1788. Gradual emancipation was established in Connecticut and Rhode Island in 1784, New York in 1799, Pennsylvania in 1780, and New Jersey in 1804. New York instituted immediate emancipation in 1827.

[18] Kathryn Grover, *The Fugitive's Gibraltar: Escaping Slaves and Abolitionism in New Bedford, Massachusetts* (Amherst: University of Massachusetts Press, 2001), 68–69; James Oliver Horton and Lois E. Horton, *In Hope of Liberty: Culture, Community and Protest among Northern Free Blacks, 1700–1860* (New York: Oxford University Press, 1997), 71–76; Lois E. Horton, "From Class to Race in Early America: Northern Post-Emancipation Racial Reconstruction," *Journal of the Early Republic* 19 (Winter 1999): 631–51.

[19] The first black Masonic lodge was founded by Prince Hall in Boston after the American Revolution. Subsequent American black lodges became Prince Hall lodges. See James Oliver Horton and Lois E. Horton, *Black Bostonians: Family Life and Community Struggle in the Antebellum North*, 2nd ed. (New York: Holmes & Meier, 1999), 30.

[20] W. Jeffrey Bolster, *Black Jacks: African American Seamen in the Age of Sail* (Cambridge, Mass.: Harvard University Press, 1997), 191, 235–39; Horton and Horton, *In Hope of Liberty*, 235.

[21] R. J. M. Blackett, "'Freemen to the Rescue!': Resistance to the Fugitive Slave Law of 1850," in *Passages to Freedom: The Underground Railroad in History and Memory*, ed. David W. Blight (Washington, D.C.: Smithsonian Books, 2004), 133–47.

[22] John Hope Franklin and Loren Schweninger, *Runaway Slaves: Rebels on the Plantation* (New York: Oxford University Press, 1999), 210–11.

[23] John Michael Vlach, "Above Ground on the Underground Railroad: Places of Flight and Refuge," in *Passages to Freedom*, ed. David W. Blight, 95–115, 99, 101; Herbert Aptheker, "Maroons within the Present Limits of the United States," *Journal of Negro History* 24 (April 1939): 167–84, 168.

[24] James Brewer Stewart, *Holy Warriors: The Abolitionists and American Slavery* (New York: Hill & Wang, 1997), 95–96, 120–21; Richard S. Newman, *The Transformation of American Abolitionism: Fighting Slavery in the Early Republic* (Chapel Hill: University of North Carolina Press, 2002), 152.

[25] Stanley Harrold, *Subversives: Antislavery Community in Washington, D.C., 1828–1865* (Baton Rouge: Louisiana State University Press, 2003), 64–93.

26 C. Peter Ripley, Roy E. Finkenbine, Michael F. Hembree, and Donald Yacovone, eds., *The Black Abolitionist Papers* (Chapel Hill: University of North Carolina Press, 1991), 3:39–40; Lois E. Horton, "Kidnapping and Resistance: Antislavery Direct Action in the 1850s," in *Passages to Freedom*, ed. David W. Blight, 149–73, 155.

27 James Oliver Horton, "A Crusade for Freedom: William Still and the Real Underground Railroad," in *Passages to Freedom*, ed. David W. Blight, 175–93; William Still, *The Underground Rail Road* (1872; repr., Chicago: Johnson, 1970), 18–19.

28 Horton, "A Crusade for Freedom," 175–93, 188–91.

29 Horton and Horton, *Slavery and the Making of America*, 146–47; Horton and Horton, *In Hope of Liberty*, 252–53.

30 Wm. Henry Seward to Gerrit Smith, October 11/12, 1850, Gerrit Smith Papers, Syracuse University Library, Syracuse, N.Y.

31 Horton and Horton, *Black Bostonians*, 112.

32 Still, *Underground Rail Road*, 382.

33 Horton, "Kidnapping and Resistance," 160–61. See also William Craft, *Running a Thousand Miles for Freedom* (London: 1860; repr., New York: Arno, 1969).

34 Larson, *Bound for the Promised Land*, 89–90.

35 Robert J. Brugger, *Maryland: A Middle Temperament, 1634–1980* (Baltimore: Johns Hopkins University Press, 1996), 265; Fields, *Slavery and Freedom*, 62.

36 Stanley W. Campbell, *The Slave Catchers* (Chapel Hill: University of North Carolina Press, 1968), 199–207.

37 Larson, *Bound for the Promised Land*, 90, 239–40; Clinton, *Harriet Tubman*, 83; Humez, *Harriet Tubman*, 183–85.

38 Horton, "Kidnapping and Resistance," 167; Julia Griffith to G. Smith, September 24, 1851, Gerrit Smith Papers, Syracuse University Library, Syracuse, N.Y. Douglass published two other autobiographies, *My Bondage and My Freedom* in 1855 and *The Life and Times of Frederick Douglass* in 1881.

39 Larson, *Bound for the Promised Land*, 90–91; Clinton, *Harriet Tubman*, 84; Conrad, *General Harriet Tubman*, 45–49; *Frederick Douglass' Paper*, June 24, 1852.

40 "The 150th Anniversary Celebration of the Longwood Progressive Friends Meeting House, Kennett Square, Pennsylvania, May 22, 2005," Kennett Underground Railroad Center, http://undergroundrr.kennett.net/densmorelongwood2005.html, accessed May 27, 2008.

41 Purvis-Forten ties were further cemented in 1838 when Robert Purvis's brother Joseph married Harriet Purvis's sister Sarah Forten. Margaret Hope Bacon, *But One Race: The Life of Robert Purvis* (Albany: State University of New York Press, 2007), 8–10, 22.

42 James A. McGowan, *Station Master on the Underground Railroad: The Life and Letters of Thomas Garrett*, rev. ed. (Jefferson, N.C.: McFarland, 2005), 103.

43 Campbell, *Slave Catchers*, 199–207; Conrad, *General Harriet Tubman*, 80. The next-greatest numbers of arrests were thirty-seven in Indiana and thirty-four in Illinois. Larson reports being unable to find evidence to corroborate Sarah Bradford's claim of the $12,000 reward for Tubman (*Bound for the Promised Land*, 334, n. 23).

44 [Ednah Dow Cheney], "Moses," *Freedmen's Record*, March 1865, 36.

45 McGowan, *Station Master*, 103; Horton and Horton, *In Hope of Liberty*, 32–33; LeRoy Moore Jr., "The Spiritual Soul of Black Religion," *American Quarterly* 23, no. 5 (December 1971): 658–76, 674, 670.

46 Jean McMahon Humez, ed., *Gifts of Power: The Writings of Rebecca Jackson, Black Visionary, Shaker Eldress* (Amherst: University of Massachusetts Press, 1981), 312; Jean M. Humez, "In Search of Harriet Tubman's Spiritual Autobiography," *NWSA Journal* 5, no. 2 (Summer 1993): 162–82.

47 William Wells Brown, *The Rising Son, or The Antecedents and Advancement of the Colored Race* (1874; repr., Miami, Fla.: Mnemosyne, 1969), 538.

48 Thomas Garrett to Eliza Wigham and Mary Edmundson, August 28, 1854, in McGowan, *Station Master*, 167–68.

[49] Larson, *Bound for the Promised Land*, 128–29.

[50] Sarah H. Bradford, *Scenes in the Life of Harriet Tubman* (Auburn, N.Y.: W. J. Moses, 1869), 53, 50; Sarah H. Bradford, *Harriet Tubman: The Moses of Her People* (1886; repr., New York: Citadel Press, 1994), 6; McGowan, *Station Master*, 106; Larson, *Bound for the Promised Land*, xvii; Clinton, *Harriet Tubman*, 86–87; Conrad, *General Harriet Tubman*, 111; E. C. B. Galvin, "The Lore of the Negro in Central New York State" (Ph.D. diss., Cornell University, 1943), New-York Historical Society. Milton C. Sernett meticulously weighed the available evidence and recent scholarly work but came to no firm conclusions, although he seems to agree with Kate Larson's lower numbers. See Milton C. Sernett, *Harriet Tubman: Myth, Memory, and History* (Durham, N.C.: Duke University Press, 2007), 62.

[51] McGowan, *Station Master*, 162, 171.

[52] Joan D. Hedrick, *Harriet Beecher Stowe* (New York: Oxford University Press, 1994), 223.

[53] Humez, *Harriet Tubman*, 23.

[54] Horton and Horton, *Black Bostonians*, 118; *Annual Report of Edinburgh Ladies Emancipation Society, 1854*, in McGowan, *Station Master*, 164.

[55] Bradford, *Harriet Tubman*, 61–64.

[56] Conrad, *General Harriet Tubman*, 50–53.

[57] Robert Ross became John Stewart, Benjamin Ross became James Stewart, and Henry Ross first became Levin Stewart, then William Henry Stewart. Benjamin's fiancée, Jane, became Catherine. John Chase changed his name to Daniel Lloyd, and Peter Jackson became Tench Tilghman (Larson, *Bound for the Promised Land*, 114–15). There is some confusion in the historical record about the time of this escape, but a diary entry made by William Still dated December 29, 1854, provides detailed information about these runaways. See Humez, *Harriet Tubman*, 289–90; Still, *Underground Rail Road*, 305–8; and Larson, *Bound for the Promised Land*, 114–16. On the white John Stewart, see Clinton, *Harriet Tubman*, 22–23.

[58] Horton and Horton, *Slavery and the Making of America*, 209.

[59] Larson, *Bound for the Promised Land*, 117–18.

[60] Bradford, *Harriet Tubman*, 57–61.

[61] Larson, *Bound for the Promised Land*, 132.

[62] James Freeman Clarke, *Anti-Slavery Days: A Sketch of the Struggle Which Ended in the Abolition of Slavery in the United States* (New York: R. Worthington, 1884), 82–83.

[63] Conrad, *General Harriet Tubman*, 78–82; Larson, *Bound for the Promised Land*, 133–35.

[64] Conrad, *General Harriet Tubman*, 80–82.

[65] *Dred Scott v. Sandford* (1857), 19 Howard 393.

[66] James O. Horton and Lois E. Horton, "Violence, Protest, and Identity: Black Manhood in Antebellum America," in James Oliver Horton, *Free People of Color* (Washington, D.C.: Smithsonian Press, 1993), 80–97.

[67] Larson, *Bound for the Promised Land*, 138–43.

[68] Reeder, *Reports, Speeches, and Fragmentary Reflections*, 38, 15, 16.

[69] Larson, *Bound for the Promised Land*, 141–43.

[70] Ibid., 145–49.

[71] Brown, *Rising Son*, 536.

[72] Horton and Horton, *Black Bostonians*, 58–59.

[73] John Stewart Rock is identified in some documents as John Swett Rock. Horton and Horton, *Black Bostonians*, 63–64.

[74] Bradford, *Scenes*, 54–55. Bronson and Abigail Alcott were the parents of the famous writer Louisa May Alcott.

[75] Humez, *Harriet Tubman*, 168–69; Bradford, *Harriet Tubman*, 81–82.

[76] Horton and Horton, *Black Bostonians*, 70–71.

[77] "The Fourth at Framingham," *Liberator*, July 8, 1859, 106, col. 3; William S. McFeely, *Frederick Douglass* (New York: W. W. Norton, 1991), 95.

[78] "New England Convention of Colored Citizens," *Liberator*, August 26, 1859, 134, col. 3; Larson, *Bound for the Promised Land*, 173.

[79] Larson, *Bound for the Promised Land*, 156; McFeely, *Frederick Douglass*, 149.

[80] John Stauffer, *The Black Hearts of Men: Radical Abolitionists and the Transformation of Race* (Cambridge, Mass.: Harvard University Press, 2001), 14–15; Benjamin Quarles, *Allies for Freedom: Blacks and John Brown* (New York: Oxford University Press, 1974), 23; Horton and Horton, *In Hope of Liberty*, 243. Gerrit Smith donated 120,000 acres of land in the Adirondacks to African Americans so that they might satisfy a property requirement that applied only to black voters in New York.

[81] Quarles, *Allies for Freedom*, 32; Edward J. Renehan Jr., *The Secret Six: The True Tale of the Men Who Conspired with John Brown* (New York: Crown, 1995), 93, 95. Other contributors included minister Henry Ward Beecher and businessmen Amos Lawrence and Samuel Cabot. After the Harpers Ferry raid the government identified Parker, Howe, Smith, Stearns, Sanborn, and Thomas Wentworth Higginson as co-conspirators.

[82] Brown's son Frederick was killed in a second engagement in Kansas at Osawatomie in August 1856. Stauffer, *Black Hearts of Men*, 194–97, 236–38; Renehan, *Secret Six*, 112–14.

[83] Quarles, *Allies for Freedom*, 40; Jermain Wesley Loguen, *The Rev. J. W. Loguen as a Slave and as a Freeman: A Narrative of Real Life* (Syracuse, N.Y.: J. G. K. Truair, 1859), available online at http://docsouth.unc.edu/neh/loguen/loguen.html.

[84] Humez, *Harriet Tubman*, 242.

[85] Renehan, *Secret Six*, 144; John Brown to John Brown Jr., April 8, 1858, in Humez, *Harriet Tubman*, 295.

[86] The radical abolitionist, black nationalist, and Canadian resident Martin R. Delany did participate in the meeting. Milton C. Sernett, *North Star Country: Upstate New York and the Crusade for African American Freedom* (Syracuse, N.Y.: Syracuse University Press, 2002), 205; Larson, *Bound for the Promised Land*, 161.

[87] Larson, *Bound for the Promised Land*, 162. Burrell Smith, a laborer born in either Virginia or Massachusetts, lived at 168 Cambridge Street with his wife and son. When the North's first black Civil War regiment, the Fifty-Fourth Massachusetts Infantry, was formed, Smith enlisted, although he was in his late forties or early fifties at the time. *Boston City Directory*, 1855, 1859; U.S. Census, 1850, 1860.

[88] Frederick Douglass to the Ladies' Irish Anti-Slavery Association, January 8, 1859, in Humez, *Harriet Tubman*, 30.

[89] Stephen B. Oates, *To Purge This Land with Blood: A Biography of John Brown* (New York: Harper & Row, 1970), 261–62; W. E. Burghardt Du Bois, *John Brown* (1909; repr., New York: International Publishers, 1962), 192–94; Fergus M. Bordewich, *Bound for Canaan: The Epic Story of the Underground Railroad, America's First Civil Rights Movement* (New York: HarperCollins, 2005), 419–20.

[90] Oates, *To Purge This Land*, 265; Du Bois, *John Brown*, 197–98. Allan Pinkerton, a Scottish immigrant and abolitionist, was the first police detective in Chicago. In 1850 he founded what would become the famous Pinkerton National Detective Agency.

[91] Larson, *Bound for the Promised Land*, 163–64; Humez, *Harriet Tubman*, 28.

[92] Oates, *To Purge This Land*, 282–83; McFeely, *Frederick Douglass*, 196.

[93] "John Brown's Raid, 1859," EyeWitness to History, 2004, www.eyewitnesstohistory.com/johnbrown.htm, accessed August 28, 2008.

[94] Bradford, *Harriet Tubman*, 119; Du Bois, *John Brown*, 360, 282, 336; Renehan, *Secret Six*, 199–200.

[95] McFeely, *Frederick Douglass*, 198–99; Stauffer, *Black Hearts*, 247, 250.

[96] Stauffer, *Black Hearts*, 245–46, 261–62.

[97] A Native of the Old Dominion to John Brown, November 21, 1859, Governor Henry A. Wise Executive Papers, 1856–1859, State Government Records Collection, misc.

microfilm, accession 36710, reel 4219, 0147, Library of Virginia; W.L.G. to John Brown, November 1, 1859, Executive Papers, reel 4220, 0586. Theodore Parker, another of Brown's backers, ill with tuberculosis, had embarked on a cruise and extended vacation in 1858, before the raid, and died in Italy two years later. Renehan, *Secret Six*, 226, 232, 261.

[98] Du Bois, *John Brown*, 365; Stauffer, *Black Hearts*, 242. All six men captured with Brown were tried, convicted, and hanged. Four of the five escapees later fought in U.S. Civil War regiments, and the fifth, Brown's son Owen, settled first in Ohio and then in California.

[99] [Cheney], "Moses," 37; Bordewich, *Bound for Canaan*, 426; Oates, *To Purge This Land*, 318–19.

[100] Conrad, *General Harriet Tubman*, 142; [Cheney], "Moses," 38; Bradford, *Harriet Tubman*, 92–93.

[101] Oates, *To Purge This Land*, 319; "Speech of Dr. Rock," *Liberator*, March 12, 1858; Horton and Horton, *Black Bostonians*, 129.

[102] "A Fugitive Slave Case in Troy—Rescue of the Fugitive," *Douglass' Monthly*, June 1860; *Troy Whig*, April 28, 1860, in Emma C. Brown, "The Lore of the Negro in Central New York State" (Ph.D. diss., Cornell University, 1943), 39–40, New-York Historical Society; Horton, "Kidnapping and Resistance," 149–73; Larson, *Bound for the Promised Land*, 179–83.

[103] William Wells Brown, *The Negro in the American Rebellion: His Heroism and His Fidelity* (1867; repr., Miami, Fla.: Mnemosyne, 1969), 41–42.

[104] "Women's Rights Meeting," *Liberator*, July 6, 1860, 106.

[105] Eric Foner, *The Fiery Trial: Abraham Lincoln and American Slavery* (New York: W. W. Norton, 2010), 139–40, 143. The electoral vote count was 180 for Lincoln, 72 for the Southern Democrat John C. Breckinridge, 39 for the Constitutional Unionist John Bell, and 12 for the Northern Democrat Stephen A. Douglas.

[106] Larson, *Bound for the Promised Land*, 185–87.

[107] Ibid., 186; Humez, *Harriet Tubman*, 231–32.

[108] Larson, *Bound for the Promised Land*, 188.

[109] Bradford, *Harriet Tubman*, 38.

[110] Ibid., 36–37.

[111] Still, *Underground Rail Road*, 554–55.

[112] McFeely, *Frederick Douglass*, 208–11; Horton and Horton, *Black Bostonians*, 135.

[113] McFeely, *Frederick Douglass*, 211.

[114] Horton and Horton, *In Hope of Liberty*, 267.

[115] Larson, *Bound for the Promised Land*, 190, 191–92.

[116] "The Fall of Sumter," *Frederick Douglass' Monthly*, May 1861, in *The Life and Writings of Frederick Douglass*, ed. Philip S. Foner (New York: International Publishers, 1952), 3:91.

[117] Humez, *Harriet Tubman*, 49.

[118] Willie Lee Rose, *Rehearsal for Reconstruction: The Port Royal Experiment* (1964; repr.: University of Georgia Press, 1999), 20; Ira Berlin, Barbara J. Fields, Steven F. Miller, Joseph P. Reidy, and Leslie S. Rowland, *Slaves No More: Three Essays on Emancipation and the Civil War* (New York: Cambridge University Press, 1992), 93–96.

[119] Larson, *Bound for the Promised Land*, 197–202; Clinton, *Harriet Tubman*, 117–23; Conrad, *General Harriet Tubman*, 74–75.

[120] Mrs. Alexander D. Brickler Jr., August 14, 1939, in Conrad, *General Harriet Tubman*, 75.

[121] Butler's action, and later Congress's, called escaping slaves contraband on the presumption that they were a resource, like armaments and other materiel, for the rebels and thus could legally be taken into federal possession. Rose, *Rehearsal for Reconstruction*, 13–14; Foner, *Fiery Trial*, 175–78; Lydia Maria Child to Gerrit Smith, December 29, 1861, box 7, Gerrit Smith Papers, Syracuse University Library, Syracuse, N.Y.

122 Larson, *Bound for the Promised Land*, 204. A different version has her traveling by military ship directly from New York to Beaufort, South Carolina. The details in the version that has her traveling alone, however, make this account more credible. It could also help explain why Tubman had such trouble later attempting to prove to government pension authorities that she went to South Carolina on official military business.

123 Benjamin Guterman, "Doing 'Good Brave Work': Harriet Tubman's Testimony at Beaufort, South Carolina," *Prologue* 32, no. 3 (Fall 2000): 154–65, 156, 158.

124 Thomas Leonard Livermore, *Numbers and Losses in the Civil War in America, 1861–1865* (New York: Houghton Mifflin, 1900), 77–80.

125 The first official black U.S. troops were raised among the free black population of New Orleans by General Benjamin F. Butler. Hunter's remaining company was later incorporated into the First South Carolina Regiment. Noah Andre Trudeau, *Like Men of War: Black Troops in the Civil War, 1862–1865* (Boston: Little, Brown, 1998), 14, 15–16; Thomas Wentworth Higginson, *Army Life in a Black Regiment* (1870; repr., East Lansing: Michigan State University Press, 1960), 1; James M. McPherson, *The Negro's Civil War: How American Negroes Felt and Acted during the War for the Union* (New York: Vintage, 1965), 164–65.

126 Livermore, *Numbers and Losses*, 77–88.

127 Trudeau, *Like Men of War*, 17; Higginson, *Army Life*, 280–84. T. W. Higginson to Mary Channing Higginson, December 10, 1862, in *The Complete Civil War Journal and Selected Letters of Thomas Wentworth Higginson*, ed. Christopher Looby (Chicago: University of Chicago Press, 2000), 250–51.

128 Bradford, *Harriet Tubman*, 97–98.

129 Harriet Tubman Davis, Civil War Pension Records, RG 233, National Archives. Gullah is a creole language, combining Elizabethan English and African languages, that arose as a trading language on Africa's west coast and was spoken on the Sea Islands and in the coastal areas of South Carolina and Georgia.

130 McFeely, *Frederick Douglass*, 215–16.

131 Brown, *Negro in the American Rebellion*, 111–19, 119.

132 Higginson, *Army Life*, 30–31.

133 Harriet Tubman Davis, Civil War Pension Records, supporting documents; Larson, *Bound for the Promised Land*, 210. Tubman listed the names of the scouts she led in a statement for her pension application: Isaac Hayward, Arnott Blake, Gabriel Cahern, Sandy Sellers, George Chrisholm, Solomon Gregory, Peter Burns, Charles Simmons, Samuel Hayward, and Walter D. Plowden.

134 Trudeau, *Like Men of War*, 73.

135 Bradford, *Harriet Tubman*, 99–102; Larson, *Bound for the Promised Land*, 212–17; Higginson, *Army Life*, 127.

136 Emma Paddock Telford, "Harriet: The Modern Moses of Heroism and Visions," typescript, n.d. [circa 1905], in Humez, *Harriet Tubman*, 245–47.

137 Higginson, *Army Life*, 130–31.

138 Humez, *Harriet Tubman*, 246, 60–61; Larson, *Bound for the Promised Land*, 213.

139 "Harriet Tubman," *Commonwealth*, July 10, 1863, typescript, Earl Conrad Collection, Schomburg Center for Research in Black Culture, New York Public Library.

140 Guterman, "Doing 'Good Brave Work,'" 159.

141 Charlotte Forten Grimké, *The Journals of Charlotte Forten Grimké*, ed. Brenda Stevenson (New York: Oxford University Press, 1988), 442.

142 Larson, *Bound for the Promised Land*, 221; Trudeau, *Like Men of War*, 74–76.

143 Trudeau, *Like Men of War*, 78–85; Larson, *Bound for the Promised Land*, 220.

144 J. Rickard, "Battle of Fort Wagner, 11 and 18 July 1863," September 3, 2007, www.historyofwar.org/articles/battles_fort_wagner.html, accessed May 15, 2012; Trudeau, *Like Men of War*, 86, 85; John David Smith, "Let Us All Be Grateful That We Have Colored Troops That Will Fight," in *Black Soldiers in Blue: African American Troops in the Civil War Era*, ed. John David Smith (Chapel Hill: University of North Carolina Press, 2002), 47; Sernett, *North Star Country*, 241.

[145] Harriet Tubman, interview by Albert Bushnell Hart, in *Slavery and Abolition, 1831–1841* (New York: Harper & Brothers, 1906), 209. Hart recorded Tubman's last words in dialect, as "git in the craps" rather than "get in the crops."

[146] Larson, *Bound for the Promised Land*, 224.

[147] Ibid., 208, 226. Wendell and George Garrison were sons of William Lloyd Garrison.

[148] Trudeau, *Like Men of War*, 254.

[149] Mary A. Livermore, *My Story of the War: A Woman's Narrative of Four Years of Personal Experience* (1887; repr., New York: Da Capo, 1995), 599. The U.S. Sanitary Commission was formed during the Civil War to care for sick and wounded soldiers and veterans.

[150] Thomas Wentworth Higginson, letter to the editor, *New York Tribune*, August 12, 1864, in Higginson, *Army Life*, 289; Trudeau, *Like Men of War*, 254–55.

[151] Conrad, *General Harriet Tubman*, 183. Sojourner Truth, a well-known antislavery speaker, was born into slavery in New York and was a generation older than Tubman. She and Tubman were both friends and houseguests of Gerrit Smith and also met each other when in Boston. Nell Irvin Painter, *Sojourner Truth: A Life, a Symbol* (New York: W. W. Norton, 1996), 201–7.

[152] Larson, *Bound for the Promised Land*, 227.

[153] Bruce Levine, "In Search of a Usable Past: Neo-Confederates and Black Confederates," in *Slavery and Public History: The Tough Stuff of American Memory*, ed. James Oliver Horton and Lois E. Horton (New York: New Press, 2006), 187–211. For more on this topic, see Bruce Levine, *Confederate Emancipation: Southern Plans to Free and Arm Slaves during the Civil War* (New York: Oxford University Press, 2006), 146–47, 154–55.

[154] Frank A. Rollin, *Life and Public Services of Martin R. Delany* (1868; repr., New York: New York Public Library, 1997), 176–78; Horton and Horton, *In Hope of Liberty*, 156, 261; Dorothy Sterling, *The Making of an Afro-American: Martin Robeson Delany, 1812–1885* (New York: Da Capo, 1996), 169. Douglass had also broached this idea with Lincoln. Delany, along with the black ministers Henry Highland Garnet and Alexander Crummell, was a founder of the African Civilization Society, which sought to encourage African Americans to emigrate to Africa. He spent a year in Africa exploring settlement prospects and visited the Niger River valley, where his grandparents had been captured into slavery and then sent to America.

[155] Abraham Lincoln, "Second Inaugural Address," in *Collected Works of Abraham Lincoln*, ed. Roy P. Basler (New Brunswick, N.J.: Rutgers University Press, 1953), 8:332–33.

[156] Larson, *Bound for the Promised Land*, 65; Humez, *Harriet Tubman*, 65; "From Camp Wm. Penn," *Christian Recorder*, April 15, 1865.

[157] Foner, *Fiery Trial*, 328–29; *Christian Recorder*, April 22, 1865, in William Robert Forstchen, "The 28th United States Colored Troops: Indiana's African Americans Go to War, 1863–1865" (Ph.D. diss., Purdue University, 1994), 193–95; Nelson Lankford, *Richmond Burning: The Last Days of the Confederate Capital* (New York: Penguin, 2002), 127.

[158] Elizabeth Keckley, *Behind the Scenes* (New York: G. W. Carleton, 1868), 183–84. Pockets of Confederate resistance continued in the West, formally ending with the final surrender in June 1865.

[159] Martha Coffin Wright to Marianne Pelham Mott, November 7, 1865, in Humez, *Harriet Tubman*, 301–2.

[160] Larson, *Bound for the Promised Land*, 232.

[161] Ibid., 233–34; Dorothy Sterling, ed., *We Are Your Sisters: Black Women in the Nineteenth Century* (New York: W. W. Norton, 1984), 411. In 1868 the Fourteenth Amendment to the Constitution gave black men the vote. Women did not receive the vote until the ratification of the Nineteenth Amendment in 1920.

[162] Claudia Linares, "The Civil War Pension Law" (Working Paper 2001-6, Center for Population Economics, University of Chicago), 8–9, www.cpe.uchicago.edu/publication/lib/pension_cpe.pdf, accessed September 30, 2011; Larson, *Bound for the Promised Land*, 242; Bradford, *Scenes*; Clinton, *Harriet Tubman*, 196; Douglass, *Narrative*;

Solomon Northup, *Twelve Years a Slave*, ed. David Wilson (Auburn, N.Y.: Derby & Miller, 1853); Harriet Jacobs, *Incidents in the Life of a Slave Girl*, ed. Lydia Maria Child (Boston, 1861); Sojourner Truth, *Narrative of Sojourner Truth*, ed. Olive Gilbert (Boston, 1850).

[163] Bradford, *Scenes*, 21.

[164] Nelson G. Charles, military service record, National Archives, Washington, D.C.; General Affidavit, January 7, 1895, by Charles H. Peterson, and Neighbors' Affidavit, June 15, 1893, by Thornton Newton and Maggie Lucas, Harriet Tubman Davis, Civil War Pension Records.

[165] Harriet Tubman Davis, Civil War Pension Records.

[166] "Westminster Presbyterian Church of Auburn, New York: The Legacy Campaign, Celebrating 150 Years, 1862–2012," www.westminsterauburn.org/TiffanyWindow/tabid /53024/Default.aspx, April 8, 2009.

[167] Larson, *Bound for the Promised Land*, 252–53; Conrad, *General Harriet Tubman*, 205.

[168] James Oliver Horton and Lois E. Horton, *Hard Road to Freedom: The Story of African America* (New Brunswick, N.J.: Rutgers University Press, 2001), 194. Jay Cooke and Company made money selling bonds to finance the Civil War and the transcontinental railroad but collapsed when it had difficulty financing a new railroad. With Cooke's failure, the stock exchange closed for ten days, banks called in loans, foreclosures on houses and farms increased, factories laid off workers, and other banks failed, wiping out most of their depositors' savings.

[169] "The Gold Swindle and the Greenback Robbery," *Auburn Daily Bulletin*, October 6, 1873, reprinted in Humez, *Harriet Tubman*, 310–14; Larson, *Bound for the Promised Land*, 256–57.

[170] Larson, *Bound for the Promised Land*, 258–59.

[171] Ibid., 260; Affidavit of Maggie Lucas, Harriet Tubman widow's pension application, June 3, 1892, Harriet Tubman Davis, Civil War Pension Records.

[172] "Petition from Auburn Residents," Harriet Tubman Davis, Civil War Pension Records, supporting documents. The signatories, primarily from Auburn, also included a few from Syracuse, New York City, and Boston, including Mrs. William Lloyd Garrison and Ednah Dow Cheney. They replaced the destroyed house with a structure built of bricks from their brickyard. Larson, *Bound for the Promised Land*, 261.

[173] Humez, *Harriet Tubman*, 260–63.

[174] "Wendell Phillips Buried," *New York Times*, February 7, 1884; Conrad, *General Harriet Tubman*, 213.

[175] Harkless Bowley to Earl Conrad, November 26, 1939, in Humez, *Harriet Tubman*, 272; Larson, *Bound for the Promised Land*, 275–76; Humez, *Harriet Tubman*, 299; Linares, "The Civil War Pension Law," 11–13; Conrad, *General Harriet Tubman*, 223. Katie is probably the child Kate Larson lists in the Ross-Stewart family tree as Evelyn K. Stewart, born in 1899 to John Isaac Stewart, son of William H. Stewart, and Helena. Katie Stewart was one of three people, along with Tubman's friend Frances R. Smith, matron of the Harriet Tubman Home, and Tubman's niece Mary Gaston, named as heirs in Tubman's will.

[176] Harriet Tubman Davis, Civil War Pension Records; Larson, *Bound for the Promised Land*, 277–78; Humez, *Harriet Tubman*, 277. In 1867 Harriet learned that John Tubman had been shot and killed in an argument with a neighbor, a white man named Robert Vincent. John was apparently murdered, but the only witness was his thirteen-year-old son, whose testimony was unlikely to be credited in postwar Maryland. The men had quarreled earlier in the day, and Vincent claimed that when they met that afternoon, John physically threatened him. He said that he shot John in the head in self-defense. The jury acquitted Vincent after deliberating for only ten minutes.

[177] National Association of Colored Women's Clubs, *Official Minutes*, 1902, and "The Fight for the Ballot," *Rochester Democrat and Chronicle*, November 19, 1896, in

Humez, *Harriet Tubman*, 316–19, 320; Conrad, *General Harriet Tubman*, 215. Wheatley was an enslaved African in colonial Boston who became a well-known poet, and Garner was a runaway slave who famously killed her child in Ohio rather than allow her to be reenslaved.

[178] Larson, *Bound for the Promised Land*, 282.

[179] U.S. House, Committee on Invalid Pensions, Report No. 1774, 55th Cong., 3rd sess., January 19, 1899, and U.S. Senate, Committee on Pensions, Report No. 1619, 55th Cong., 3rd sess., February 7, 1899, Harriet Tubman Davis, Civil War Pension Records. Only a few nurses' pensions were more than $12 a month.

[180] Sernett, *Harriet Tubman*, 258–59.

[181] Handwritten note, January 1, 1903, title page, Sarah H. Bradford, *Harriet: The Moses of Her People* (New York:, J. J. Little, 1901), Susan B. Anthony Collection, Rare Book and Special Collections Division, Library of Congress, Washington, D.C.; Larson, *Bound for the Promised Land*, 287.

[182] Sernett, *Harriet Tubman*, 175, 176, 180; Larson, *Bound for the Promised Land*, 288–89; "Harriet Tubman Is Dead," *Auburn Citizen*, March 11, 1913, typescript, Earl Conrad Collection, box 2, Schomburg Center for Research in Black Culture, New York Public Library.

[183] Sarah H. Bradford, *Harriet: The Moses of Her People* (New York: George R. Lockwood & Son, 1886), 9; Larson, *Bound for the Promised Land*, 266–67; Sernett, *Harriet Tubman*, 107. Later printings of Bradford's book in 1897 and 1901 (see n. 181) also contributed to Tubman's income.

[184] "Harriet Tubman Dying," *New York Times*, March 11, 1913, 17; "Harriet Tubman Davis," *New York Times*, March 14, 1913, 9, col. 2.

[185] Sernett, *Harriet Tubman*, 178–82; "A Race of Harriets," *Auburn Citizen*, March 14, 1913, typescript, Conrad Collection, box 2, Schomburg Center for Research in Black Culture, New York Public Library.

[186] Sernett, *Harriet Tubman*, 186–90; "Let All Display Flags on the Morrow!" *Auburn Citizen*, June 11, 1914; David W. Blight, *Race and Reunion: The Civil War in American Memory* (Cambridge, Mass.: Belknap Press of Harvard University Press, 2001), 332.

[187] Blight, *Race and Reunion*, 221.

[188] Edward Tabor Linenthal, *Sacred Ground: Americans and Their Battlefields*, 2nd ed. (Urbana: University of Illinois Press, 1993), 95; Thomas Cripps, *Slow Fade to Black: The Negro in American Film, 1900–1942* (New York: Oxford University Press), 26, 52.

[189] Larson, *Bound for the Promised Land*, 290; Sernett, *Harriet Tubman*, 222, 293. Lawrence, a native of Harlem, studied with Alain Locke, a specialist in African American culture and chair of the philosophy department at Howard University.

[190] Dorothy Sterling, *Freedom Train: The Story of Harriet Tubman* (New York: Doubleday, 1954); Ann Petry, *Harriet Tubman: Conductor on the Underground Railroad* (New York: Thomas Y. Crowell, 1955); Joan Bacchus (Maynard) and Francis Taylor, *Golden Legacy: Illustrated History Magazine: The Saga of Harriet Tubman: "The Moses of Her People,"* vol. 2 (Dix Hills, N.Y.: Fitzgerald, 1967); Clinton, *Harriet Tubman*, 220.

[191] Alan Schroeder and Jerry Pinkney, *Minty: A Story of Young Harriet Tubman* (New York: Puffin, 2000); Courtni C. Wright, *Journey to Freedom: A Story of the Underground Railroad* (New York: Holiday House, 1994); Faith Ringgold, *Aunt Harriet's Underground Railroad in the Sky* (New York: Crown, 1992); Greg Toppo, "High Schoolers Name Women, Black Americans 'Most Famous,'" *USA Today*, February 4, 2008. The survey conducted by Sam Wineburg and Chauncey Monte-Sano, professors at Stanford University and the University of Maryland, respectively, found the most famous Americans, excluding presidents and first ladies, to be, in order, Martin Luther King Jr., Rosa Parks, Harriet Tubman, Susan B. Anthony, Benjamin Franklin, Amelia Earhart, Oprah Winfrey, Marilyn Monroe, Thomas Alva Edison, and Albert Einstein.

PART TWO

The Documents

1

U.S. CONSTITUTION

Provision regarding Fugitive Slaves
1787

---

*Slavery was a contentious issue from the very beginning of the United
States. Immediately after the Revolution, some northern states ended
slavery, and others provided for its gradual abolition. But southern states
wanted to protect their property in slaves from interference by the federal
government. The Constitution, approved in 1787 and ratified by the req-
uisite nine states in 1788, did not use the word* slavery, *but its intended
focus on slaveholders' rights to their slaves' labor is nonetheless clear. The
issue of slavery continued to aggravate North-South relations and was
the subject of a series of legislative compromises until slavery was finally
abolished after the Civil War.*

No person held to service or labour in one State under the laws thereof,
escaping into another, shall, in consequence of any law or regulation
therein, be discharged from such service or labour, but shall be delivered up on claim of the party to whom such service or labour may
be due.

U.S. Constitution, Article IV, Section II. Constitutional Convention, September 17, 1787.

2

Fugitive Slave Law

1793

*With this law Congress added enforcement provisions to the article of the
U.S. Constitution concerning fugitives from slavery, adding penalties for
aiding a slave's escape. As throughout the Constitution, the word* slavery
*is not used here. Instead, escaping from slavery is called escaping from
service or labor owed and is classed with treason, felonies, and other
crimes. Ironically, such fugitives were included in the phrase "fugitive
from justice." Aiding an escaped slave at first carried lesser penalties than
aiding other fugitives from the law, but as the Underground Railroad
grew, harsher penalties were added for people who helped freedom seekers.*

An Act Respecting Fugitives from Justice, and Persons Escaping from the Service of Their Masters

Sec. 1. *Be it enacted by the Senate and House of Representatives of the
United States of America in Congress assembled,* That whenever the
executive authority of any State in the Union, or of either of the territories northwest or south of the river Ohio, shall demand any person
as a fugitive from justice, of the executive authority of any such state
or territory to which such person shall have fled, and shall moreover
produce the copy of an indictment found, or an affidavit made before a
magistrate of any state or territory as aforesaid, charging the person so
demanded, with having committed treason, felony or other crime, certified as authentic by the governor or chief magistrate of the state or territory from whence the person so charged fled, it shall be the duty of the
executive authority of the state or territory to which such person shall
have fled, to cause him or her to be arrested and secured, and notice of
the arrest to be given to the executive authority making such demand,
or to the agent of such authority appointed to receive the fugitive, and
to cause the fugitive to be delivered to such agent when he shall appear:
But if no such agent shall appear within six months from the time of

From "Proceedings and Debates of the House of Representatives of the United States at
the Second Session of the Second Congress, Begun at the City of Philadelphia, November 5, 1792," *Annals of the Congress of the United States,* 2nd Cong., 2nd sess., November
5, 1792, to March 2, 1793, 1414–15.

the arrest, the prisoner may be discharged. And all costs or expenses incurred in the apprehending, securing, and transmitting such fugitive to the state or territory making such demand, shall be paid by such state or territory.

Sec. 2. *And be it further enacted*, That any agent appointed as aforesaid, who shall receive the fugitive into his custody, shall be empowered to transport him or her to the state or territory from which he or she shall have fled. And if any person or persons shall by force set at liberty, or rescue the fugitive from such agent while transporting, as aforesaid, the person or persons so offending shall, on conviction, be fined not exceeding five hundred dollars, and be imprisoned not exceeding one year.

Sec. 3. *And be it also enacted*, That when a person held to labor in any of the United States, or in either of the territories on the northwest or south of the river Ohio, under the laws thereof, shall escape into any other part of the said states or territory, the person to whom such labor or service may be due, his agent or attorney, is hereby empowered to seize or arrest such fugitive from labor, and to take him or her before any judge of the Circuit or District Courts of the United States, residing or being within the state, or before any magistrate of a county, city or town corporate, wherein such seizure or arrest shall be made, and upon proof to the satisfaction of such judge or magistrate, either by oral testimony or affidavit taken before and certified by a magistrate of any such state or territory, that the person so seized or arrested, doth, under the laws of the state or territory from which he or she fled, owe service or labor to the person claiming him or her, it shall be the duty of such judge or magistrate to give a certificate thereof to such claimant, his agent or attorney, which shall be sufficient warrant for removing the said fugitive from labor, to the state or territory from which he or she fled.

Sec. 4. *And be it further enacted*, That any person who shall knowingly and willingly obstruct or hinder such claimant, his agent or attorney when so arrested pursuant to the authority herein given and declared: or shall harbor or conceal such person after notice that he or she was a fugitive from labor, as aforesaid, shall, for either of the said offences, forfeit and pay the sum of five hundred dollars. Which penalty may be recovered by and for the benefit of such claimant, by action of debt, in any court proper to try the same; saving moreover to the person claiming such labor or service, his right of action for or on account of the said injuries or either of them. . . .

Approved February 12th, 1793.

3

Fugitive Slave Law

1850

When this fugitive slave law was passed, many African Americans who had escaped slavery and lived in the North for many years felt endangered. Harriet Tubman and her family were among the many blacks who settled on safer ground in Canada. By making the recovery process easier and denying the accused the right of self-defense, it also exacerbated free blacks' fears of being kidnapped into slavery. This law was one of five acts that made up the Compromise of 1850. It strengthened the provisions of the 1793 law (Document 2) by removing the requirement that the fugitive be brought before a judge, adding a prison term to the monetary penalty for aiding a fugitive, and requiring the help of bystanders in a fugitive's capture. Some provisions were designed to nullify state laws giving fugitives more rights and prohibiting state officials from participating in returning fugitives to slavery.

Other parts of the Compromise of 1850 admitted the free state of California to the Union under the doctrine of popular sovereignty, settled the boundaries of Texas, acquired the debt of the former Republic of Texas, established the territories of Utah and New Mexico, and abolished the slave trade (but not slavery) in the District of Columbia. When President Millard Fillmore signed the Fugitive Slave Act into law in September 1850, it further inflamed sectional tensions. It seemed so biased in favor of slaveholders and in violation of basic rights that it helped abolitionists recruit some northerners to the antislavery cause.

An Act to amend, and supplementary to, the Act entitled "An Act respecting Fugitives from Justice, and Persons escaping from the Service of their Masters," approved February twelfth, one thousand seven hundred and ninety-three.

From Resolution introduced by Senator Henry Clay in relation to the adjustment of all existing questions of controversy between the states arising out of the institution of slavery (the resolution later became known as the Compromise of 1850), January 29, 1850; Senate Simple Resolutions, Motions, and Orders of the 31st Congress, ca. 03/1849– ca. 03/1851, RG 46, National Archives.

Be it enacted by the Senate and House of Representatives of the United States of America in congress assembled, That the persons who have been, or may hereafter be, appointed commissioners, in virtue of any act of Congress, by the Circuit Courts of the United States and who, in consequence of such appointment, are authorized to exercise the powers that any justice of the peace, or other magistrate of any of the United States, may exercise in respect to offenders for any crime or offence against the United States, by arresting, imprisoning, or bailing the same . . . are hereby, authorized and required to exercise and discharge all the powers and duties conferred by this act. . . .

Sec. 4. *And be it further enacted,* That the commissioners above named shall have concurrent jurisdiction with the judges of the Circuit and District Courts of the United States . . . and shall grant certificates to such claimants, upon satisfactory proof being made, with authority to take and remove such fugitives from service or labor, under the restrictions herein contained, to the State or Territory from which such persons may have escaped or fled.

Sec. 5. *And be it further enacted,* That it shall be the duty of all marshals and deputy marshals to obey and execute all warrants and precepts issued under the provisions of this act, when to them directed; and should any marshal or deputy marshal refuse to receive such warrant, or other process, when tendered, or to use all proper means diligently to execute the same, he shall, on conviction thereof, be fined in the sum of one thousand dollars, to the use of such claimant, on the motion of such claimant, by the Circuit or District Court for the district of such marshal; and after arrest of such fugitive, by such marshal or his deputy, or whilst at any time in his custody under the provisions of this act, should such fugitive escape, whether with or without the assent of such marshal or his deputy, such marshal shall be liable, on his official bond, to be prosecuted for the benefit of such claimant, for the full value of the service or labor of said fugitive . . . and the better to enable the said commissioners . . . to execute their duties faithfully and efficiently, . . . they are hereby authorized and empowered . . . to appoint . . . any one or more suitable persons, from time to time, to execute all such warrants and other process . . . with authority to such commissioners, or the persons to be appointed by them, . . . to summon and call to their aid the bystanders, or *posse comitatus* of the proper county . . . ; and all good citizens are hereby commanded to aid and assist in the prompt and efficient execution of this law, whenever their services may be required. . . .

Sec. 6. *And be it further enacted*, That when a person held to service or labor in any State or Territory of the United States, has heretofore or shall hereafter escape into another State or Territory of the United States, the person or persons to whom such service or labor may be due, or his, her, or their agent or attorney . . . may pursue and reclaim such fugitive person, either by procuring a warrant from some one of the courts, judges, or commissioners aforesaid, of the proper circuit, district, or county, for the apprehension of such fugitive from service or labor, or by seizing and arresting such fugitive, where the same can be done without process, and by taking, or causing such person to be taken, forthwith before such court, judge, or commissioner, whose duty it shall be to hear and determine the case of such claimant in a summary manner; and upon satisfactory proof being made, by deposition or affidavit, in writing, to be taken and certified by such court, judge, or commissioner, or by other satisfactory testimony . . . of the identity of the person whose service or labor is claimed to be due as aforesaid, that the person so arrested does in fact owe service or labor to the person or persons claiming him or her . . . and that said person escaped, to make out and deliver to such claimant, his or her agent or attorney, a certificate setting forth the substantial facts . . . with authority to such claimant, or his or her agent or attorney, to use such reasonable force and restraint as may be necessary, under the circumstances of the case, to take and remove such fugitive person back to the State or Territory whence he or she may have escaped. . . . In no trial or hearing under this act shall the testimony of such alleged fugitive be admitted in evidence; and the certificates . . . shall be conclusive of the right of the person or persons in whose favor granted, to remove such fugitive to the State or Territory from which he escaped, and shall prevent all molestation of such person or persons by any process issued by any court, judge, magistrate, or other person whomsoever.

Sec. 7. *And be it further enacted*, That any person who shall knowingly and willingly obstruct, hinder, or prevent such claimant, his agent or attorney, or any person or persons lawfully assisting him, her, or them, from arresting such a fugitive from service or labor . . . or shall rescue, or attempt to rescue, such fugitive . . . ; or shall aid, abet, or assist such person . . . , directly or indirectly, to escape . . . ; or shall harbor or conceal such fugitive, so as to prevent the discovery and arrest of such person, . . . shall, for either of said offences, be subject to a fine not exceeding one thousand dollars, and imprisonment not exceeding six months . . . ; and shall moreover forfeit and pay, by way of civil damages to the party injured by such illegal conduct, the sum of one thousand dollars, for each fugitive so lost. . . .

Sec. 8. *And be it further enacted*, That . . . in all cases where the proceedings are before a commissioner, he shall be entitled to a fee of ten dollars in full for his services in each case, upon the delivery of the said certificate to the claimant, his or her agent or attorney; or a fee of five dollars in cases where the proof shall not, in the opinion of such commissioner, warrant such certificate and delivery. . . .

Sec. 9. *And be it further enacted*, That, upon affidavit made by the claimant of such fugitive, his agent or attorney, after such certificate has been issued, that he has reason to apprehend that such fugitive will be rescued by force from his or their possession before he can be taken beyond the limits of the State in which the arrest is made, it shall be the duty of the officer making the arrest to retain such fugitive in his custody, and to remove him to the State whence he fled, and there to deliver him to said claimant, his agent, or attorney. And to this end, the officer aforesaid is hereby authorized and required to employ so many persons as he may deem necessary to overcome such force, and to retain them in his service so long as circumstances may require. The said officer and his assistants, while so employed, to receive the same compensation, and to be allowed the same expenses, as are now allowed by law for transportation of criminals, to be certified by the judge of the district within which the arrest is made, and paid out of the treasury of the United States. . . .

Approved September 18, 1850.

4

AUSTIN BEARSE

Reminiscences of Fugitive-Slave Law
Days in Boston
1818–1830

Austin Bearse was a white shipmaster in Boston from 1818 to 1830 and a member of the city's vigilance committee dedicated to aiding fugitives from slavery. Before becoming an abolitionist, Bearse had worked on Boston ships that plied the southern coast in the winter and had witnessed slavery firsthand. Later, as a ship captain, he rescued runaways and in his memoir recounted slave rescues and attempted rescues in Boston. His recollection of New England ships' involvement in the South paints a vivid picture of the internal slave trade that disrupted so many slave communities, took Harriet Tubman's sisters, and threatened Tubman herself and other family members. The fear of being sold away from one's family to the Deep South, where conditions for slaves were generally even harsher than in the upper South, prompted many escape attempts.

I am a native of the State of Massachusetts. Between 1818 and 1830, I was from time to time mate on board of different vessels engaged in the coasting trade on the coast of South Carolina. It is well known that many New England vessels are in the habit of spending their winters on the Southern coast, in pursuit of this business—for vessels used to run up the rivers for the rough rice and cotton of the plantations, which we took to Charleston. We often carried gangs of slaves to the plantations as they had been ordered. These slaves were generally collected by slave-traders in Charleston, brought there by various causes, such as the death of owners and the division of estates, which threw them into the market. Some were sent as punishment for insubordination, or because the domestic establishment was too large; or because persons moving to the North and West preferred selling their slaves to the trouble of carrying them. We had on board our vessels, from

From Austin Bearse, *Reminiscences of Fugitive-Slave Law Days in Boston* (Boston: Warren Richardson, 1880), 8–9.

time to time, numbers of these slaves—sometimes two or three, and sometimes as high as seventy or eighty. They were separated from their families and connections with as little concern as calves and pigs are selected out of a lot of domestic animals. Our vessel used to lie at a place called Poor Man's Hole, not far from the city. We used to allow the relatives and friends of the slaves to come on board and stay all night with their friends, before the vessel sailed. In the morning it used to be my business to pull off the hatches and warn them that it was time to separate, and the shrieks and cries at these times were enough to make anybody's heart ache. In the year 1828, while mate of the brig "Milton," of Boston, bound from Charleston, S.C., to New Orleans, the following incident occurred, which I shall never forget. The traders brought on board four quadroon men[1] in handcuffs. An old negro woman, more than eighty years of age, came screaming after them, "My son! Oh, my son!" She seemed almost frantic, and when we had got more than a mile out in the harbor, we heard her screaming yet. When we were in the Gulf Stream, I came to the men and took off their handcuffs. They were resolute fellows, and they told me I would see they would never live to be slaves in New Orleans. One of them was a carpenter and one a blacksmith. We brought them into New Orleans, and consigned them over to the agent. The agent told the captain that in forty-eight hours afterwards they were all dead men, having every one killed himself as they said they should. One of them I know was bought for a fireman on the steamer "Post Boy," that went down to the Balize.[2] He jumped overboard and was drowned.

[1] African Americans identified as having one-quarter African ancestry.
[2] In Central America.

5

SOLOMON NORTHUP

Kidnapped into Slavery

1853

In 1841 Solomon Northup, a black musician born free in New York State, was offered a job in Washington, D.C., by two white men, who drugged him and sold him to a slave trader. Northup spent twelve years in slavery in Louisiana before he finally got word to his wife and New York authorities rescued him. He recounted his kidnapping in his 1853 memoir, Twelve Years a Slave, *which he dedicated to Harriet Beecher Stowe, the author of the influential* Uncle Tom's Cabin. *The popularity of Stowe's book, Northup's narrative, and other slave autobiographies increased abolitionist sentiment and greatly facilitated Tubman's fundraising for her rescues and other antislavery work. Northup's book also showed that kidnapping was a common danger for free blacks, especially in the border areas between slave and free states.*

The pain in my head had subsided in a measure, but I was very faint and weak. I was sitting upon a low bench, made of rough boards, and without coat or hat. I was hand-cuffed. Around my ankles also were a pair of heavy fetters. One end of a chain was fastened to a large ring in the floor, the other to the fetters on my ankles. I tried in vain to stand upon my feet. Waking from such a painful trance, it was some time before I could collect my thoughts. Where was I? What was the meaning of these chains? . . . What had I done to deserve imprisonment in such a dungeon? I could not comprehend. There was a blank of some indefinite period, preceding my awakening in that lonely place, the events of which the utmost stretch of memory was unable to recall. I listened intently for some sign or sound of life, but nothing broke the oppressive silence, save the clinking of my chains, whenever I chanced to move. I spoke aloud, but the sound of my voice startled me. I felt of my pockets, so far as the fetters would allow—far enough, indeed, to ascertain that I had not only been robbed of liberty, but that my money and free

From Solomon Northup, *Twelve Years a Slave*, ed. Sue Eakin and Joseph Logsdon (Baton Rouge: Louisiana State University Press, 1968), 19–20, 23, 25–26, 38, 41–42.

papers were also gone! Then did the idea begin to break upon my mind, at first dim and confused, that I had been kidnapped. But that I thought was incredible. There must have been some misapprehension—some unfortunate mistake. It could not be that a free citizen of New-York, who had wronged no man, nor violated any law, should be dealt with thus inhumanly. The more I contemplated my situation, however, the more I became confirmed in my suspicions. It was a desolate thought, indeed. I felt there was no trust or mercy in unfeeling man; and commending myself to the God of the oppressed, bowed my head upon my fettered hands, and wept most bitterly. . . .

"Well, my boy, how do you feel now?" said [slave dealer James H.] Burch, as he entered through the open door. I replied that I was sick, and inquired the cause of my imprisonment. He answered that I was his slave—that he had bought me, and that he was about to send me to New-Orleans. I asserted, aloud and boldly, that I was a free man—a resident of Saratoga, where I had a wife and children, who were also free, and that my name was Northup. I complained bitterly of the strange treatment I had received, and threatened, upon my liberation, to have satisfaction for the wrong. He denied that I was free, and with an emphatic oath, declared that I came from Georgia. Again and again I asserted I was no man's slave, and insisted upon his taking off my chains at once. He endeavored to hush me, as if he feared my voice would be overheard. But I would not be silent, and denounced the authors of my imprisonment, whoever they might be, as unmitigated villains. Finding he could not quiet me, he flew into a towering passion. With blasphemous oaths, he called me a black liar, a runaway from Georgia, and every other profane and vulgar epithet that the most indecent fancy could conceive. . . .

. . . With the paddle, Burch commenced beating me. Blow after blow was inflicted upon my naked body. When his unrelenting arm grew tired, he stopped and asked if I still insisted I was a free man. I did insist upon it, and then the blows were renewed, faster and more energetically, if possible, than before. When again tired, he would repeat the same question, and receiving the same answer, continue his cruel labor. All this time, the incarnate devil was uttering most fiendish oaths. At length the paddle broke, leaving the useless handle in his hand. Still I would not yield. All his brutal blows could not force from my lips the foul lie that I was a slave. Casting madly on the floor the handle of the broken paddle, he seized the rope.[3] This was far more painful than

---

[3] The rope was a whip called a cat-o'-nine-tails, with the end unraveled and a knot tied at the end of each strand.

the other. I struggled with all my power, but it was in vain. I prayed for mercy, but my prayer was only answered with imprecations and with stripes. I thought I must die beneath the lashes of the accursed brute. Even now the flesh crawls upon my bones, as I recall the scene. I was all on fire. My sufferings I can compare to nothing else than the burning agonies of hell!

At last I became silent to his repeated questions. I would make no reply. In fact, I was becoming almost unable to speak. Still he plied the lash without stint upon my poor body, until it seemed that the lacerated flesh was stripped from my bones at every stroke. A man with a particle of mercy in his soul would not have beaten even a dog so cruelly. At length [Burch's jail keeper Ebenezer] Radburn said that it was useless to whip me any more—that I would be sore enough. Thereupon Burch desisted, saying, with an admonitory shake of his fist in my face, and hissing the words through his firm-set teeth, that if ever I dared to utter again that I was entitled to my freedom, that I had been kidnapped, or any thing whatever of the kind, the castigation I had just received was nothing in comparison with what would follow. He swore that he would either conquer or kill me. With these consolatory words, the fetters were taken from my wrists, my feet still remaining fastened to the ring; the shutter of the little barred window, which had been opened, was again closed, and going out, locking the great door behind them, I was left in darkness as before. . . .

. . . [After the slaves were transported and confined to a slave pen in Richmond, Virginia, Burch admonished Northup], "If ever I hear you say a word about New-York, or about your freedom, I will be the death of you—I will kill you; you may rely on that." . . .

I doubt not he understood then better than I did, the danger and the penalty of selling a free man into slavery. He felt the necessity of closing my mouth against the crime he knew he was committing. Of course, my life would not have weighed a feather, in any emergency requiring such a sacrifice. Undoubtedly, he meant precisely what he said.

Under the shed on one side of the yard, there was constructed a rough table, while overhead were sleeping lofts—the same as in the pen at Washington. After partaking at this table of our supper of pork and bread, I was hand-cuffed to a large yellow man, quite stout and fleshy, with a countenance expressive of the utmost melancholy. He was a man of intelligence and information. Chained together, it was not long before we became acquainted with each other's history. His name was Robert. Like myself, he had been born free, and had a wife and two children in Cincinnati. He said he had come south with two men, who had hired him in the city of his residence. Without free papers, he had been seized at Fredericksburgh [*sic*], placed in confinement, and beaten until he had learned, as I had, the necessity and the policy of silence. He had been in [the slave trader's] pen about three weeks. To this man I became much attached. We could sympathize with, and understand each other. It was with tears and a heavy heart, not many days subsequently, that I saw him die, and looked for the last time upon his lifeless form! . . .

After we were all on board, the brig Orleans proceeded down James River. Passing into Chesapeake Bay, we arrived next day opposite the city of Norfolk. While lying at anchor, a lighter[4] approached us from the town, bringing four more slaves. Frederick, a boy of eighteen, had been born a slave, as also had Henry, who was some years older. They had both been house servants in the city. Maria was a rather genteel looking colored girl, with a faultless form, but ignorant and extremely vain. The idea of going to New-Orleans was pleasing to her. She entertained an extravagantly high opinion of her own attractions. Assuming a haughty mien, she declared to her companions, that immediately on our arrival in New-Orleans, she had no doubt, some wealthy single gentleman of good taste would purchase her at once!

But the most prominent of the four, was a man named Arthur. As the lighter approached, he struggled stoutly with his keepers. It was with main force that he was dragged aboard the brig. He protested, in a loud voice, against the treatment he was receiving, and demanded to be released. His face was swollen, and covered with wounds and bruises, and, indeed, one side of it was a complete raw sore. He was forced, with all haste, down the hatchway into the hold. I caught an outline of his story as he was borne struggling along, of which he afterwards gave me a more full relation, and it was as follows: He had long resided in the city of Norfolk, and was a free man. He had a family living there, and was a mason by trade. Having been unusually detained, he was returning late one night to his house in the suburbs of the city, when he was attacked by a gang of persons in an unfrequented street. He fought until his strength failed him. Overpowered at last, he was gagged and bound with ropes, and beaten, until he became insensible. For several days they secreted him in the slave pen at Norfolk—a very common establishment, it appears, in the cities of the South. The night before, he had been taken out and put on board the lighter, which, pushing out from shore, had awaited our arrival. For some time he continued his protestations, and was altogether irreconcilable. At length, however, he became

[4] A flat-bottomed cargo boat.

silent. He sank into a gloomy and thoughtful mood, and appeared to be counseling with himself. There was in the man's determined face, something that suggested the thought of desperation.

6

ELIZA ANN BRODESS

Runaway Advertisement

1849

Slaveowners often placed advertisements for escaped slaves in newspapers, offering rewards and enlisting virtually the entire white population in their capture. Eliza Ann Brodess, Edward Brodess's widow, placed this runaway ad for Harriet Tubman (called Minty) and her brothers Ben and Henry (called Harry) in October 1849. The advertisement ran in the local Cambridge (Md.) Democrat *and in the* Delaware Gazette, *published in Delaware City. Situated south of Wilmington, across Delaware Bay from New Jersey, Delaware City was located on a water route from Delaware to Philadelphia.*

THREE HUNDRED DOLLARS REWARD.

RAN AWAY from the subscriber on Monday the 17th ult., three negroes, named as follows: HARRY, aged about 19 years, has on one side of his neck a wen,[5] just under the ear, he is of a dark chestnut color, about 5 feet 8 or 9 inches hight [*sic*]; BEN, aged aged [*sic*] about 25 years, is very quick to speak when spoken to, he is of a chestnut color, about six feet high; MINTY, aged about 27 years, is of a chestnut color, fine looking, and about 5 feet high. One hundred dollars reward will be given for each of the above named negroes, if taken out of the State, and $50

---

[5] A cyst or swelling.

Eliza Ann Brodess, "Three Hundred Dollars Reward," *Cambridge Democrat*, October 3, 1849.

each if taken in the State. They must be lodged in Baltimore, Easton or Cambridge Jail, in Maryland.

ELIZA ANN BRODESS,
Near Bucktown, Dorchester county, Md.
Oct. 3d, 1849.

The Delaware Gazette will please copy the above three weeks, and charge this office.

7

LIBERATOR

Slave-Hunters in Boston
November 1, 1850

Harriet Tubman began her Underground Railroad career just a few months after the Fugitive Slave Law of 1850 (Document 3) made rescues more difficult and dangerous. Shortly after its passage, slave catchers demonstrated the law's reach far into the North. Their attempt in 1850 to return William and Ellen Craft to slavery from Boston also revealed the growing conflict the law exacerbated. Among the Bostonians who hid the Crafts were two federal commissioners charged with enforcing the fugitive slave law. Boston abolitionists protected the Crafts from capture and sent them to freedom in England. This account from William Lloyd Garrison's antislavery newspaper, the Liberator, *reveals the sympathy of local residents, including officials, for escaped slaves and shows African American defiance of the law. It also attempts to discredit one of the slave catchers, quoting him directly to demonstrate his lack of education.*

Our city, for a week past, has been thrown into a state of intense excitement by the appearance of two prowling villains, named Hughes and Knight, from Macon, Georgia, for the purpose of seizing William and Ellen Craft, under the infernal Fugitive Slave Bill, and carrying them

From "Slave-Hunters in Boston," *Liberator*, November 1, 1850.

back to the hell of Slavery. Since the day of '76, there has not been such a popular demonstration on the side of human freedom in this region. The humane and patriotic contagion has infected all classes. Scarcely any other subject has been talked about in the streets, or in the social circle. On Thursday, of last week, warrants for the arrest of William and Ellen were issued by Judge Levi Woodbury, but no officer has yet been found ready or bold enough to serve them. In the meantime, the Vigilance Committee, appointed at the Faneuil Hall meeting, has not been idle. Their number has been increased to upwards of a hundred "good men and true," including some thirty or forty members of the bar; and they have been in constant session, devising every legal method to baffle the pursuing bloodhounds, and relieve the city of their hateful presence. On Saturday placards were posted up in all directions, announcing the arrival of these slave-hunters, and describing their persons. On the same day, Hughes and Knight were arrested on the charge of slander against William Craft. The [(Boston) Daily] Chronotype says, the damages being laid at $10,000; bail was demanded in the same sum, and was promptly furnished. . . .

Hughes and Knight have since been twice arrested and put under bonds of $10,000 (making $30,000 in all), charged with a conspiracy to kidnap and abduct William Craft, a peaceable citizen of Massachusetts, etc. . . .

The following (says the Chronotype), is a *verbatim et literatim* copy of one letter sent by Knight to Craft, to entice him to the U.S. Hotel, in order to kidnap him. It shows, that the school-master owes Knight more "service and labor" than it is possible for Craft to:

BOSTON, OCT. 22, 1850, 11 OCLK P.M.

WM. CRAFT—SIR—I have to leave so Eirley in the morning that I cold not call according to promis, so if you want me to carry a letter home with me, you must bring it to the United States Hotel to morrow and leave it in box 44, or come your self to morro eavening after tea and bring it. Let me no if you come your self by sending a note to box 44 U. S. Hotel so that I may know whether to wate after tea or not by the Bearer. If your wife wants to see me you cold bring her with you, if you come your self.

JOHN KNIGHT.

P.S. I shall leave for home eirley a Thursday moring.   J.K.

At a meeting of colored people, held in Belknap Street Church, on Friday evening, the following resolutions were unanimously adopted:

Resolved, That God willed us free; man willed us slaves. We will as God wills; God's will be done.

Resolved, That our oft repeated determination to resist oppression is the same now as ever, and we pledge ourselves, at all hazards, to resist unto death any attempt upon our liberties.

Resolved, That as South Carolina seizes and imprisons colored seamen from the North, under the plea that it is to prevent insurrection and rebellion among her colored population, the authorities of this State, and city in particular, be requested to lay hold of, and put in prison, immediately, any and all fugitive slave-hunters who may be found among us, upon the same ground, and for similar reasons. . . .

Telegraphic intelligence is received, that President Fillmore has announced his determination to sustain the Fugitive Slave Bill, at all hazards. Let him try!

The fugitives, as well as the colored people generally, seem determined to carry out the spirit of the resolutions to their fullest extent.

8

THOMAS GARRETT

Sending Underground Railroad Passengers to Philadelphia

1854

In Wilmington, Delaware, Harriet Tubman's friend Thomas Garrett operated one of the most active stations on the Underground Railroad. Tubman frequently stopped there en route from Maryland to the North. This note on Tubman's behalf to the Philadelphia Anti-Slavery Society office shows both the hardships of escaping from slavery and the need for an extensive network of trustworthy people to help freedom seekers along the way.

From William Still, *The Underground Rail Road* (1872; repr., Chicago: Johnson, 1970), 305.

WILMINGTON, 12 Mo. 29TH, 1854

Esteemed Friend, J. Miller McKim:

We made arrangements last night, and sent away Harriet Tubman, with six men and one woman to Allen Agnew's, to be forwarded across the country to the city. Harriet, and one of the men had worn their shoes off their feet, and I gave them two dollars to help fit them out, and directed a carriage to be hired at my expense, to take them out, but do not yet know the expense. I now have two more from the lowest county in Maryland, on the Peninsula, upwards of one hundred miles. I will try to get one of our trusty colored men to take them to-morrow morning to the Anti-slavery office. You can then pass them on.

THOMAS GARRETT.

9

WILLIAM STILL

Moses Arrives with Six Passengers

1854

William Still, chair of the Philadelphia Vigilance Committee and one of Tubman's most important contacts, kept an extensive record of the fugitives who came through his Underground Railroad station, including detailed descriptions of them, their lives in slavery, and their reasons for escaping. In this passage from his book The Underground Rail Road, *published in 1872, he documents Tubman's arrival in 1854 with six fugitives and describes her indomitability. Such accounts helped construct the mythology of Tubman's nearly superhuman powers.*

Harriet Tubman had been their "Moses." . . . She had faithfully gone down into Egypt, and had delivered these six bondmen by her own heroism. Harriet was a woman of no pretensions, indeed, a more ordinary specimen of humanity could hardly be found among the most unfortunate-looking farm hands of the South. Yet, in point of courage,

From William Still, *The Underground Rail Road* (1872; repr., Chicago: Johnson, 1970), 305–8.

shrewdness and disinterested exertions to rescue her fellow-men, by making personal visits to Maryland among the slaves, she was without her equal.

Her success was wonderful. Time and again she made successful visits to Maryland on the Underground Rail Road, and would be absent for weeks at a time, running daily risks while making preparations for herself and passengers. Great fears were entertained for her safety, but she seemed wholly devoid of personal fear. The idea of being captured by slave-hunters or slave-holders, seemed never to enter her mind. She was apparently proof against all adversaries. While she thus manifested such utter personal indifference, she was much more watchful with regard to those she was piloting. Half of her time, she had the appearance of one asleep, and would actually sit down by the road-side and go fast asleep when on her errands of mercy through the South, yet, she would not suffer one of her party to whimper once, about "giving out and going back," however wearied they might be from hard travel day and night. She had a very short and pointed rule or law of her own, which implied death to any who talked of giving out and going back. Thus, in an emergency she would give all to understand that "times were very critical and therefore no foolishness would be indulged in on the road." That several who were rather weak-kneed and faint-hearted were greatly invigorated by Harriet's blunt and positive manner and threat of extreme measures, there could be no doubt.

After having once enlisted, "they had to go through or die." Of course Harriet was supreme, and her followers generally had full faith in her, and would back up any word she might utter. So when she said to them that "a live runaway could do great harm by going back, but that a dead one could tell no secrets," she was sure to have obedience. Therefore, none had to die as traitors on the "middle passage." It is obvious enough, however, that her success in going into Maryland as she did, was attributable to her adventurous spirit and utter disregard of consequences. . . .

. . . Although these travelers were all of the field-hand order, they were, nevertheless, very promising, and they anticipated better days in Canada. Good advice was proffered them on the subject of temperance, industry, education, etc. Clothing, food and money were also given them to meet their wants, and they were sent on their way rejoicing.

10

BOSTON VIGILANCE COMMITTEE

Fugitive Slaves Aided by the Vigilance Committee since the Passage of the Fugitive Slave Bill 1850
1850–1858

Harriet Tubman had strong ties to abolitionists in the Boston area, and many contributed money to support her antislavery work. The success of the Boston Vigilance Committee demonstrates the strength of anti-slavery sentiment there after the passage of the Fugitive Slave Law of 1850. Of the 407 people they aided from 1850 to 1858, an average of 45 per year, only 3—Thomas Sims, Anthony Burns, and Sandy Swan—were captured and returned to the South. Recording such illegal activity also shows abolitionists' sense that they were safe in Boston. The entries from 1850 to 1852 excerpted here include the fugitives' names, number of accompanying family members, and sometimes destination. Francis Jackson, committee treasurer, kept the account books and probably also recorded the list of fugitives they helped.

1850

John Thomas & Wife	2	Canada
Shadrach	1	do [ditto]
B. Hall	1	—
Thos Johnson & another	2	Plymouth
James Williams	1	Providence
James Dale, Wife & children &		
Mrs. Henderson	4	Halifax
Henry Garnet & Geo Johnson	2	Westminster
David Brown & Henry Richardson	2	Westminster
Ely Baney, Wife & Catherine Jones	3	Westfield
Henry Williams & Henry Lewis	2	Westminster
Jones & Henry Long	2	—

From "Fugitive Slaves Aided by the Vigilance Committee since the Passage of the Fugitive Slave Bill 1850," Massachusetts Anti-Slavery Society, Manuscript Department, New-York Historical Society, New York.

Joseph Truet, Wife, son & daughter	4	Hopedale[6]
John Simmons & Wm Miller	2	—
James Jackson & George Reason	2	Worcester
Solomon Banks	1	Plymouth
Isaac Mason & Wife	2	Worcester
George Newton	1	—
James Tompson	1	Canada
Mr. Jno. Thomas[,] Wife & 2 children	4	Canada
William Crafts & Wife	2	England
Peter Truett	1	Hopedale
Andrew Jones	1	New Bedford
Edward Gray & Wm. Stuart	2	Westminster
Elizabeth Higgerman	1	S. Braintree
James Cork	1	New York
James Brown, John Armistead	2	—

1851

Henry Watson[,] Wife & Child	3	St. Johns[,] N.B.
4 Fugitive Slaves	4	Plymouth
Wm Ringold, Isaac Gaiter & Wm Peters	3	Southboro
James Harris	1	Halifax
. . .		
Mrs. Ringle & 3 children	4	Canada
Charles Remond	1	St. Johns
Mr. Brown	1	—
Rosanna	1	—
Samuel Russell	1	Canada
James Hall	1	—
Wm Talbot	1	—
Ann Albeck	1	Canada
Thos Clark[,] Wife & child	3	New Bedford
William H. Fisher	1	Wareham
B. Collins	1	—
Mrs. Callings	1	Canada

[6] A utopian socialist community committed to abolition, temperance, women's rights, and nonviolence, founded in 1841 in south-central Massachusetts.

1852

Fielding Banks	1	—
Charles Williams	1	—
John Bennett	1	Vermont
Mrs. Cooley & Child	2	—
Mr. Macks	1	—
John Wesley & Wife	2	Plymouth
Charles H. Williams	1	—
Mrs. Andy Long	1	Cambridge
Mr. Juniper	1	—
William Attucks	1	—
Mrs. Dunlap & Child	2	—
Elizabeth Howard	1	Canada
John Bonnett	1	do
Fugitive at Wm Clark's	1	—
David Smith	1	—
William Brown	1	—
Mrs. Taylor	1	Canada
Mr. Cooper, Mary Brown & 5 children	7	do
John Williams	1	do

11

JOHN BROWN

Letter to John Brown Jr.
April 8, 1858

The radical white abolitionist John Brown wrote this letter to his son after he met Harriet Tubman for the first time. He hoped to recruit her for his planned raid on the federal arsenal at Harpers Ferry, Virginia, and the slave insurrection he wanted to inspire, so that she could rally enslaved

John Brown to John Brown Jr., April 8, 1858, Boyd B. Stutler Collection, West Virginia State Archives, Charleston, W.V.

people from the countryside to his cause. The black minister Jermain W.
Loguen took him to meet Tubman in Canada, and Brown was so im-
pressed with her Underground Railroad experiences and strength that
he referred to her in this letter with masculine pronouns. In this way he
conveyed how Tubman — at least in his eyes — defied nineteenth-century
concepts of gender.

St Catharines, Canada West. 8th April, 1858

Dear Son John:

I came on here direct with J. W. Loguen the day after you left Rochester. I am succeeding *to all appearances* beyond my expectations. Hariet
[*sic*] Tubman hooked on *his* whole team at once. He *Hariet* is the most of
a *man* naturally; that *I ever* met with. There is the most abundant material; & *of the right quality*: in this quarter; beyond all doubt. Do not forget
to write Mr Case (near Rochester) at once about hunting up every *person*
& family of the reliable Kind; about at, or near, Bedford, Chambersburg,
Gettysburg, & Carlisle in Pa; & also Hagerstown, & vicinity Maryland; &
Harpers Ferry Va. The names; & residence of all I want to have sent *me*
at [Lyndonville] *enclosed* to Alex E. Fobes. Any thing you want to say to
me before you leave; *write* so that it may be sent at once; when I direct
where: or be kept by Mr Fobes till I call for it. I shall write you where to
direct to me as soon as I can fix on any point. Shall direct to you at North
Elba after a few days; when I write. I shall probably be about this region
some days yet. May God bless You all.

Your Affectionate Father
John Brown

12

LIBERATOR

Tubman Addresses Fourth of July Meeting
July 8, 1859

Thousands of Massachusetts abolitionists traveled to Framingham for a day of antislavery speeches and resolutions to commemorate the Fourth of July 1859. The Reverend Thomas Wentworth Higginson, Unitarian minister and antislavery firebrand, introduced Tubman to the crowd as an Underground Railroad conductor, called Moses in the South. After telling her story with what the newspaper indicated was a powerful authenticity, she accepted the proceeds of a collection to help her house and support her parents and to continue her Underground Railroad activity. Though not introduced by her real name for her protection, such appearances built Tubman's fame in the North.

"Moses," the deliverer, then stood up before the audience, who greeted her with enthusiastic cheers. She spoke briefly, telling the story of her sufferings as a slave, her escape, and her achievements on the Underground Railroad, in a style of quaint simplicity, which excited the most profound interest in her hearers. The mere words could not do justice to the speaker, and therefore we do not undertake to give them; but we advise all our readers to take the earliest opportunity to see and hear her.

Mr. Higginson stated that this brave woman had never asked for a cent from the Abolitionists, but that all her operations had been conducted at her own cost, with money earned by herself. Now, however, having brought her father and mother out of slavery, she found that the labor required for their support rendered her incapable of doing any thing in the way of business, and she therefore desired to raise a few hundred dollars to enable her to buy a little place where her father and mother could support themselves, and enable her to resume the practice of her profession! (Laughter and applause.)

From "The Fourth at Framingham," *Liberator*, July 8, 1859, 106–7.

A collection was taken in her behalf, amounting to thirty-seven dollars, for which at the conclusion of the meeting, in a few earnest and touching words, she spoke her thanks.

13

LEWIS HAYDEN

Letter to John Brown
September 16, 1859

A month before John Brown's raid on Harpers Ferry, the black abolitionist Lewis Hayden promised to send Harriet Tubman to Brown via Franklin Sanborn ("our friend at Concord") as soon as she returned to Boston. In their communications about Brown's plans, the correspondents took great pains to conceal their identities; Hayden used only his initials in the signature. This letter was found at Harpers Ferry after the raid and published in the New York Herald *as part of the coverage of Brown's conspiracy and during the government's efforts to uncover the names of co-conspirators. Apparently, the references here were not enough to identify Tubman or to make her a target of the investigation.*

MY DEAR SIR—I received your very kind letter, and would state that I have sent a note to Harriet requesting her to come to Boston, saying to her in the note that she must come right on as soon as she received the note, which I think she will do, and when she does come I think we will find some way to send her on. I have seen our friend at Concord; he is a true man. I have not yet said anything to anybody except him. I do not think it is wise for me to do so. I shall, therefore, when Harriet comes, send for our Concord friend, who will attend to the matter. Have you all the hands you wish? Write soon.

Yours, L. H.
Boston, Sept. 16, 1859.

Lewis Hayden to John Brown, September 16, 1859, *New York Herald*, October 25, 1859.

14

DOUGLASS' MONTHLY

Charles Nalle Rescue

June 1860

Charles Nalle escaped from slavery in Culpepper, Virginia, and was betrayed when he tried to arrange to bring his wife and two children to freedom in the North. Tubman played a central role in Nalle's rescue in Troy, New York, in April 1860. In the middle of the fray and essentially directing the rescue, she courageously extricated Nalle from the authorities and ushered him away under a hail of gunfire. She was not mentioned, however, in the local newspaper accounts reprinted by Frederick Douglass in his newspaper. It could be that local reporters did not know her, that an apparently elderly black woman was unremarkable, or that the reporters were protecting her identity. In the same issue, Douglass reported Nalle's safe arrival at St. Catharines, Canada (a subterfuge), and noted that people in Troy had raised $1,000 to buy his freedom.

An excited crowd of some thousand persons had gathered about the Commissioner's office, threatening a rescue. When [Nalle] was brought down to be taken before Judge Gould, the crowd surrounded the officers. . . .

. . . The Sheriff was knocked down. One of the rescuers seized the fugitive's arm from behind, others grasped hold of the first, forming a long single file . . . and this column, running at full speed and swaying from side to side, pushed him rapidly down to the River. Others running before and on either side "cleared the track," and prevented any attempt at seizure from being made. . . .

. . . Arrived at the Ferry, it was found that the Ferry Boat had just left the slip. No time was to be lost. The Fugitive was instantly run down to the beach, and put into a skiff, and the man in charge bid to ply his oars vigorously. . . .

Meanwhile a large number of the rescuers from this side, apprehending what had occurred, crowded upon the steam ferry boat to the

---

From "A Fugitive Slave Case in Troy—Rescue of the Fugitive," *Douglass' Monthly*, June 1860.

number of two hundred or more, as soon as it touched the dock, and were transported to the new theater of war. On finding that the fugitive was in the office of Mr. Stewart, the building was at once placed in a state of siege. Led by several persons from this side of the river, and others, the colored men made two vigorous assaults upon the stairway, which were repelled; [Officer] Becker, standing at the head of the stairs, and firing at the crowd without effect—the only damage being a bullet-hole in the hat of a barber in the employ of Mr. Peter Baltimore. Mr. Morrison says that over twenty shots were fired during this melee; the officers reloading their revolvers. That no one was killed is a fact attributable only to an astounding lack of accuracy in aim. After two repulses, the attacking party rallied, armed with brickbats, clubs and the like, and carrying a small dry-goods box as a shield, which was propped near the foot of the stairs.

Mr. Kissellburgh preceded the crowd, and effected an ingress to the office, although fired at twice. A powerful colored man named Martin followed him, and was pushing through the doorway, when Mr. A. J. Morrison, who defended it, struck him upon the forehead violently with the back of a hatchet. The blow stunned him, and he fell in the doorway in such manner as to prevent its closure, and to enable those just behind to rush over and seize the fugitive, who stood near the door. Mr. Morrison was unable to withold [*sic*] him from their grasp. They hurried him down stairs, one or two bullets following them. Amid the exclamations of the crowd, Nalle was hurried off down the street. Near the Post-Office an unwilling farmer was stopped and obliged to take him on board. But his wagon soon broke down. Again the party harried [*sic*] off toward the Shaker road on foot, until near the rear of the Arsenal wall, when they were overtaken by a fleet horse provided for the purpose by a colored man named Hank York. With this and a good supply of firearms, Nalle was harried off "toward the North star and freedom," Hank York and Andrew Parker, another resolute colored man, accompanying him. When last heard from he was about four miles west of the village, and going at a good rate of speed.

15

WILLIAM WELLS BROWN

Emancipation Eve
December 31, 1862

Slave songs, hymns, and improvised freedom songs were important to spiritual life and inspired commitment and courage in both enslaved and free black communities. They were also powerful tools used by Tubman to transmit coded messages to the Underground Railroad about her rescue efforts, scheduled missions, and charges. Antislavery activist and former fugitive William Wells Brown recorded some of the songs he heard in a Washington, D.C., contraband camp on December 31, 1862, the eve of Lincoln's Emancipation Proclamation. The second song excerpted here uses the traditional African and African American call-and-response pattern: The improvised verses sung by one man were punctuated by the chorus "Free forever! Forever free!"

The first of January next, eighteen sixty-three,—
So says the Proclamation,—the slaves will all be free!
To every kindly heart 'twill be the day of jubilee;
     For the bond shall all go free!

John Brown, the dauntless hero, with joy is looking on;
From his home among the angels he sees the coming dawn;
Then up with Freedom's banners, and hail the glorious morn
     When the slaves shall all go free! . . .

No more from crushed and bleeding hearts we hear the broken sigh;
No more from brothers bound in chains we'll hear the pleading cry;
For the happy day, the glorious day, is coming by and by,
     When the slaves shall all go free! . . .

From William Wells Brown, *The Negro in the American Rebellion: His Heroism and His Fidelity* (Boston: Lee & Shepard, 1867), 113–14, 117–18.

"NO COMPROMISE WITH SLAVERY!" we hear the cheering sound,
The road to peace and happiness "Old Abe" at last has found:
With earnest hearts and willing hands to stand by him we're bound,
   While he sets the bondmen free! . . .

And when we on the "other side" do all together stand,
As children of one family we'll clasp the friendly hand:
We'll be a band of brothers in that brighter, better land,
   Where the bond shall all be free!

Free Forever! Forever Free!

Ring, ring! O Bell of Freedom, ring!
And to the ears of bondmen bring
Thy sweet and freeman-thrilling tone.
On Autumn's blast, from zone to zone,
The joyful tidings go proclaim,
In Liberty's hallowed name:
Emancipation to the slave,
The rights which his Creator gave,
To live with chains asunder riven,
To live free as the birds of heaven,
To live free as the air he breathes,
Entirely free from galling greaves;
The right to act, to know, to feel,
That bands of iron and links of steel
Were never wrought to chain the mind,
Nor human flesh in bondage bind;
That Heaven, in its generous plan,
Gave like and equal rights to man.
Go send thy notes from shore to shore,
Above the deep-voiced cannon's roar;
Go send Emancipation's peal
Where clashes North with Southern steel,
And nerve the Southern bondmen now
To rise and strike the final blow,
To lay Oppression's minions low.
Oh! Rouse the mind and nerve the arm
To brave the blast and face the storm;
And, ere the war-cloud passes by,
We'll have a land of liberty.

Our God has said, "Let there be light
Where Error palls the land with night."
Then send forth now, O Freedom's bell,
Foul Slavery's last and fatal knell!
Oh! Speed the tidings o'er the land,
That tells that stern Oppression's hand
Has yielded to the power of Right:
That Wrong is weak, that Truth is might!
. . . .

Then Union shall again return,
And Freedom's fires shall brightly burn;
and PEACE and JOY, sweet guests, shall come,
And dwell in every heart and home.

16

COMMONWEALTH

Account of Combahee River Raid

July 10, 1863

During the Civil War, Harriet Tubman served the Union as a nurse, a military scout, and a spy. Franklin Sanborn, a John Brown supporter and Tubman's friend, published this account of her role in a June 1863 military raid up the Combahee River in South Carolina that rescued hundreds of slaves from upriver plantations. When they returned to Beaufort, Colonel James Montgomery and Tubman addressed the freed people, celebrating their new life in freedom and urging them to meet its responsibilities. Tubman's wartime bravery only added to her Underground Railroad legend.

Col. Montgomery and his gallant Band of 300 black soldiers, under the guidance of a black woman, dashed into the enemies' country, struck a bold and effective blow, destroying millions of dollars' worth of

From "Harriet Tubman," *Commonwealth*, July 10, 1863.

commissary stores, cotton and lordly dwellings, and striking terror to the heart of rebeldom, brought off nearly 800 slaves and thousands of dollars' worth of property, without losing a man or receiving a scratch. It was a glorious consummation.

After they were all fairly disposed of in the Beaufort church, they were addressed in strains of thrilling eloquence by their gallant deliverer, to which they responded in a song—

"There is a white robe for thee."

A song so appropriate and so heartfelt and cordial as to bring unbidden tears.

The Colonel was followed by a speech from the black woman, who led the raid and under whose inspiration it was originated and conducted. For sound sense and real native eloquence, her address would do honor to any man, and it created a great sensation.

17

COMMONWEALTH

Solicitation of Aid for Harriet Tubman
August 12, 1864

Most of Tubman's activities with the U.S. Army during the Civil War were unpaid. She earned money for her own subsistence and also provided aid to freed people and supported her family at home. Her antislavery friends provided as much assistance as they could. Franklin Sanborn published this advertisement soliciting money and clothing for her in his Boston newspaper, Commonwealth.

This heroic woman whose career we described last summer, when she was engaged in the military service, in the Department of the South, has lately arrived in Boston, where her numerous friends will be glad to see her. She left Florida to come North in the latter part of June,

"Harriet Tubman," *Commonwealth*, August 12, 1864.

and went from New York where she landed directly to the home of her aged parents in Auburn, whence she has come to this city. Her services to her people and to the army seem to have been very inadequately recompensed by the military authorities, and such money as she has received, she has expended for others as her custom is. Any contributions of money or clothing sent to her at this office will be received by her, and the givers may be assured that she will use them with fidelity and discretion for the good of the colored race. Her address is "care of Dr. J. S. Rock, Boston."

18

FREEDMEN'S RECORD

Moses

March 1865

Ednah Dow Cheney, a friend of Harriet Tubman, wrote this short biography for the New England Freedmen's Aid Society publication, Freedmen's Record, *to introduce supporters to Tubman and explain why the society had hired her as a teacher. Published near the end of the war, it gave the most complete description of her and her life up to that time, including her Underground Railroad and wartime activities. This account began to solidify the important stories that would often be repeated in later Tubman biographies.*

One of the teachers lately commissioned by the New-England Freedmen's Aid Society is probably the most remarkable woman of this age. That is to say, she has performed more wonderful deeds by the native power of her own spirit against adverse circumstances than any other. She is well known to many by the various names which her eventful life has given her; Harriet Garrison, Gen. Tubman, &c.; but among the slaves she is universally known by her well-earned title of Moses,—Moses the deliverer. She is a rare instance, in the midst of high civilization and intellectual culture, of a being of great native powers, working power-fully, and to beneficent ends, entirely unaided by schools or books.

Her maiden name was Araminta Ross. She is the granddaughter of a native African, and has not a drop of white blood in her veins. She was born in 1820 or 1821, on the Eastern Shore of Maryland. Her parents were slaves, but married and faithful to each other, and the family affection is very strong. She claims that she was legally freed by a will of her first master, but his wishes were not carried into effect. . . .

When quite young she lived with a very pious mistress; but the slaveholder's religion did not prevent her from whipping the young girl for every slight or fancied fault. Araminta found that this was usually a morning exercise; so she prepared for it by putting on all the thick clothes she could procure to protect her skin. She made sufficient out-cry, however, to convince her mistress that her blows had full effect; and in the afternoon she would take off her wrappings, and dress as well as she could. When invited into family prayers, she preferred to stay on the landing, and pray for herself; "and I prayed to God," she says, "to make me strong and able to fight, and that's what I've allers prayed for ever since." It is in vain to try to persuade her that her prayer was a wrong one. She always maintains it to be sincere and right, and it has certainly been fully answered. In her youth she received a severe blow on her head from a heavy weight thrown by her master at another slave, but which accidentally hit her. The blow produced a disease of the brain which was severe for a long time, and still makes her very lethargic. She cannot remain quiet fifteen minutes without appearing to fall asleep. It is not refreshing slumber; but a heavy, weary condition which exhausts her. She therefore loves great physical activity, and direct heat of the sun, which keeps her blood actively circulating. She was married about 1844 to a free colored man named John Tubman, but never had any children. Owing to changes in her owner's family, it was determined to will her and some other slaves; but her health was so much injured, that a purchaser was not easily found. At length she became convinced that she would soon be carried away, and she decided to escape. Her broth-ers did not agree with . . . her plans; and she walked off alone, following the guidance of the brooks, which she had observed to run North. The evening before she left, she wished very much to bid her companions farewell, but was afraid of being betrayed, if any one knew of her inten-tions; so she passed through the street singing, —

Good bye, I'm going to leave you,
Good bye, I'll meet you in the kingdom, —

and similar snatches of Methodist songs[.] As she passed on singing, she saw her master, Dr Thompson standing at his gate, and her native humor breaking out, she sung yet louder, bowing down to him,—

Good bye, I'm going for to leave you

He stopped and looked after her as she passed on, and he afterwards said, that, as her voice came floating back in the evening air it seemed as if—

A wave of trouble never rolled
Across her peaceful breast.

Wise judges are we of each other!—She was only quitting home, husband, father, mother, friends, to go out alone, friendless and penniless into the world.

She remained two years in Philadelphia working hard and carefully hoarding her money. Then she hired a room, furnished it as well as she could, bought a nice suit of men's clothes, and went back to Maryland for her husband. But the faithless man had taken to himself another wife. Harriet did not dare venture into her presence, but sent word to her husband where she was. He declined joining her. At first her grief and anger were excessive. She said, "she did not care what massa did to her, she thought she would go right in and make all the trouble she could, she was determined to see her old man once more," but finally she thought "how foolish it [w]as just for temper to make mischief," and that, "if he could do without her, she could without him," and so "he dropped out of her heart," and she determined to give her life to brave deeds. . . . Seven or eight times she has returned to the neighborhood of her former home, always at the risk of death in the most terrible forms, and each time has brought away a company of fugitive slaves, and led them safely to the free States, or to Canada. Every time she went, the dangers increased. In 1857 she brought away her old parents, and, as they were too feeble to walk, she was obliged to hire a wagon, which added greatly to the hazards of the journey. In 1860 she went for the last time, and among her troop was an infant whom they were obliged to keep stupefied with laudanum to prevent its outcries. . . . She has shown in [her journeys] all the characteristics of a great leader, courage, foresight, prudence, self-control, ingenuity, subtle perception, command over others' minds. Her nature is at once profoundly practical and highly imaginative. . . . She would never allow more to join her than she could properly care for though she often gave others direction by which they succeeded in escaping. She always came in the winter when the nights are long and dark, and people who have homes stay in them. She was never seen on the plantation herself; but appointed a rendezvous for her company eight or ten miles distant, so that if they were discovered at the first start she was not compromised.... She resorted to various devices, she had confidential friends all along the road. She would hire a man to follow the one who put up the notices, and take them down as soon as his back was turned. She crossed creeks on railroad bridges by night, she hid her company in the woods while she herself not being advertised went into the towns in search of information. If met on the road, her face was always to the south, and she was always a very respectable looking darkey, not at all a poor fugitive. She would get into the cars near her pursuers, and manage to hear their plans. By day they lay in the woods; then she pulled out her patchwork, and sewed together little bits, perhaps not more than inch square, which were afterwards made into comforters for the fugitives in Canada.

The expedition was governed by the strictest rules. If any man gave out, he must be shot. "Would you really do that?" she was asked. "Yes," she replied, "if he was weak enough to give out, he'd be weak enough to betray us all, and all who had helped us; and do you think I'd let so many die just for one coward man." "Did you ever have to shoot any one" was asked. "One time," she said, "a man gave out the second night; his feet were sore and swollen, he couldn't go any further; he'd rather go back and die, if he must." They tried all arguments in vain, bathed his feet, tried to strengthen him, but it was of no use, he would go back. Then she said, "I told the boys to get their guns ready, and shoot him. They'd have done it in a minute; but when he heard that, he jumped right up and went; on as well as any body." ...

When going on these journeys she often lay alone in the forests all night. Her whole soul was filled with awe of the mysterious Unseen Presence, which thrilled her with such depths of emotion, that all other care and fear vanished. Then she seemed to speak with Her Maker "as a man talketh with his friend"; her childlike petitions had direct answers, and beautiful visions lifted her up above all doubt and anxiety into serene trust and faith....

She loves to describe her visions, which are very real to her; but she must tell them word for word as they lie in her untutored mind, with endless repetitions and details; she cannot shorten or condense them, whatever be your haste. She has great dramatic power; the scene rises before you as she saw it, and her voice and language change with her different actors....

Her efforts were not confined to the escape of slaves. She conducted them to Canada, watched over their welfare, collected clothing, organized them into societies, and was always occupied with plans for their benefit. She first came to Boston in the spring of 1859, to ask aid of the friends of her race to build a house for her aged father and mother. She brought recommendations from Gerrit Smith, and at once won many friends who aided her to accomplish her purpose. Her parents are now settled in Auburn, and all that Harriet seems to desire in reward for her labors is the privilege of making their old age comfortable. She has a very affectionate nature, and forms the strongest personal attachments. She has great simplicity of character; she states her wants very freely, and believes you are ready to help her; but if you have nothing to give, or have given to another, she is content. She is not sensitive to indignities to her color in her own person; but knows and claims her rights. She will eat at your table if she sees you really desire it; but she goes as willingly to the kitchen. She is very abstemious in her diet, fruit being the only luxury she cares for. Her personal appearance is very peculiar. She is thoroughly negro, and very plain. She has needed disguise so often, that she seems to have command over her face, and can banish all expression from her features, and look so stupid that nobody would suspect her of knowing enough to be dangerous; but her eye flashes with intelligence and power when she is roused. She has the rich humor and the keen sense of beauty which belong to her race. She would like to dress handsomely. Once an old silk dress was given her among a bundle of clothes, and she was in great delight. "Glory!" she exclaimed; "didn't I say when I sold my silk gown to get money to go after my mother, that I'd have another some day?" She is never left in a room with pictures or statuary that she does not examine them and ask with interest about them.

I wish it were possible to give some of her racy stories; but no report would do them justice. She gives a most vivid description of the rescue of a slave in Troy. She fought and struggled so that her clothes were torn off her; but she was successful at last. Throughout all she shouted out her favorite motto. "Give me liberty or give me death," to which the popular heart never fails to respond. When she was triumphantly bearing the man off, a little boy called out, "Go it, old aunty! you're the best old aunty the fellow ever had." She is perfectly at home in such scenes; she loves action. . . .

She was deeply interested in John Brown; and it is said, that she was fully acquainted with his plans, and approved them. On the day when his companions were executed, she came to my room. Finding me occupied, she said, "I am not going to sit down, I only want you to give me an address"; but her heart was too full, she must talk. "I've been studying and studying upon it," she said, "and its clar to me, it wasn't John Brown that died on that gallows. When I think how he gave up his life for our people, and how he never flinched, but was so brave to the end; its clar to me it wasn't mortal man, it was God in him. When I think of all the groans and tears and prayers I've heard on the plantations, and remember that God is a prayer-hearing God, I feel that his time is drawing near." . . .

When the war broke out Harriet was very anxious to go to South Carolina to assist the contrabands. The only condition she made was, that her old parents should be kept from want. It was wonderful to see with what shrewd economy she had planned all their household arrangements. She concluded that thirty dollars would keep them comfortable through the winter. She went to Port Royal, and was employed by Gen. Hunter, in scouting service, and accompanied Col. Montgomery in his expedition up the Combahee river. She was afterwards engaged by Gen. Saxton, to take a number of freed women under her charge, and teach them to do the soldiers' washing. She has also been making herb-medicine for the soldiers, which she gives away gratuitously, feeling it to be impossible to receive money from sick soldiers; and she has made cakes and pies for sale, in the intervals of other work.

She has had no regular support from Government; and she feels that she must have some certain income, which she wishes to apply to her parents' support. This society consider her labors too valuable to the freedmen to be turned elsewhere, and have therefore taken her into their service, paying her the small salary of ten dollars per month that she asks for.

19

THOMAS GARRETT

Memories of Harriet Tubman and the Underground Railroad

June 1868

Tubman's friend Thomas Garrett, who operated an Underground Railroad station in Wilmington, Delaware, assisted thousands of enslaved people on their flight to freedom. Sarah Bradford solicited his reminiscences for her first biography of Tubman, Scenes in the Life of Harriet Tubman, *published in 1869. She included the letter excerpted here both in that book and in her expanded biography,* Harriet: The Moses of Her People, *published in 1886. Here Garrett attests to the danger of Tubman's Underground Railroad work and her unshakable faith in God's guidance. Evidence of Tubman's faith would have been especially appealing to Bradford's readers, many of whom were religiously motivated reformers, and it was a powerful contribution to the Tubman legend.*

WILMINGTON, 6TH MO., 1868.

My Friend:

Thy favor of the 12th reached me yesterday, requesting such reminiscences as I could give respecting the remarkable labors of Harriet Tubman, in aiding her colored friends from bondage. I may begin by saying, living as I have in a slave State, and the laws being very severe where any proof could be made of any one aiding slaves on their way to freedom, I have not felt at liberty to keep any written word of Harriet's or my own labors, except in numbering those whom I have aided. For that reason I cannot furnish so interesting an account of Harriet's labors as I otherwise could, and now would be glad to do; for in truth I never met with any person, of any color, who had more confidence in the voice of God, as spoken direct to her soul. She has frequently told me that she talked with God, and he talked with her every day of her life, and she has declared to me that she felt no more fear of being arrested by her

---

From Sarah H. Bradford, *Harriet: The Moses of Her People* (New York: George R. Lockwood & Son, 1886), 83–88.

former master, or any other person, when in his immediate neighborhood, than she did in the State of New York, or Canada, for she said she never ventured only where God sent her, and her faith in a Supreme Power truly was great.

. . . I think she must have brought from the neighborhood where she had been held as a slave, from 60 to 80 persons, from Maryland, some 80 miles from here. No slave who placed himself under her care, was ever arrested that I have heard of; she mostly had her regular stopping places on her route; but in one instance, when she had two stout men with her, some 30 miles below here, she said that God told her to stop, which she did; and then asked him what she must do. He told her to leave the road, and turn to the left; she obeyed, and soon came to a small stream of tide water; there was no boat, no bridge; she again inquired of her Guide what she was to do. She was told to go through. It was cold, in the month of March; but having confidence in her Guide, she went in; the water came up to her armpits; the men refused to follow till they saw her safe on the opposite shore. They then followed, and if I mistake not, she had soon to wade a second stream; soon after which she came to a cabin of colored people, who took them all in, put them to bed, and dried their clothes, ready to proceed next night on their journey. Harriet had run out of money, and gave them some of her underclothing to pay for their kindness. When she called on me two days after, she was so hoarse she could hardly speak, and was also suffering with violent toothache. The strange part of the story we found to be, that the master of these two men had put up the previous day, at the railroad station near where she left, an advertisement for them, offering a large reward for their apprehension; but they made a safe exit. She at one time brought as many as seven or eight, several of whom were women and children. She was well known here in Chester County and Philadelphia, and respected by all true abolitionists. I had been in the habit of furnishing her and those that accompanied her, as she returned from her acts of mercy, with new shoes; and on one occasion when I had not seen her for three months, she came into my store. I said, "Harriet, I am glad to see thee! I suppose thee wants a pair of new shoes." Her reply was "I want more than that." I, in jest, said, "I have always been liberal with thee, and wish to be; but I am not rich, and cannot afford to give much." Her reply was: "God tells me you have money for me." I asked her "if God never deceived her?" She said, "No!" "Well! how much does thee want?" After studying a moment, she said: "About twenty-three dollars." I then gave her twenty-four dollars and some odd cents, the net proceeds of five pounds sterling, received through Eliza Wigham, of Scotland, for her. I had given some accounts of Harriet's labor to the Anti-Slavery Society of Edinburgh, of which Eliza Wigham was Secretary. On the reading of my letter, a gentleman present said he would send Harriet four pounds if he knew of any way to get it to her. Eliza Wigham offered to forward it to me for her, and that was the first money ever received by me for her. Some twelve months after, she called on me again, and said that God told her I had some money for her, but not so much as before. I had, a few days previous, received the net proceeds of one pound ten shillings from Europe for her. To say the least, there was something remarkable in these facts, whether clairvoyance, or the divine impression on her mind from the source of all power, I cannot tell; but certain it was she had a guide within herself other than the written word, for she never had any education. . . .

Thy friend,
THOS. GARRETT.

20

FREDERICK DOUGLASS AND WENDELL PHILLIPS

Testimonials

June and August 1868

The white abolitionist Wendell Phillips and the black abolitionist Frederick Douglass provided these letters of endorsement about Tubman for Sarah Bradford's 1869 biography. It was common for prominent people to attest to the authenticity of published narratives of former slaves and for their endorsements to be printed in the books. The endorsement from Douglass, the most accomplished and famous black abolitionist and former slave in America, added credibility to Tubman's story and prestige to Bradford's biography and provides a glimpse into his relationship with Tubman. Phillips's letter recalls her association with John Brown, who was revered by abolitionists.

From Sarah H. Bradford, *Scenes in the Life of Harriet Tubman* (Auburn, N.Y.: W. J. Moses, 1869), 5–8.

JUNE 16, 1868.

Dear Madame:

The last time I ever saw John Brown was under my own roof, as he brought Harriet Tubman to me, saying: "Mr. Phillips, I bring you one of the best and bravest persons on this continent—*General* Tubman, as we call her."

He then went on to recount her labors and sacrifices in behalf of her race. After that, Harriet spent some time in Boston, earning the confidence and admiration of all those who were working for freedom. With their aid she went to the South more than once, returning always with a squad of self-emancipated men, women, and children, for whom her marvelous skill had opened the way of escape. After the war broke out, she was sent with indorsements from Governor Andrew and his friends to South Carolina, where in the service of the Nation she rendered most important and efficient aid to our army.

In my opinion there are few captains, perhaps few colonels, who have done more for the loyal cause since the war began, and few men who did before that time more for the colored race, than our fearless and most sagacious friend, Harriet.

Faithfully yours,
WENDELL PHILLIPS.

ROCHESTER, AUGUST 29, 1868.

Dear Harriet:

I am glad to know that the story of your eventful life has been written by a kind lady, and that the same is so soon to be published. You ask for what you do not need when you call upon me for a word of commendation. I need such words from you far more than you can need them from me, especially where your superior labors and devotion to the cause of the lately enslaved of our land are known as I know them. The difference between us is very marked. Most that I have done and suffered in the service of our cause has been in public, and I have received much encouragement at every step of the way. You on the other hand have labored in a private way. I have wrought in the day—you in the night. I have had the applause of the crowd and the satisfaction that comes of being approved by the multitude, while the most that you have done has been witnessed by a few trembling, scarred, and foot-sore bondmen and women, whom you have led out of the house of bondage, and whose heartfelt "*God bless you*" has been your only reward. The midnight sky and the silent stars have been the witnesses of your devotion to freedom and of your heroism. Excepting John Brown—of sacred memory—I

know of no one who has willingly encountered more perils and hardships to serve our enslaved people than you have. Much that you have
done would seem improbable to those who do not know you as I know
you. It is to me a great pleasure and a great privilege to bear testimony
to your character and your works, and to say to those to whom you may
come, that I regard you in every way truthful and trustworthy.

Your friend,

FREDERICK DOUGLASS.

21

WILLIAM WELLS BROWN

Moses

1874

*William Wells Brown, fugitive slave and Underground Railroad con-
ductor in western New York, became an internationally renowned antislavery speaker and an accomplished author. A decade after the Civil
War, he published a scholarly history that celebrated the accomplishments
of notable African Americans and showed their exertions in creating
black freedom. Included in that book was the following biographical
sketch of Harriet Tubman.*

For eight or ten years previous to the breaking out of the Rebellion,
all who frequented anti-slavery conventions, lectures, picnics, and fairs,
could not fail to have seen a black woman of medium size, upper front
teeth gone, smiling countenance, attired in coarse, but neat apparel, with
an old-fashioned reticule, or bag, suspended by her side, and who, on
taking her seat, would at once drop off into a sound sleep. This woman
was Harriet Tubman, better known as "Moses."

    She first came to Boston in 1854, and was soon a welcome visitor
to the homes of the leading Abolitionists, who were always attentive
listeners to her strange and eventful stories. Her plantation life, where
she was born a slave at the South, was cruelly interesting. Her back

From William Wells Brown, *The Rising Son, or The Antecedents and Advancement of the
Colored Race* (1874; repr., Miami, Fla.: Mnemosyne, 1969), 536–38.

and shoulders, marked with the biting lash, told how inhuman was the institution from which she had fled. . . . Moses had no education, yet the most refined person would listen for hours while she related the intensely interesting incidents of her life, told in the simplest manner, but always seasoned with good sense.

. . . Men from Canada, who had made their escape years before, and whose families were still in the prison-house of slavery, would seek out Moses, and get her to go and bring their dear ones away. How strange! This woman,—one of the most ordinary looking of her race; unlettered; no idea of geography; asleep half of the time,—would penetrate the interior slave states, hide in the woods during the day, feed on the bondsman's homely fare at night, bring off whole families of slaves, and pilot them to Canada, after running the gauntlet of the most difficult parts of the Southern country. . . .

While in Canada, in 1860, we met several whom this woman had brought from the land of bondage, and they all believed that she had supernatural power. Of one man we inquired, "Were you not afraid of being caught?"

"O, no," said he, "Moses is got de charm."

"What do you mean?" we asked.

He replied, "De whites can't catch Moses, kase you see she's born wid de charm. De Lord has given Moses de power."

22

SARAH H. BRADFORD

Harriet Tubman Biographies
1869 and 1886

Sarah Bradford, an author of sentimental fiction, published Scenes in the Life of Harriet Tubman *in 1869 to raise money for Tubman and her work. In 1886 she published a substantially revised and expanded version titled* Harriet: The Moses of Her People. *Both promoted the lone, heroic legendary figure known to generations of children and adults,*

From Sarah H. Bradford, *Scenes in the Life of Harriet Tubman* (1869; repr., Salem, N.H.: Ayer, 1992), 9–10, 19–20; Sarah H. Bradford, *Harriet: The Moses of Her People* (1886; repr., New York: Citadel Press, 1994), 13–14, 29–32.

but a comparison of the two reveals changing attitudes toward race in post–Civil War America. The first two excerpts here compare how the two books began Tubman's story; the second two excerpts compare how they handled the story of her escape from slavery.

Scenes in the Life of Harriet Tubman, 1869

Harriet Tubman, known at various times, and in various places, by many different names, such as "Moses," in allusion to her being the leader and guide to so many of her people in their exodus from the Land of Bondage; "the Conductor of the Underground Railroad"; and "Moll Pitcher,"[7] for the energy and daring by which she delivered a fugitive slave who was about to be dragged back to the South; was for the first twenty-five years of her life a slave on the eastern shore of Maryland. Her own master she represents as never unnecessarily cruel; but as was common among slaveholders, he often hired out his slaves to others, some of whom proved to be tyrannical and brutal to the utmost limit of their power.

She had worked only as a field-hand for many years, following the oxen, loading and unloading wood, and carrying heavy burdens, by which her naturally remarkable power of muscle was so developed that her feats of strength often called forth the wonder of strong laboring men. Thus was she preparing for the life of hardship and endurance which lay before her, for the deeds of daring she was to do, and of which her ignorant and darkened mind at that time never dreamed.

Harriet: The Moses of Her People, 1886

On a hot summer's day, perhaps sixty years ago, a group of merry little darkies were rolling and tumbling in the sand in front of the large house of a Southern planter. Their shining skins gleamed in the sun, as they rolled over each other in their play, and their voices, as they chattered together, or shouted in glee, reached even to the cabins of the negro quarter, where the old people groaned in spirit, as they thought of the future of those unconscious young revelers; and their cry went up, "O, Lord, how long!"

---

[7] A folk hero of the American Revolution who fought alongside her husband in the Battle of Monmouth, New Jersey.

Apart from the rest of the children, on the top rail of a fence, holding tight on to the tall gate post, sat a little girl of perhaps thirteen years of age; darker than any of the others, and with a more decided *woolliness* in the hair; a pure unmitigated African. She was not so entirely in a state of nature as the rollers in the dust beneath her; but her only garment was a short woolen skirt, which was tied around her waist, and reached about to her knees. She seemed a dazed and stupid child, and as her head hung upon her breast, she looked up with dull blood-shot eyes towards her young brothers and sisters, without seeming to see them. Bye and bye the eyes closed, and still clinging to the post, she slept. The other children looked up and said to each other, "Look at Hatt, she's done gone off agin!" Tired of their present play ground they trooped off in another direction, but the girl slept on heavily, never losing her hold on the post, or her seat on her perch. Behold here, in the stupid little negro girl, the future deliverer of hundreds of her people; the spy, and scout of the Union armies; the devoted hospital nurse; the protector of hunted fugitives; the eloquent speaker in public meetings; the cunning eluder of pursuing man-hunters; the heaven guided pioneer through dangers seen and unseen; in short, as she has well been called, "The Moses of her People."

Scenes in the Life of Harriet Tubman, 1869

And she started on her journey, "not knowing whither she went," except that she was going to follow the north star, till it led her to liberty. Cautiously and by night she traveled, cunningly feeling her way, and finding out who were friends; till after a long and painful journey she found, in answer to careful inquiries, that she had at last crossed that magic "line" which then separated the land of bondage from the land of freedom. . . .

"When I found I had crossed dat *line,*" she said, "I looked at my hands to see if I was de same pusson. There was such a glory ober ebery ting; de sun came like gold through the trees, and ober the fields, and I felt like I was in Heaben."

. . . "I had crossed the line. I was *free*; but there was no one to welcome me to the land of freedom. I was a stranger in a strange land; and my home, after all, was down in Maryland; because my father, my mother, my brothers, and sisters, and friends were there. But I was free, and *they* should be free. I would make a home in the North and bring them there, God helping me. Oh, how I prayed then," she said; "I said to de Lord, 'I'm gwine to hole stiddy on to *you,* an' I *know* you'll see me through.'"

Harriet: The Moses of Her People, 1886

Harriet was now left alone, but after watching the retreating forms of her brothers, she turned her face toward the north, and fixing her eyes on the guiding star, and committing her way unto the Lord, she started again upon her long, lonely journey. . . . And so, with only the North Star for her guide, our heroine started on the way to liberty. "For," said she, "I had reasoned dis out in my mind; there was one of two things I had a *right* to, liberty, or death; if I could not have one, I would have de oder; for no man should take me alive; I should fight for my liberty as long as my strength lasted, and when de time came for me to go, de Lord would let dem take me."

And so without money, and without friends, she started on through unknown regions; walking by night, hiding by day, but always conscious of an invisible pillar of cloud by day, and of fire by night, under the guidance of which she journeyed or rested.[8] Without knowing whom to trust, or how near the pursuers might be, she carefully felt her way, and by her native cunning, or by God given wisdom, she managed to apply to the right people for food, and sometimes for shelter; though often her bed was only the cold ground, and her watchers the stars of night.

After many long and weary days of travel, she found that she had passed the magic line, which then divided the land of bondage from the land of freedom. But where were the lovely white ladies whom in her visions she had seen, who, with arms outstretched, welcomed her to their hearts and homes. All these visions proved deceitful: she was more alone than ever; but she had crossed the line; no one could take her now, and she would never call any man "Master" more.

"I looked at my hands," she said, "to see if I was de same person now I was free. Dere was such a glory ober eberything, de sun came like gold trou de trees, and ober de fields, and I felt like I was in heaven." But then came the bitter drop in the cup of joy. She was alone, and her kindred were in slavery, and not one of them had the courage to dare what she had dared. Unless she made the effort to liberate them she would never see them more, or even know their fate. . . .

. . . "I had crossed de line of which I had so long been dreaming. I was free; but dere was no one to welcome me to de land of freedom, I was a stranger in a strange land, and my home after all was down in de old cabin quarter, wid de ole folks, and my brudders and sisters. But to

---

[8] Here Bradford compares Tubman to Moses and the Israelites, whom, according to the book of Exodus, God led out of bondage in Egypt with a pillar of cloud by day and of fire by night.

dis solemn resolution I came; I was free, and dey should be free also; I would make a home for dem in de North, and de Lord helping me, I would bring dem all dere. Oh, how I prayed den, lying all alone on de cold, damp ground; 'Oh, dear Lord,' I said, 'I haint got no friend but *you*. Come to my help, Lord, for I'm in trouble!' "

23

HARRIET TUBMAN DAVIS

Affidavit
May 28, 1892

Harriet Tubman made this statement as one of the many documents accompanying her application for a pension as the widow of a Civil War soldier. Prior to this, she had tried unsuccessfully for decades to obtain a pension for her service as a Union nurse, scout, and spy. She finally received support under an 1890 law providing aid to widows of military veterans of the war. Her husband Nelson Davis's different names complicated her claim, and she had to prove not only that he was her spouse but also that the name he enlisted under, the name he married under, and the name on his death certificate all referred to the same man. Among African Americans at the time, multiple names were common: New slaveowners conferred new names on slaves, some people were called one name by friends and family and another by their masters, and many people chose new names to mark their freedom.

The correct name of her late husband was *Nelson Davis*. He was born in Slavery, his master's Surname being *Charles*. *Nelson was known and called, while in Slavery, as Nelson Charles* after the surname of his master.[9] The said *Nelson Davis* who also went by the name of *Nelson Charles* escaped from his master and Slavery after he was grown up, and sometime before the late war of the rebellion, and came North, still

---

[9] His father's name was Milford Davis.

From Harriet Tubman Davis, Civil War Pension Records, RG 233, National Archives.

holding and known under the name of *Nelson Charles*. He was enrolled (Drafted she thinks), served, and discharged under the name of *Nelson Charles*. When he came to Auburn, N.Y. to live (after his discharge) in or about 1866 or early in 1867 he was known and recognized both as *Nelson Charles* and *Nelson Davis* but generally as *Nelson Davis*, as he said *Davis* was his *correct name*.

When affiant and said Davis were married, it appears from the church record of marriage that he gave his name to the Rev. Henry Fowler as *Charles Nelson Davis*. Affiant cannot assign any reason why he gave his name as he did, except that he wanted all three of the names to appear upon the church record.

Affiant positively and unequivocally swears that the *Nelson Davis* who was married under the name *Charles Nelson Davis*, and who died as *Nelson Davis*, was the identical person who served in Co. "G" 8th U.S.C. Infty as *Nelson Charles*.

her
HARRIET X DAVIS
mark

24

HARRIET TUBMAN DAVIS

Affidavit

November 10, 1894

Harriet Tubman's application for a pension as the widow of a Civil War veteran required extensive paperwork. This document is noteworthy as one of the few biographical accounts in Tubman's own words. A clerk transcribed this for her, since she could neither read nor write.

In the matter of orign'l Pension no 449.592 of Harriet Davis as Widow of Nelson Davis late of Co "G" 8th Reg't U.S.C.T. on this 10 day of Nov 1894 personally appeared before me Harriet Davis who is well known to me

From Harriet Tubman Davis, Civil War Pension Records, RG 233, National Archives.

to be entitled to full credit and belief and who being by me duly sworn
deposes and says in relation to the aforesaid case as follows.

I was born at Cambridge, Dorchester County, Md. My residence at the
time I became acquainted with the above named Soldier was in the town
of Fleming, Cayuga Co., N.Y. (adjoining the city of Auburn, N.Y.). . . . I
had known the soldier before my marriage to him a little over three
years. I was married to the soldier in the city of Auburn, N.Y. March
18th 1869 by the Rev. Henry Fowler. See proof of my marriage on file.

I was a slave in the state of Maryland before the war. My owner's
name was Edward Broadice [*sic*]. I escaped from Slavery before the
war and came North. I was not a slave at the time of my marriage to the
soldier, I having been freed by the Proclamation of President Lincoln.
My name before I married my first husband, *John Tubman*, was Harriet
Ross. After my marriage to him my name was Harriet Tubman and so
continued and I was known and recognized by that name until my marriage to Nelson Davis. See my affidavit of Nov. 28, 1892 and proof of
Tubman's death dated Nov. 22nd 1892 all on file with my claim. I have
had no husband since the death of the soldier Nelson Davis. . . . I never
had any children nor child by the soldier nor by John Tubman.

The soldier was born (as he informed me) *in or near Elizabeth City,
North Carolina.* His actual residence when I became acquainted with
him was at my house in the town of Fleming, Cayuga C., N.Y. as a
boarder. . . . His occupation was that of a brickmaker and laborer. His
age as given in his certificate of discharge is 21, and in the record of his
death it is 44. See proof of death on file. His height 5 ft 11 inches, color
of skin black. The name of his owner (when a Slave) was Fred *Charles.
His father's name was Milford Davis.* The soldier was not a slave at the
time of his marriage to me, nor at the time of his Enrollment, he having been freed from Slavery by the proclamation of President Lincoln
Sept. 22, 1862 which gave him his freedom on January 1st 1863. *He was
known as Nelson Charles and Nelson Davis.* He never had any other wife
but me. . . .

her
HARRIET X DAVIS
mark

C. G. ADAMS
Clerk of County Court of
Cayuga County New York.

25

WILBUR H. SIEBERT

Letter to Earl Conrad

September 4, 1940

When Earl Conrad was researching his 1943 biography of Tubman, Gen-eral Harriet Tubman, *he wrote to Wilbur Siebert seeking information. Siebert, a white professor at Ohio State University, had gathered volu-minous material on the Underground Railroad, soliciting reminiscences from people involved and from others who had known them or knew about their involvement. Siebert published* The Underground Railroad *in 1898 but continued collecting material into the mid-twentieth century. This account of his conversation with Tubman in Cambridge, Mas-sachusetts, sometime in late 1894 provides a vivid picture of her at age seventy-two.*

Dear Mr. Conrad:

I have your letter of August 19th about the biography you are prepar-ing of Harriet Tubman, the fugitive slave and abductor of several hun-dred of her fellows from slavery.

My wife and I met Harriet Tubman in the home of Dr. Harriet Cobb on the west side of Massachusetts Avenue near Shepard Street, Cam-bridge, Mass., I think, in the autumn of 1894.

A friend of ours was boarding there who also knew Miss [Sarah H.] Bradford, and as I was then working on my Underground Railroad book our friend succeeded in having Harriet come out to Cambridge when she came to Boston.

Harriet was a small, kindly faced, sharp eyed woman with woolly hair showing a little grey. I knew a good deal about her from the Bradford biography of her but was very glad to meet her and get a first-hand impression of her personality. Although she was considerably aged and worn, her mind was still clear and she talked well, telling her methods in leading parties of slaves out of the land of bondage. She required them to obey her orders, and said she would have used her revolver on any

Wilbur H. Siebert to Earl Conrad, September 4, 1940, Earl Conrad Collection, box 1, Schomburg Center for Research in Black Culture, New York Public Library, New York.

who did not. When pursuers were tracking them they must hide and be silent, and a dose of paregoric kept babies from crying. Much she explained in answer to my questions.

When she first began to talk, she said that as a girl of perhaps twelve years of age she had been sent to the store on an errand. In a quarrel between the storekeeper and another man, one of them had thrown a weight lying on the counter and it had hit her on the head and left a permanent dent. She had me feel it. This caused her at frequent intervals (say of half an hour or so) to lose consciousness for three or four minutes. She explained that her head would drop and she would become silent, but I was not to become alarmed; she would arouse and continue her talk without losing the thread of her conversation.

Harriet Tubman was undoubtedly a remarkable person, shrewd in outwitting the planters whose slaves she stole, resourceful in leading her parties of blacks through woods and wilderness, and acquainted with certain lines of [the] Underground Railroad that would best serve her purpose. Some very noted abolitionists were her friends, as were also some distinguished generals of the Union army during the War Between the States.

Yours cordially,
W. H. SIEBERT.

26

U.S. SENATE

Committee on Pensions Report
1899

By 1898 Tubman had been receiving a small pension as the widow of a Civil War veteran for several years. In her pension application that year, she claimed that the government owed her $1,800 for her own military service. Although the letters of endorsement quoted in this document mention her military service, the Senate committee report refers to "her alleged *[emphasis added] services to the Government" and concentrates on*

U.S. Senate, Committee on Pensions, Report No. 1619, 55th Cong., 3rd sess., February 7, 1899, 1–2.

her role as a nurse and cook. The Senate agreed to increase her widow's pension but reduced the amount that had been granted by the House of Representatives. The following document provides a glimpse of the process Tubman endured to obtain this increase.

The Committee on Pensions, to whom was referred the bill (H.R. 4982) granting a pension to Harriet Tubman Davis, have examined the same and report:

The report of the Committee on Invalid Pensions of the House of Representatives is as follows:

The effect of this bill is to increase from $8 to $25 per month the pension of the beneficiary, Harriet T. Davis, of Auburn, N.Y.

Mrs. Davis is the widow of Nelson Davis, who served under the name of Nelson Charles as a private in Company G, Eighth United States Colored Infantry, from September 25, 1863, to November 10, 1865, and was honorably discharged. She also served long and faithfully as an army nurse.

Soldier died October 14, 1888, and the widow filed a claim as such July 24, 1890, under the act of June 27, 1890, and is now pensioned under said act at $8 per month. It is not shown that the soldier's death was due to his military service. It is shown, however, by evidence filed with this committee, that the claimant was sent to the front by Governor Andrew, and acted as nurse, cook in hospital, and spy during nearly the whole period of the war.

The following is a copy of the letter from Secretary Seward:

WASHINGTON, D.C., JULY 25, 1865

My Dear Sir:

Harriet Tubman, a colored woman, has been nursing our soldiers during nearly all the war. She believes she has claims for faithful service to the command in South Carolina with which you are connected, and she believes you would be disposed to see her claim justly settled. I have known her long as a noble high spirit, as true as seldom dwells in the human form. I commend her, therefore, to your kind attention.

Faithfully, your friend,
WILLIAM H. SEWARD.

. . . Gen. Rufus Saxton, in a letter referring to Mrs. Tubman, says:

"She was employed by General Hunter, and I think both by Generals Stephens and Sherman, and is as deserving of a pension from the Government for her service as any other of its faithful servants."

In a letter to Brigadier-General Gilmore, from Headquarters Colored Brigade, St. Helena Island, South Carolina, July 6, 1863, Col. James Montgomery, commanding brigade, said:

"I would respectfully recommend to your attention Mrs. Harriet Tubman, a most remarkable woman, invaluable as a scout."

These testimonials sufficiently show the character and value of the service rendered by Mrs. Davis during the war.

She now is about 75 years of age, physically broken down, and poor.

This woman has a double claim on the Government. She went into the field and hospitals and cared for the sick and wounded. She saved lives. In her old age and poverty a pension of $25 per month is none too much.

The bill is reported back with the recommendation that it pass.

The papers in this case show that a claim for this woman was once presented to the House of Representatives and referred to the Committee on War Claims. Manifestly that would be the better way to reimburse her for her alleged services to the Government, but her advanced years and necessitous condition lead your committee to give the matter consideration. There is, however a strong objection to the bill in its present form. The number of nurses on the pension roll at a rate higher than $12 per month is very few indeed, and there are no valid reasons why this claimant should receive a pension of $25 per month as a nurse, thus opening a new avenue for pension increases. She is now drawing [a] pension at the rate of $8 per month as the widow of a soldier, and in view of her personal services to the Government Congress is amply justified in increasing that pension.

The passage of the bill is recommended after being amended as follows:

Strike out all after the enacting clause and insert:

That the Secretary of the Interior be, and he is hereby, authorized and directed to place on the pension roll, subject to the provisions and limitations of the pension laws, the name of Harriet Tubman Davis, widow of Nelson Davis, late a private in Company G, Eighth Regiment United States Colored Infantry, and pay her a pension at the rate of twenty dollars per month in lieu of that she is now receiving.

27

SYRACUSE HERALD

To End Days in Home She Founded
June 4, 1911

This article recounting the story of Tubman's life appeared in the Syracuse (N.Y.) Herald *just two years before her death. It was accompanied by a photograph, taken some years before, identifying her as Harriet Tubman-Davis. This relatively accurate summary of her life repeated much of the legend first crafted by Sarah Bradford and later embellished by Tubman and her admirers.*

WAS AN ESCAPED SLAVE

Piloted Hundreds of Slaves From the South to Free States of the North by the "Underground Railway" and Served as a Spy Within Confederate Lines During the Civil War.

Auburn, June 3.—Harriet Tubman, the aged negress, known as the "Moses of her people," was last Thursday taken to the Harriet Tubman home, penniless, to end her days. Her age is past 90 years.[10] She was born in slavery, but ran away from her Maryland home about the year 1849, and between that time and the outbreak of the civil war piloted nearly 400 escaped slaves to the Northern States and Canada. She was befriended by William H. Seward, Gerrit Smith, Wendell Phillips, William Lloyd Garrison and other distinguished abolitionists and was an aid and admirer of John Brown. Harriet Beecher Stowe planned to write a story of Harriet Tubman's life. Since the civil war she has resided in a small house on the outskirts of Auburn and devoted her interests to the work

---

[10]Tubman, like many enslaved people, was uncertain about the exact year of her birth. She was actually eighty-nine years old when this article was written, and she was twenty-two when she married John Tubman.

From "To End Days in Home She Founded: Remarkable Story of the Career of Harriet Tubman of Auburn," *Syracuse Herald*, June 4, 1911.

of establishing an institution for aged colored men and women, and upon this home she is now dependent. . . . Harriet's name was originally Arimenia [*sic*] Ross. At the age of 24 she married a free Maryland colored man named Tubman. When Harriet escaped from slavery she lost track of Tubman, but learned afterward that he had married again. Harriet also married. Her second husband was an Auburn colored man named Nelson Davis. . . .

She was born about 1820 in Dorchester county, on the eastern shore of Maryland, near Cambridge. She has all the characteristics of the pure African race strongly marked upon her and is believed to be directly descended from a tribe of Felietas on the Guinea coast. She is naturally shrewd and blunt of speech, but her simplicity and ignorance have caused her in many cases to be imposed upon. For years her household has consisted of several old black people and some forlorn and wandering women. From the effects of a blow upon her head received in childhood she has a stupid, half-witted look, but she also has a pair of sharp black eyes and a ready wit that have carried her through many trying places.

Her flight from slavery was occasioned by the belief that she was about to be sold and separated from her mother and father and ten brothers and sisters. After undergoing severe privations she reached the free States, obtained work and saved her wages with the idea of going back South eventually to lead more of her people out of bondage. . . . Up to the time the war broke out she had made nineteen trips across the Mason and Dixon line and piloted between 300 and 400 slaves to freedom. A high price was set upon the head of the mysterious colored woman who appeared occasionally on the plantations and always managed to disappear in company with a band of valuable slaves.

Among those people she led away were her mother and father and nine of their children. One of her sisters died in the South. During the war she was sent South by Governor Andrews [*sic*] of Massachusetts as a spy and scout for the Fifty-fourth Massachusetts colored infantry. During this time she received no pay and drew but twenty rations from the government in four years, yet a plan to secure a pension for her was rejected as coming under no recognized law. She worked in the army hospitals as an attendant by day and at night baked pies, which she peddled in the Confederate area and at the same time managed to pick up valuable information. Harriet is deeply religious and is a firm believer that the Lord will provide for the deserving. When in deepest distress she said she never lost hope "but just got down an' prayed hard an' something was boun' to turn up." She is an interesting storyteller and relates many thrilling tales in her matter of fact way, of slavery days and the times of John Brown and the great war which followed.

28

NEW YORK TIMES

Harriet Tubman Davis Obituary
March 14, 1913

Four days after Tubman's death, the New York Times *published this obituary. In it the newspaper repeated common beliefs that became part of the Tubman mythology, including those about her age, the number of slaves she rescued, and the high rewards slaveholders offered for her. The misspelling of Frederick Douglass's name shows how far he had faded from public memory.*

Harriet Tubman Davis, an ex-slave, known as the "Moses of her People," who before the civil war took 300 slaves to Canada through her "underground railroad," died on Monday night at the home she founded for aged and indigent Negroes at Auburn, New York. She was said to be 98 years old, and her death was caused by pneumonia.

Harriet Tubman Davis was esteemed by such men as Ralph Waldo Emerson, William Lloyd Garrison, Phillips Brooks, Horace Mann, Ferderick [*sic*] Douglas [*sic*], Gerrit Smith, and John Brown, while on the other hand planters and slave owners offered rewards of from $12,000 to $40,000 for her capture during the fifties, at the time when she was taking slaves out of the United States. She had served as a scout, nurse, and spy in the Union Army.

"Harriet Tubman Davis," *New York Times*, March 14, 1913, 9, col. 2.

29

AUBURN CITIZEN

Harriet Tubman Memorialized

June 11, 1914

The year after Tubman died, this contradictory characterization of her appeared in the mayor of Auburn's announcement of a day to honor her. Tubman undoubtedly would have been outraged to see herself described as a "faithful old slave." This phrase reflects the revision of the Civil War taking place in American popular culture in the early twentieth century. According to this recreation, contented slaves were treated like members of slaveholders' families, and the Confederates fought a doomed but principled struggle not to preserve slavery, but for citizenship rights. The depiction of Tubman is congruent with the era's tolerance of racial segregation and efforts to promote national healing by ignoring racial inequality and injustice and by looking forward to a prosperous and powerful future.

**LET ALL DISPLAY FLAGS ON THE MORROW! IS THE OFFICIAL WISH OF
MAYOR BRISTER, THAT THE MEMORY OF FAITHFUL OLD SLAVE
HARRIET TUBMAN MAY BE HONORED**

The citizens of Auburn have very properly seen fit to erect a public monument to the memory of Harriet Tubman, a tribute for her faithful services to the Nation, during the Civil War, and to her own people in the cause of freedom. At [*sic*] a further mark of respect and as a token of appreciation for her loyal and patriotic service to our country and flag, as Auburn's Chief Executive Officer I direct that on tomorrow June 12, the date of the unveiling of the memorial, the flags be displayed on the municipal buildings, and suggest as there are many of our loyal citizens who may wish to honor the memory of this faithful old slave who was willing to die for her race, if need be that they also, at the same time, cooperate and display the national emblem from their homes and places of business.

"Let All Display Flags on the Morrow!" *Auburn Citizen*, June 11, 1914.

If the stars and stripes could float from every home in Auburn we believe that it would inspire patriotism and demonstrate that we are not forgetful of those who suffered so much for the cause of freedom and were willing to die that we might have one country and one flag.

CHARLES W. BRISTER,
Mayor.
Auburn, N.Y., June 11, 1914.

A Chronology of the Life and Times of Harriet Tubman (1822–1913)

ca.
1822   Harriet, known as Araminta, born to Harriet Green and Benjamin Ross, both enslaved on Maryland's Eastern Shore.

1827   New York abolishes slavery.

1831   Radical white abolitionist William Lloyd Garrison begins publishing antislavery newspaper, the *Liberator*, in Boston.

ca.
1837   Harriet suffers life-threatening head injury when overseer throws lead weight at another slave and hits her instead.

1838   Frederick Bailey, later Frederick Douglass, escapes from slavery in Maryland.

1844   Harriet Ross marries John Tubman, a free black man.

1848   New York governor William H. Seward elected to the U.S. Senate.

1849   Harriet escapes from slavery in Maryland to freedom in the North.

1850   Congress passes stronger fugitive slave law, one of five acts constituting Compromise of 1850, which also admits California as free state and outlaws slave trading in District of Columbia.

Harriet makes first return trip to Maryland to rescue her niece, Kessiah Bowley, and Kessiah's two children.

1851   John Tubman refuses to leave Maryland; Harriet conducts group of ten fugitives to Canada.

1852   Harriet Beecher Stowe publishes *Uncle Tom's Cabin*.

1854   Republican party formed.

Kansas-Nebraska Act sparks armed conflict in Kansas between antislavery and proslavery forces.

1857   In *Dred Scott v. Sandford* U.S. Supreme Court refuses to free Scott, upholds expansion of slavery, and denies African Americans' right to citizenship.

Harriet Tubman brings her parents from Maryland to Canada.

1858   Tubman and John Brown first meet in Canada.

1859   Tubman establishes home in Auburn, New York.

Brown, thirteen whites, and five blacks conduct ill-fated raid on Harpers Ferry, Virginia.

1860   Tubman participates in Charles Nalle's rescue in Troy, New York.

Tubman addresses annual women's rights meeting in Boston.

Abraham Lincoln elected president.

South Carolina secedes from the United States.

1861   Mississippi, Florida, Alabama, Georgia, Louisiana, and Texas join South Carolina to form Confederate States of America; later joined by Virginia, Arkansas, Tennessee, and North Carolina.

1861–1865   Civil War; more than 180,000 African Americans serve in combat.

1862–1865   Tubman serves as wartime spy, scout, nurse, and cook.

1863   Lincoln issues Emancipation Proclamation.

Tubman leads Combahee River raid, freeing about seven hundred people from slavery.

1864   Congress equalizes pay for some African American soldiers.

1865   Lincoln assassinated.

Thirteenth Amendment to U.S. Constitution abolishes slavery.

1867   John Tubman killed.

1869   Sarah Bradford publishes *Scenes in the Life of Harriet Tubman*.

Tubman marries Nelson Davis.

1886   Bradford publishes *Harriet: The Moses of Her People*.

1888   Nelson Davis dies of tuberculosis.

1895   Tubman receives Civil War widow's pension.

1896   Tubman addresses first meeting of National Association of Colored Women in Washington, D.C., and Susan B. Anthony's National American Woman Suffrage Association.

1899   Tubman's pension increased in recognition of her work as Civil War nurse.

1908   AME Zion Church in Auburn officially opens Harriet Tubman Home on land she transferred to it.

1913   Tubman dies and is buried in Auburn, New York.

Questions for Consideration

1. How did Harriet Tubman learn of freedom, and what motivated her to seek freedom when she did?
2. What led Tubman to undertake the risk of going back into the slave South to bring people to the North?
3. Why did Tubman believe she could rescue people from slavery despite the dangers involved?
4. Why might people have changed their names when they escaped from slavery or became free?
5. What made Harriet Tubman, an illiterate former slave, so popular among elite white northern antislavery advocates?
6. Did Tubman's religious views help or hinder her antislavery mission?
7. Abolitionists were divided over the question of whether the U.S. Constitution was a proslavery or potentially an antislavery document. How was this important for the antislavery movement's tactics?
8. What were the differences between the fugitive slave laws of 1793 and 1850? How might they have affected public opinion about slavery?
9. Some abolitionists argued that the Fugitive Slave Law of 1850 was unconstitutional. What parts of the law might they have cited to make this argument?
10. Why did many free blacks move to Canada, particularly after the passage of the Fugitive Slave Law of 1850?
11. Antislavery activists often invoked the memory of the heroes of the American Revolution. Why might they have seen themselves as engaged in a similar struggle?
12. Many Underground Railroad participants were Quakers and other pacifists. What evidence is there that Tubman believed or did not believe in nonviolence as a principle of antislavery action?
13. Describe how the capture of fugitive slaves and their trials might actually have helped the antislavery cause.
14. What was Tubman's relationship with John Brown and his raid on the federal arsenal at Harpers Ferry, Virginia?

15. Why did Brown describe Tubman as "the most of a *man*" he had ever met?

16. What might we learn from African Americans' songs about their conception of freedom?

17. Discuss Tubman's role in the Civil War. Why did she have such trouble obtaining a pension from the U.S. government?

18. In what ways did Tubman violate traditional gender expectations in regard to women? Were such expectations different for black and white women?

19. What was Tubman's role in the women's rights movement, and why might she have considered the movement important?

20. Was Tubman a feminist? Explain.

21. How did postwar Reconstruction events influence changes in Sarah H. Bradford's biography of Tubman?

22. How did the reality of Tubman's life differ from the myth and legend?

23. What had changed in society to lead the mayor of Auburn, New York, to recall Tubman as a "faithful old slave" after her death? What does this reveal about history and memory?

24. How and why did the memory of Tubman change during the twentieth century?

Selected Bibliography

HARRIET TUBMAN

Bradford, Sarah H. *Harriet: The Moses of Her People*. New York: George R. Lockwood & Son, 1886.

———. *Scenes in the Life of Harriet Tubman*. Auburn, N.Y.: W. J. Moses, 1869.

Clinton, Catherine. *Harriet Tubman: The Road to Freedom*. New York: Little, Brown, 2004.

Conrad, Earl. *General Harriet Tubman*. Washington, D.C.: Associated Publishers, 1990. First published 1943.

Humez, Jean M. *Harriet Tubman: The Life and the Life Stories*. Madison: University of Wisconsin Press, 2003.

Larson, Kate Clifford. *Bound for the Promised Land: Harriet Tubman: Portrait of an American Hero*. New York: Ballantine, 2004.

Sernett, Milton C. *Harriet Tubman: Myth, Memory, and History*. Durham, N.C.: Duke University Press, 2007.

Siebert, Wilbur H., to Earl Conrad. September 4, 1940. Earl Conrad/Harriet Tubman Research Collection (Sc Micro R 906), Manuscripts, Archives and Rare Books Division, Schomburg Center for Research in Black Culture, The New York Public Library.

HARRIET TUBMAN IN CHILDREN'S LITERATURE

Bacchus (Maynard), Joan and Francis Taylor. *Golden Legacy: Illustrated History Magazine: The Saga of Harriet Tubman; "The Moses of Her People,"* vol. 2. Dix Hills, N.Y.: Fitzgerald, 1967.

McGovern, Ann. *Runaway Slave: The Story of Harriet Tubman*. New York: Four Winds, 1965.

Petry, Ann. *Harriet Tubman: Conductor on the Underground Railroad*. New York: Thomas Y. Crowell, 1955.

Ringgold, Faith. *Aunt Harriet's Underground Railroad in the Sky*. New York: Crown, 1992.

Sadlier, Rosemary. *Tubman: Harriet Tubman and the Underground Railroad*. Toronto: Umbrella, 1997.

Schroeder, Alan, and Jerry Pinkney. *Minty: A Story of Young Harriet Tubman.* New York: Puffin, 2000.

Sterling, Dorothy. *Freedom Train: The Story of Harriet Tubman.* New York: Doubleday, 1954.

Wright, Courtni C. *Journey to Freedom: A Story of the Underground Railroad.* Illustrated by Gershom Griffith. New York: Holiday House, 1994.

CHESAPEAKE BAY SLAVERY AND BLACK FREEDOM

Berlin, Ira. *Slaves without Masters: The Free Negro in the Antebellum South.* New York: Random House, 1974.

Breen, T. H., and Stephen Innes. *"Myne Owne Ground": Race and Freedom on Virginia's Eastern Shore, 1640–1676.* 2nd ed. New York: Oxford University Press, 2004.

Douglass, Frederick. *Narrative of the Life of Frederick Douglass, an American Slave, Written by Himself.* Edited by David W. Blight. Boston: St. Martin's Press, 1997.

Fields, Barbara Jeanne. *Slavery and Freedom on the Middle Ground: Maryland during the Nineteenth Century.* New Haven, Conn.: Yale University Press, 1985.

Kulikoff, Allan. *Tobacco and Slaves: The Development of Southern Cultures in the Chesapeake, 1680–1800.* Chapel Hill: University of North Carolina Press, 1986.

Morgan, Philip D. *Slave Counterpoint: Black Culture in the Eighteenth-Century Chesapeake and Lowcountry.* Chapel Hill: University of North Carolina Press, 1998.

Whitman, T. Stephen. *The Price of Freedom: Slavery and Manumission in Baltimore and Early National Maryland.* Lexington: University Press of Kentucky, 1997.

CHRISTIANITY AND AFRICAN BELIEFS

Creel, Margaret Washington. *"A Peculiar People": Slave Religion and Community-Culture among the Gullahs.* New York: New York University Press, 1989.

Raboteau, Albert J. *Slave Religion: The "Invisible Institution" in the Antebellum South.* New York: Oxford University Press, 2004.

Sobel, Mechal. *"Trabelin' On": The Slave Journey to an Afro-Baptist Faith.* Princeton, N.J.: Princeton University Press, 1988.

Stuckey, Sterling. *Slave Culture: Nationalist Theory and the Foundations of Black America.* New York: Oxford University Press, 1987.

Young, Jason. *Rituals of Resistance: African Atlantic Religion in Kongo and the Low Country South in the Era of Slavery.* Baton Rouge: Louisiana State University Press, 2007.

ANTISLAVERY AND THE UNDERGROUND RAILROAD

Blight, David W., ed. *Passages to Freedom: The Underground Railroad in History and Memory.* Washington, D.C.: Smithsonian Books, 2004.

Blue, Frederick J. *No Taint of Compromise: Crusaders in Antislavery Politics.* Baton Rouge: Louisiana State University Press, 2005.

Bordewich, Fergus M. *Bound for Canaan: The Epic Story of the Underground Railroad, America's First Civil Rights Movement.* New York: HarperCollins, 2005.

Brown, William Wells. *The Rising Son, or The Antecedents and Advancement of the Colored Race.* Miami, Fla.: Mnemosyne Publishing, Inc., 1969. First published 1874.

Camp, Stephanie. *Closer to Freedom: Enslaved Women and Everyday Resistance in the Plantation South.* Chapel Hill: University of North Carolina Press, 2005.

Gara, Larry. *The Liberty Line: The Legend of the Underground Railroad.* Lexington: University of Kentucky Press, 1961.

Grover, Kathryn. *The Fugitive's Gibraltar: Escaping Slaves and Abolitionism in New Bedford, Massachusetts.* Amherst: University of Massachusetts Press, 2001.

Hepburn, Sharon A. Roger. *Crossing the Border: A Free Black Community in Canada.* Urbana: University of Illinois Press, 2007.

Horton, James Oliver, and Lois E. Horton. *Black Bostonians: Family Life and Community Struggle in the Antebellum North.* 2nd ed. New York: Holmes & Meier, 1999.

———. *In Hope of Liberty: Culture, Community and Protest among Northern Free Blacks, 1700–1860.* New York: Oxford University Press, 1997.

Jacobs, Harriet A. *Incidents in the Life of a Slave Girl.* Edited by Jean Fagan Yellin. Cambridge, Mass.: Harvard University Press, 1987.

Johnson, Walter. *Soul by Soul: Life inside the Antebellum Slave Market.* Cambridge, Mass.: Harvard University Press, 1999.

Kaye, Anthony. *Joining Places: Slave Neighborhoods in the Old South.* Chapel Hill: University of North Carolina Press, 2007.

Mayer, Henry. *All on Fire: William Lloyd Garrison and the Abolition of Slavery.* New York: St. Martin's, 1998.

McFeely, William S. *Frederick Douglass.* New York: W. W. Norton, 1991.

McGowan, James A. *Station Master on the Underground Railroad: The Life and Letters of Thomas Garrett.* Rev. ed. Jefferson, N.C.: McFarland & Company, Inc., 2005.

Pacheco, Josephine F. *The Pearl: A Failed Slave Escape on the Potomac.* Chapel Hill: University of North Carolina Press, 2005.

Rael, Patrick. *Black Identity and Black Protest in the Antebellum North.* Chapel Hill: University of North Carolina Press, 2002.

Siebert, Wilbur H. *The Underground Railroad: From Slavery to Freedom.* New York: The Macmillan Company, 1898.

Stauffer, John. *The Black Hearts of Men: Radical Abolitionists and the Transformation of Race.* Cambridge, Mass.: Harvard University Press, 2001.

Stewart, James Brewer. *Holy Warriors: The Abolitionists and American Slavery.* Rev. ed. New York: Hill & Wang, 1997.

Still, William. *The Underground Rail Road.* Chicago: Johnson, 1970. First published 1872.

Yee, Shirley J. *Black Women Abolitionists: A Study in Activism, 1828–1860.* Knoxville: University of Tennessee Press, 1992.

CIVIL WAR AND EMANCIPATION

Adams, Virginia M., ed. *On the Altar of Freedom: A Black Soldier's Civil War Letters from the Front.* Amherst: University of Massachusetts Press, 1991.

Blight, David W. *Race and Reunion: The Civil War in American Memory.* Cambridge, Mass.: Belknap Press of Harvard University Press, 2001.

Foner, Eric. *Forever Free: The Story of Emancipation and Reconstruction.* New York: Alfred A. Knopf, 2005.

Glatthaar, Joseph T. *Forged in Battle: The Civil War Alliance of Black Soldiers and White Officers.* New York: Free Press, 1990.

Glymph, Thavolia. *Out of the House of Bondage: The Transformation of the Plantation Household.* Cambridge: Cambridge University Press, 2008.

Higginson, Thomas Wentworth. *Army Life in a Black Regiment.* East Lansing: Michigan State University Press, 1960. First published 1870.

Hunter, Tera. *To 'Joy My Freedom: Southern Black Women's Lives after the Civil War.* Cambridge, Mass.: Harvard University Press, 1998.

Kachun, Mitchell A. *Festivals of Freedom: Memory and Meaning in African American Emancipation Celebrations, 1808–1915.* Amherst: University of Massachusetts Press, 2003.

Manning, Chandra. *What This Cruel War Was Over: Soldiers, Slavery, and the Civil War.* New York: Alfred A. Knopf, 2007.

McPherson, James. *The Negro's Civil War: How American Negroes Felt and Acted during the War for the Union.* New York: Vintage, 1965.

Oates, Stephen B. *To Purge This Land with Blood: A Biography of John Brown.* New York: Harper & Row, 1970.

Quarles, Benjamin. *Allies for Freedom: Blacks and John Brown.* New York: Oxford University Press, 1974.

———. *The Negro in the Civil War.* Boston: Little, Brown, 1969. First published 1953.

Vorenberg, Michael. *The Emancipation Proclamation: A Brief History with Documents.* Boston: Bedford/St. Martin's, 2010.

WOMEN'S RIGHTS

Ginzberg, Lori D. *Untidy Origins: A Story of Women's Rights in Antebellum New York.* Chapel Hill: University of North Carolina Press, 2005.

Griffith, Elisabeth. *In Her Own Right: The Life of Elizabeth Cady Stanton.* New York: Oxford University Press, 1984.

Jones, Martha. *All Bound Up Together: The Woman Question in African American Public Culture, 1830–1900.* Chapel Hill: University of North Carolina Press, 2007.

Painter, Nell Irvin. *Sojourner Truth: A Life, a Symbol.* New York: W. W. Norton, 1996.

Sklar, Kathryn Kish. *Women's Rights Emerges within the Antislavery Movement, 1830–1870: A Brief History with Documents.* Boston: Bedford/St. Martin's, 2000.

Wellman, Judith. *The Road to Seneca Falls: Elizabeth Cady Stanton and the First Woman's Rights Convention.* Urbana: University of Illinois Press, 2004.

Acknowledgments (*continued from p. ii*)

Figure 1. Ambrotype of Thomas Garrett, Wilmington, Delaware, ca. 1850, courtesy of the Trustees of the Boston Public Library.

Figure 2. Engraving of William Still by J. Sartain, courtesy of the Chester County Historical Society.

Figure 3. Photograph of American Abolitionist Frederick Douglass, © Bettmann/Corbis.

Figure 4. Photograph of Abolitionist John Brown, © Bettmann/Corbis.

Figure 5. Portrait of Abolitionist Harriet Tubman, © Bettmann/Corbis.

Figure 6. Photograph of Harriet Tubman, late 1886, courtesy of the Ohio Historical Society.

Document 10. Excerpt from "Fugitive Slaves Aided by the Vigilance Committee since the Passage of the Fugitive Slave Bill 1850," Massachusetts Anti-Slavery Society Records, The New-York Historical Society. Reprinted by permission of the New-York Historical Society.

Document 11. John Brown. Letter to John Brown Jr., April 8, 1858, Boyd B. Stutler Collection, West Virginia State Archives. Reprinted by permission of the West Virginia State Archives.

Document 25. Wilbur H. Siebert. Letter to Earl Conrad, September 4, 1940, Earl Conrad/Harriet Tubman Research Collection (Sc Micro R 906), Manuscripts, Archives and Rare Books Division, Schomburg Center for Research in Black Culture, The New York Public Library. Courtesy of the New York Public Library.

Index

abolitionists
  aid to black soldiers by, 70
  aid to runaway slaves, 9–10
  Bleeding Kansas and, 42
  in Boston, 54–55, 122
  deaths of, 80–81
  Douglass and, 20
  Dred Scott decision and, 34
  fugitive slave laws and, 18, 106, 122
  Harpers Ferry raid and, 49, 54–55
  Kansas-Nebraska Act and, 34
  philosophical differences among, 40
  runaway slaves as, 10
  Sea Islands and, 57
  Tubman endorsed by, 142–44
  Underground Railroad and, 21
  western Virginia and, 42
  women, 44
"Account of Combahee River Raid" (*Commonwealth*), 132–33
Adams, C. G., 151
advertisements, for runaway slaves, 5–6, 33, 116–17, 137
"Affidavit" (Tubman), 149–51
African Americans. *See also* free blacks; slaves
  American Revolution and, 49
  antiblack sentiment and, 74
  army salaries, 69–71
  black history, 88–89
  colonization proposals for, 10, 14, 15, 97n154
  Confederate Army and, 67, 72
  Emancipation Proclamation and, 61–62
  freed slaves, 64–65
  indentured servants, 11
  language, 40, 61
  name changes, 31
  oral tradition, 25–26
  popular culture image of, 87, 159
  post–Civil War conditions, 78–79
  preparing for independence, 57
  racism against, 74–75, 78, 159
  religious beliefs, 25–26
  rights of, 33–34, 74, 159, 162
  soldiers, 69, 70–72, 74, 88

  testimony against whites, 65, 67
  unequal pay, 60, 69–71
  Union Army and, 56–61, 67–69, 72
  well-being of, 2–3
  women, 51
African Civilization Society, 97n154
African Meeting House, Boston, 55
African Methodist Episcopal (AME) churches, 19
African Methodist Episcopal (AME) Zion Church, Auburn, New York, 80, 84, 85, 86
African Methodist Episcopal (AME) Zion Church, New Bedford, 10
African slave raids, 90n4
Agnew, Allen, 120
Alcott, Bronson, 38
"America," 62
American Anti-Slavery Society, 14, 22, 30–31
American Revolution, 49
Andrew, John A., 38, 56, 58–59, 63, 70, 143, 154, 157
Anthony, Susan B., 24, 75, 81, 83, 84, 162
antislavery movement
  black militias, 34–35
  in Boston, 29
  Douglass and, 20
  growth of, 11–15
  networks, 14–15, 37–41
  radical, 14–17
  Tubman and, 2, 38–39
  Uncle Tom's Cabin and, 28
  Underground Railroad and, 2, 6
  violence and, 14, 15
  women in, 40
Anti-Slavery Society of Edinburgh, 142
Attucks, Crispus, Day, 49
Auburn, New York, 22, 45, 55–56, 77, 84, 86, 138, 151
Auburn Citizen, 86
  "Harriet Tubman Memorialized," 159–60
Aunt Harriet's Underground Railroad in the Sky (Ringgold), 89

Bailey, Frederick, 10, 161. *See also* Douglass, Frederick

Bailey, Josiah (Joe), 32–33
Bailey, William (Bill), 33
Baltimore, Maryland. *See also* Maryland
  free blacks in, 19, 23, 51, 57
  fugitive slaves, 10, 15
  slaves hired out in, 9
  Underground Railroad, 23, 32, 54, 59
  women's religious groups, 26
Baltimore, Peter, 129
Bearse, Austin
  "Reminiscences of Fugitive-Slave Law
    Days in Boston," 110–11
Beaufort, South Carolina, 59
Becker, Officer, 129
Beecher, Henry Ward, 94n81
Bell, John, 95n105
Bird, M. B., 39
Birth of a Nation, The, 88
black history, 88–89
black militias, 34–35, 48
  Brown and, 41, 42, 46, 63
  Civil War and, 56
  in Kansas, 63
  organization of, 34–35, 48, 49
black Shakers, 26
Bleeding Kansas, 42
Blight, David W., 87
bloomer dress, 65
"Blow Ye the Trumpet, Blow," 61
Booth, John Wilkes, 74
Boston
  abolitionists in, 12–13, 19, 22, 29, 37–38,
    39, 40, 46, 48, 49, 54–55, 67, 71, 82, 122
  antislavery movement in, 29, 51, 57, 61
  Brown in, 42, 46, 127
  Emancipation Proclamation celebration, 61
  fugitive slave laws and, 110–11
  fugitive slaves in, 12–13, 29–30, 110–11,
    122–24
  Great Awakening, 13
  slave hunters in, 117–19
  Tubman in, 31, 37, 40, 44, 51, 56, 71, 82,
    83, 84, 133–34, 138, 143, 144, 152
Boston Daily Chronotype, 118
Boston Massacre, 49
Boston Vigilance Committee, 37
  "Fugitive Slaves Aided by the Vigilance
    Committee since the Passage of the
    Fugitive Slave Bill 1850," 122–24
*Bound for the Promised Land: Harriet Tub-
  man: Portrait of an American Hero*
  (Larson), 90
Bowley, Araminta, 19
Bowley, James, 19, 21, 78–79
Bowley, John, 19, 21, 31
Bowley, Kessiah, 19, 20, 31, 161
Bradford, Sarah H., 27, 66, 75–76, 80, 83, 85,
  89, 92n43, 140, 142, 152, 156, 162
  "Harriet Tubman Biographies," 145–49
Breckenridge, John C., 95n105
Brisbane, W. H., 62

Broadice, Edward, 151. *See also* Brodess,
  Edward
Brodess, Edward, 5, 6–7, 9, 116
Brodess, Eliza Ann, 5
  "Runaway Advertisement," 116–17
Brodess, Mary Pattison, 6
Brooks, E. U. A., 85, 86
Brooks, Phillips, 158
Brooks, Preston S., 42
Brown, Frederick, 94n82
Brown, John, 2, 41f, 42–49, 63, 77, 86, 156,
  158, 162
  capture of, 47
  commemoration of, 54–55
  fundraising by, 42–43
  hanging, 48, 138–39
  Harpers Ferry raid, 46–47
  letter from Lewis Hayden to, 127
  "Letter to John Brown Jr.," 124–25
  martyrdom of, 48
  Pottawatomie Creek massacre and, 42
  significance of, 49
  slaves freed by, 44–45
  songs about, 62, 130–31
  sons, 45, 47
  trial, 48
  Tubman and, 42, 124–25, 127, 138–39,
    142–43, 158
Brown, John, Hall, 84
Brown, John, Jr., 55
  letter from John Brown to, 124–25
Brown, Owen, 95n98
Brown, William Wells, 26, 37, 39, 61–62, 130
  "Emancipation Eve," 130–32
  "Moses," 144–45
Buchanan, James, 47
Burch, James H., 113, 114
Burns, Anthony, 37, 39, 122
Butler, Andrew P., 42
Butler, Benjamin F., 58, 95n121, 96n125

Cabot, Samuel, 94n81
California, 17, 106, 161
Camp William Penn, 73
Canada
  refugee communities, 37, 44
  safety in, 12, 32, 33, 34, 36
  Tubman in, 27, 56, 145
Carney, William H., 68
Case, Mr., 125
cat-o'-nine-tails, 113n3
Cayuga County Court House, 86
Central Presbyterian Church, Auburn, New
  York, 75, 77
Charles, Fred, 77
Charles, Nelson G. (Davis), 76–78, 81,
  98n164, 149–50, 151, 154
  "Charles Nalle Rescue" (*Douglass' Monthly*),
    128–29
Charleston campaign, 67–69
Chase, John, 30, 93n57

Cheney, Ednah Dow, 44, 48, 56, 73, 98*n*172
    Tubman biography, 134–39
Chesapeake Bay area, 3–10, 29
Chicago Defender, 88
Child, Lydia Maria, 58
children
    difficulties of rescuing, 13, 24–25, 32
    infant and child mortality, 7
    Tubman's sedation of, 24–25, 136
Christianity, 25–26
Christian Recorder, 73
cimarrón, 14
citizenship, of African Americans, 34
Civil War, 56–74, 162
    African American volunteers, 56
    anticipation of, 42, 48–49
    casualties, 59, 60, 68
    Charleston campaign, 67–69
    Combahee River raid, 63–65, 67, 132–33,
        139, 162
    Confederate Army, 67, 72
    ending, 71–74
    film industry and, 87–88
    Fort Wagner, 67–68
    Fort Wagner, Battle of, 84
    nursing, 60–61, 68–69
    Olustee, Battle of, 69, 77
    reconciliation following, 87
    Shiloh, battle of, 59
    Tubman and, 1, 2, 48–49, 56–61, 60–61,
        63–67
    Union Army and, 56–61, 67–69, 72
Clinton, Catherine, 89, 90
clothing, 65
Cobb, Harriet, 152
coded messages, 27, 29–30
    songs as, 130
colonization, 10, 14, 15, 36, 97*n*154
Combahee River raid, 63–65, 67, 132–33,
    139, 162
"Committee on Pensions Report" (U.S. Sen-
    ate), 153–55
Commonwealth magazine, 71
    "Account of Combahee River Raid,"
        132–33
    "Solicitation of Aid for Harriet Tubman,"
        133–34
compensation
    pension and back pay claims, 71, 74, 80,
        81, 83, 84, 139, 149–51, 153–55
    unequal pay, 60, 69–71
Compromise of 1850, 17, 106, 161
Concord, Massachusetts, 38
conductors, 13, 21, 24, 26–28, 39
Confederate Army
    black soldiers in, 72
    Confiscation Acts and, 58
    fall of Richmond and, 73
    treatment of African Americans by, 67
Confederate States of America
    commitment to slavery by, 71–72

formation of, 56
freedom for slaves in, 59
Confiscation Acts, 58
Conrad, Earl, 88
    Siebert's letter to, 152–53
Constitution, U.S., 40
    Fourteenth Amendment, 97*n*161
    Nineteenth Amendment, 97*n*161
    "Provision regarding Fugitive Slaves," 103
    Thirteenth Amendment, 71, 162
Constitutional Union party, 52, 54–55
contraband
    equal pay and, 69
    slaves as, 58, 95*n*121, 139
contraband camps, 59, 61–62, 65, 130
Cooke, Jay, and Company, 78, 98*n*168
cotton cultivation, 3
cotton gin, 3
Craft, Ellen, 18–19, 37, 117–18
Craft, William, 18, 37, 117–18
Crummell, Alexander, 97*n*154

Dall, Caroline, 51
Daniels, Jim, 44
Darby, J. C., 66
Davis, Charles Nelson, 77, 150. *See also*
    Davis, Nelson (Charles)
Davis, Gertie, 80, 81, 83
Davis, Harriet Tubman. *See* Tubman,
    Harriet
Davis, Jefferson, 62
Davis, Milford, 77, 149*n*9, 151
Davis, Nelson (Charles), 76–78, 79, 81,
    149–50, 151, 154, 155, 157, 162
Delany, Martin R., 72, 73–74, 97*n*154
Democratic party, 52
Douglas, H. Ford, 55
Douglas, Stephen A., 95*n*105
Douglass, Annie, 47
Douglass, Frederick, 9–10, 19, 20, 40, 41*f*,
    42, 44, 55, 61, 67, 71, 76, 81, 83, 86,
    97*n*154, 128, 158, 161
    Harpers Ferry raid and, 45–46, 47
    "Testimonial," 142–44
Douglass' Monthly, 50
    "Charles Nalle Rescue," 128–29
Dover, Delaware, 34–35
Dover Eight, 35, 36
Downing, George T., 81
Dred Scott v. Sandford, 33–34, 35–36, 49,
    70, 162
dysentery, 61

Eastern Shore, Maryland
    black militias, 34–35
    slavery in, 3–10
economy
    panic of 1873, 78
    slavery and, 87
Edinburgh Ladies' Emancipation Society, 28
Edmundson, Mary, 28

Eighth Regiment United States Colored
    Infantry, 155
Eighth U.S. Colored Infantry, 154
Eighth U.S. Colored Troops, 69, 77
Elliott, Thomas, 34–35
emancipation, gradual, 3, 11, 14
"Emancipation Eve" (Brown), 130–32
Emancipation Proclamation, 60, 61–62, 162
    songs celebrating, 130–32
Emerson, Ralph Waldo, 38, 48, 158
Ennals, Maria, 52
Ennals, Stephen, 52

Fifty-Fifth Massachusetts Regiment, 69
Fifty-Fourth Massachusetts Regiment, 63,
    67–68, 69, 70, 94n87, 157
Fillmore, Millard, 106, 119
film industry, 87–88
First Confiscation Act, 58
First South Carolina Regiment, 60, 62, 63,
    70, 96n125
Florida, 12
Fobes, Alex E., 125
Forbes, Hugh, 44
Forten, Charlotte, 67
Forten, Harriet, 22
Forten, James, 22
Fort Hill Cemetery, 86
Fort Sumter, 56
Fort Wagner, Battle of, 67–68, 84
Forty-Seventh Pennsylvania Regiment, 65
Fourteenth Amendment, 97n161
Fowler, Henry, 77, 150, 151
Framingham, Massachusetts, 39
France, 60
Frederick Douglass Paper, 20
free blacks. *See also* African Americans
    aid to runaway slaves by, 12, 19, 34–36
    in Baltimore, 19
    in Chesapeake Bay area, 4–5
    colonization proposals, 10, 14, 15, 36
    communities of, 12
    enslavement of, 51
    kidnapped and sold into slavery, 6, 112–16
    limits on numbers of, 51
    marriage to slaves, 9
    in Maryland, 3, 4–5, 19, 23, 35–36, 51, 57
    rights of, 10, 34, 35–36
    sailors, 9–10, 12
    slave catchers and, 20–21
    slaves and, 9–10
    social classes, 37
    unequal pay for, 70
    well-being of, 2–3
Freedman, Peter (Steel), 15, 17, 31
Freedmen's Record, 73
    "Moses," 134–39
Freedom Train: The Story of Harriet Tubman
    (Sterling), 89
Frémont, John C., 58
Fugitive Slave Law of 1793, 12, 17
    text, 104–5

Fugitive Slave Law of 1850, 34, 161
    in Boston, 110–11
    enforcement of, 17, 19–20, 29
    fugitives arrested under, 24
    resistance to, 17–20, 117–19, 122
    slave catchers and, 18–19
    text, 106–9
fugitive slaves. *See also* runaway slaves
    arrests of, 19–20
    in Boston, 29–30, 110–11, 122–24
    legal rights of, 17–18
    name changes by, 31
    penalties for aiding, 104–5, 106–9
    in Philadelphia, 119–21
    records of, 120–24
    recovery of, 106–9
    rescue of, 50
    return to slavery, 29, 50
    reuniting families, 31
    rewards for, 34
    sympathy for, 117–19
    U.S. Constitution and, 103
"Fugitive Slaves Aided by the Vigilance
    Committee since the Passage of the
    Fugitive Slave Bill 1850" (Boston Vigi-
    lance Committee), 122–24

Garner, Margaret, 83, 99n177
Garnet, Henry Highland, 10, 43, 49, 97n154
Garrett, Rachel, 21
Garrett, Thomas, 13, 16f, 21, 22, 26, 29, 30,
    32, 33, 35, 36, 54
    "Memories of Harriet Tubman and the
    Underground Railroad," 140–42
    "Sending Underground Railroad Passen-
    gers to Philadelphia," 119–20
Garrison, Douglas, 81
Garrison, George, 69
Garrison, Harriet (Tubman), 40, 64. *See also*
    Tubman, Harriet
Garrison, Mrs. William Lloyd, 98n172
Garrison, Wendell, 69
Garrison, William Lloyd, 13, 14, 22, 38, 48,
    51, 73–74, 81, 117, 156, 158, 161
Gaston, Mary, 98n175
gender discrimination, 2
gender roles, 39, 77–78
General Harriet Tubman (Conrad), 88
get-rich-quick schemes, 78–79
Gettysburg, Pennsylvania, 87–88
Gibbs, Jacob R., 15
Gillmore, Quincy, 68
"Go Down Moses," 53, 62
Golden Legacy magazine, 89
Gorsuch, Edward, 21
Gould, Judge, 128
gradual emancipation, 3, 11, 14
Great Dismal Swamp, 14
Green, Harriet (Rit or Rittia), 6–7, 161
Green, Samuel, 36
Green, Shields, 45–46
Griffith, D. W., 88

Griffith, Gershom, 89
Gullah, 61, 96n129

Hall, Prince, 91n19
Harpers Ferry raid, 2, 41, 42, 45–48, 162
  anti-abolitionist feeling and, 54
  impacts of, 49
  planning, 45–46, 124–25
  slave uprisings and, 46–47
  Tubman and, 43–48, 124–25, 127
Harriet: The Moses of Her People (Bradford),
    85, 140, 145–48
"Harriet Tubman Biographies" (Bradford),
    145–49
*Harriet Tubman: Conductor on the Under-
    ground Railroad* (Petry), 89
"Harriet Tubman Davis Obituary" (*New
    York Times*), 158
"Harriet Tubman Memorialized" (*Auburn
    Citizen*), 159–60
*Harriet Tubman: Myth, Memory, and His-
    tory* (Sernett), 90
*Harriet Tubman: The Life and the Life
    Stories* (Humez), 90
Harriet Tubman: The Road to Freedom
    (Clinton), 90
Hayden, Lewis, 18, 19, 29, 37, 44, 46, 56
  "Letter to John Brown," 127
Henry, Robert, 19
Higginson, Thomas Wentworth, 29, 39, 43,
    47–48, 60, 62, 63, 64, 70, 81, 126
hiring out, 4, 8
Hopkins, Samuel Miles, Jr., 76
Hopkins, Samuel Miles, Sr., 75–76
Howe, Julia Ward, 81
Howe, Samuel Gridley, 38, 43, 47
Hughes (slave hunter), 117–18
Hughes, Denard, 34–35
Humez, Jean M., 90
Hunter, David, 59–60, 63, 96n125, 139,
    155

Incidents in the Life of a Slave Girl (Jacobs),
    76
indentured servants, 11
infant mortality, 7
internal slave trade, 3–7, 13, 110–16

Jackson, Francis, 122
Jackson, Jacob, 29–30
Jackson, Peter, 30, 93n57
Jackson, Rebecca Cox, 26
Jackson, William Henry, 30
Jacobs, Harriet, 76
Jayhawkers, 63
Jefferson, Thomas, 3
John (black man), 52
"John Brown's Body," 62
Johnson, Andrew, 74
Johnson, Oliver, 38
*Journey to Freedom: A Story of the Under-
    ground Railroad* (Wright), 89

Kagi, John, 45
Kane, Jane (Catherine), 30, 31, 93n57
Kansas, 42
Kansas-Missouri border, 44–45, 63
Kansas-Nebraska Act, 34, 42, 161
Keckley, Elizabeth, 70, 74
Kiah, Emily, 34–35
Kiah, William (Bill), 34–35
"Kidnapped into Slavery" (Northup), 112–16
kidnapping of free blacks, 6, 112–16
Kisselburgh, Mr., 129
Knight, John, 117–18
Ku Klux Klan, 88

Ladies' Irish Anti-Slavery Association, 44
Larson, Kate Clifford, 27, 90, 93n50, 98n175
laudanum, 136
Lawrence, Amos, 94n81
Lawrence, Jacob, 88, 99n189
Lawrence, Kansas, 42
Lee, Jarena, 26
Lee, Robert E., 47, 73
"Letter to Earl Conrad" (Siebert), 152–53
"Letter to John Brown" (Hayden), 127
"Letter to John Brown Jr." (Brown), 124–25
Levine, Bruce, 72
Liberator, 14, 39, 40, 161
  "Slave-Hunters in Boston," 117–19
  "Tubman Addresses Fourth of July Meet-
    ing," 126–27
Lincoln, Abraham, 86, 97n154, 130, 151, 162
  abolishment of slavery and, 71
  assassination of, 74
  black soldiers and, 69, 70, 72
  election of, 52, 95n105
  Emancipation Proclamation, 60, 61–62
  end of Civil War and, 72–73
  opposition to, 55
  reluctance to attack slavery, 58
Lincoln, Mary Todd, 70
Livermore, Mary, 70
Lloyd, Daniel, 93n57
Locke, Alain, 99n189
Loguen, Jermain W., 43, 44, 81, 124–25
Longfellow, Henry Wadsworth, 49
Louisiana Purchase, 3
Lucas, Henry, 79–80
lying out periods, 14

Mann, Horace, 38, 158
Manokey, Eliza, 32–33
Manokey, Mary, 32
manumission, 4, 10
maroon communities, 14
marriage
  among slaves, 7
  between slaves and free blacks, 9
  Tubman, 5, 9, 76–78, 81, 135, 157
Martin (black man), 50, 129
Martin, John Sella, 55
Maryland. *See also* Baltimore, Maryland
  black militias, 34–35

Maryland. (*cont.*)
  free blacks, 3, 4–5, 19, 23, 35–36, 51, 57
  fugitive slaves, 34–36
  slavery in, 3–10
  Tubman's trips to, 20, 21, 23, 28–33, 36,
    52, 55–57, 136
Maryland House of Delegates, 35
Massachusetts. *See also* Boston
  abolitionists in, 24, 38–39, 56, 58, 60
  fugitive slaves in, 11, 17
  slavery abolished in, 11
  Tubman in, 38–40, 44, 83
Massachusetts Anti-Slavery Society, 39
Massachusetts General Hospital, 83
May, Samuel J., 51, 81
McClellan, George B., 71
McKim, J. Miller, 30
"Memories of Harriet Tubman and the
  Underground Railroad" (Garrett),
  140–42
men
  indentured servants, 11
  runaway slaves, 13
Mendenhall, Dinah, 21
Mendenhall, Isaac, 21
Mexico, 12
militias. *See also* black militias
  African Americans barred from, 49
  slaves captured by, 29
Minty: A Story of Young Harriet Tubman
  (Schroeder and Pinkney), 89
Missouri
  slaves in, 33–34, 58
Missouri Compromise, 34
Modesty (Tubman's grandmother), 6
Montgomery, James, 63, 64, 65, 72, 132–33,
  139, 155
"moral suasion," 14
Morrison, A. J., 129
Moses, 25, 26
  Biblical story of, 54
  Tubman as, 20–33, 26, 37, 39, 51, 58, 64,
    86, 120–21, 126, 134–39, 144–45, 146,
    156, 158
"Moses" (Brown), 144–45
"Moses" (*Freedmen's Record*), 134–39
"Moses Arrives with Six Passengers" (Still),
  120–21
Mott, James, 22
Mott, Lucretia Coffin, 22, 24
Murray, Anna, 10
Museum of Modern Art, New York, 88
mysticism, 25–26

Nalle, Charles, 49–51, 128–29, 162
name changes, by fugitive slaves, 31
Narrative (Truth), 76
Narrative of the Life of Frederick Douglass
  (Douglass), 20, 76
National Association of Colored Women,
  83, 85

National Woman Suffrage Association, 83
Negro spirituals, 53–54
New Bedford, Massachusetts, 10, 11
New England Convention of Colored
  Citizens, 40
New England Freedmen's Aid Society, 57,
  73, 134
New England ships
  slave trade and, 110–11
New Mexico, 106
New York, 12–13
  abolitionists in, 12–13, 43, 44
  antislavery societies, 14, 24, 38, 40
  fugitive slaves in, 17, 18
  indentured servants, 11
  Museum of Modern Art exhibit, 88
  Nalle rescue, 49–51
  Tubman in, 46, 49–51, 56, 59, 69, 74–80,
    83–86
  Underground Railroad, 20, 21, 27, 31, 33,
    36, 44
New York Anti-Slavery Society, 38
New York Times, 85–86
  "Harriet Tubman Davis Obituary," 158
New York Tribune, 70
Nineteenth Amendment, 97n161
North Star, 20, 40
Northup, Solomon, 76
  "Kidnapped into Slavery," 112–16
Northwest Ordinance, 11

Olustee, Battle of, 69, 77
Osbornes, Eliza Wright, 84
Otwell, Thomas, 34–35

panic of 1873, 78
Parker, Andrew, 129
Parker, Theodore, 22, 43, 95n97
Parker, William, 21
Pattison, Atthow, 6
Payne, Sereno E., 80
Pennington, James W. C., 10
Pennington, Peter, 33
Pennsylvania Anti-Slavery Society, 38
Petry, Ann, 89
Philadelphia
  antislavery societies, 6, 13, 16, 17
  fugitive slaves aided in, 10, 119–21
  Tubman in, 20
  Underground Railroad, 19, 20, 21, 26,
    30–31
Philadelphia Anti-Slavery Society, 17, 119–20
Philadelphia Vigilance Committee, 16, 120
Phillips, Wendell, 39, 49, 55, 81, 156
  "Testimonial," 142–43
Pinkney, Jerry, 89
Pinkerton, Allan, 45, 94n90
Pitcher, Moll, 146
Plowden, Walter, 65n
political debate, 52–56
Poor Man's Hole, 111

Port Royal Experiment, 57, 139
Pottawatomie Creek massacre, 42
Predeaux, Henry, 34–35
Prince Hall Masonic lodges, 12, 91n19
Providence, Rhode Island, 11
"Provision regarding Fugitive Slaves" (U.S. Constitution), 103
Purvis, Harriet (Forten), 22
Purvis, Robert, 22

Quakers
    aid from, 11, 53
    ecstatic Quakerism, 26
    Underground Railroad and, 6, 21–22
Quarles, Benjamin, 89
quilts, 89, 137
Quincy, Edmund, 39

racial segregation
    in federal agencies, 88
    following Civil War, 74–75
    tolerance of, 159
racism
    film industry and, 87–88
    post–Civil War, 78, 85
    tolerance of, 159
    Washington, Booker T., on, 87
Radburn, Ebenezer, 114
radical antislavery movement, 14–17
religious beliefs, 25–26
religious revivals, 25
"Reminiscences of Fugitive-Slave Law Days in Boston" (Bearse), 110–11
Republican party, 52
Richmond, Virginia, 72, 73, 77
Ringgold, Faith, 89
ring shout, 25
Rivers, Prince, 62
Rochester, New York, 40, 41
Rock, John Stewart, 37–38, 44, 49, 71, 134
Ross, Angerine, 31–32, 51
Ross, Araminta (Harriet Tubman), 7, 135, 157. See also Tubman, Harriet
Ross, Benjamin (Ben) (Tubman's brother), 5, 7, 29, 30, 93n57, 116
Ross, Benjamin (Ben) (Tubman's father), 7, 9, 33, 36, 78, 161
Ross, Benjamin (Ben) (Tubman's nephew), 31–32, 52
Ross, George, 30
Ross, Harriet (Araminta or Minty), 7, 151. See also Tubman, Harriet
Ross, Harriet (Rit or Rittia) (Harriet's mother), 7, 30, 80
Ross, Henry (Harry), 5, 7, 29, 30, 93n57, 116
Ross, Linah, 7, 19
Ross, Mariah, 7
Ross, Moses, 7, 19
Ross, Rachel, 7, 31–32, 36, 37, 52
Ross, Robert, 7, 29, 30, 93n57
Ross, Soph, 7

Ruggles, David, 10
"Runaway Advertisement" (Brodess), 116–17
runaway slaves. See also fugitive slaves
    as abolitionists, 10
    advertisements for, 6–7, 116–17, 137
    assistance to, 11–14, 34–36
    betrayal of, 34–35
    with children, 13, 24–25
    conflicts with slave catchers, 20–21
    free blacks and, 9–11, 12
    fugitive slave laws and, 17–18
    gender of, 13
    legal rights of, 17–18
    lying out periods, 14
    punishment of, 13
    Quaker protection of, 11
    in Washington, D.C., 15

Saga of Harriet Tubman, The: The "Moses of Her People" (Quarles), 89
sailors, 9–10, 12
Sanborn, Franklin, 25, 42–43, 44, 46, 47, 48, 55, 65, 71, 127, 132, 133
Saxton, Rufus, 65, 139, 155
Scenes in the Life of Harriet Tubman (Bradford), 27, 66, 76, 85, 140, 145–47
Schimer, Anthony, 79
Schroeder, Alan, 89
Scotland, 28
Scott, Dred, 33–34
Sea Islands, 57, 59–60, 96n129
Second Confiscation Act, 58
Second Great Awakening, 13, 25
Second Presbyterian Church, Auburn, New York, 77
Second South Carolina Regiment, 63–64
Senate, U.S.
    "Committee on Pensions Report," 153–55
"Sending Underground Railroad Passengers to Philadelphia" (Garrett), 119–20
Seneca Falls, New York, 24
Sernett, Milton C., 90, 93n50
Seward, Alice, 57–58
Seward, Frances, 80
Seward, Frederick, 78
Seward, William Henry, 18, 22, 24, 45, 52, 55, 57–58, 74, 76, 78, 80, 81, 86, 154, 156, 161
Shakers, black, 26
Shaw, Robert Gould, 63, 67, 68
Shepard, Hayward, 46
Sherman, T. W., 59
Sherman, William Tecumseh, 71, 155
Shiloh, battle of, 59
Siebert, Wilbur H.
    "Letter to Earl Conrad," 152–53
Sims, Thomas, 122
slave auctions, 19
slave catchers/hunters
    abolitionists and, 19

slave catchers/hunters (*cont.*)
 fugitive slave laws and, 18–19, 55
 in the North, 6, 10, 11, 15, 19, 45, 117–19
 resistance to, 20–21
 Tubman and, 24, 33, 52–53
 Union Army and, 58
slaveholders
 capture of, 46
 Constitution and, 40
 control of slaves by, 4, 14, 35–37
 fears of, 10, 11, 12, 35–36
 fugitive slave laws and, 17–18, 28–29, 104–9
 gradual emancipation by, 3
 internal slave trade and, 3–7, 13, 110–16
 property rights of, 21–22, 35–37
 rewards posted by, 24
 of Tubman's family, 5, 9
"Slave-Hunters in Boston" (*Liberator*),
 117–19
slave marriages, 7, 9
slave names, 31
slave narratives, 76, 112, 142
slavery
 abolished in northern states, 11, 91*n17*
 abolishment of, 71
 American Revolution and, 49
 Dred Scott decision and, 33–34, 35–36
 economy and, 87
 film industry and, 87–88
 gradual abolition of, 3
 in Maryland, 3–10
 opposition to, 2
 political debate over, 52–56
 post–Civil War interpretation of, 87
 power of, 2
 proposed legislation protecting, 10
 return of fugitive slaves to, 29
slaves. *See also* African Americans
 brutality of life for, 4, 112–16
 capture of, in Africa, 90*n4*
 as contraband of war, 58
 Emancipation Proclamation, 60
 escapes, 1, 2, 3, 5–7, 9–15, 17, 18, 20, 21,
  24–27, 29, 30–41, 44, 47, 49, 50, 51, 52,
  57–59, 61, 62, 64, 65, 67, 73, 77, 111
 female, 7–8, 10
 free blacks and, 9–10
 freedom purchased for, 51
 freeing of, by U.S. Army, 64–65
 government protection sought by, 58
 hiring out, 4, 8
 infant and child mortality, 7
 manumission of, 4
 marriage, 7, 9
 ordered free by Civil War generals, 59
 punishment of, 4, 7–8, 13, 111, 113
 runaway, 4
 self-purchase by, 4
 sold away from families, 3–7, 17, 19, 29,
  32, 44, 62, 73, 110–11
 suicides of, 111

slave songs, 53–54
slave trade
 abolished in Washington, D.C., 17, 106,
  161
 internal, 3–4
 New England ships and, 110–11
 sales of family members, 5, 7
slave uprisings, 46–47
Smith, Burrell, 44, 94*n87*
Smith, Charles A., 84, 85
Smith, Frances R., 98*n175*
Smith, Gerrit, 24, 42, 43, 47, 55–56, 71, 81,
  97*n151*, 138, 156, 158
Smith, Stephen, 43
"Solicitation of Aid for Harriet Tubman"
  (*Commonwealth*), 133–34
songs
 celebrating Emancipation Proclamation,
  61, 62
 as entertainment, 38
 as signals, 53–54, 130
 "Emancipation Eve," 130–32
South Carolina, 55
Southern Rights Convention, 51
Southern states. *See also* Confederate States
  of America
 secession of, 55, 56
 slave trade in lower South, 3–4
Spain, 12
spiritual practices, 25–26
Sprague, Rosetta Douglass, 83
SS *Harriet Tubman*, 88
Stanton, Edwin M., 60, 72
Stanton, Elizabeth Cady, 24, 75
St. Catharines, Canada, 21, 31
Stearns, George, 43, 47, 56
Stearns, Mary, 56
Steel, Levin, 15, 17
Steel, Peter (Freedman), 15, 17
Steel, Sidney, 15
Stephens, General, 155
Sterling, Dorothy, 88–89
Steward, Frances, 57–58
Steward, Judge, 50
Stewart, Alice, 85
Stewart, Benjamin (Ross), 30–31
Stewart, Catherine, 93*n57*
Stewart, Charles, 85
Stewart, Charles E., Post, Grand Army of
  the Republic, 86
Stewart, Charles E., Relief Corps, 86
Stewart, Clarence, 85
Stewart, Eva, 85
Stewart, Evelyn K., 98*n175*
Stewart, Helena, 81, 98*n175*
Stewart, Henry (Ross), 30–31
Stewart, James, 93*n57*
Stewart, John, 9, 31, 45, 81, 93*n57*
Stewart, John Henry, 80
Stewart, John Isaac, 98*n175*
Stewart, Katie, 81, 98*n175*

Stewart, Levin, 93*n*57
Stewart, Margaret (Tubman), 57–58, 79–80
Stewart, Maria, 39
Stewart, Mr., 129
Stewart, Robert (Ross), 30–31
Stewart, William Henry, 93*n*57, 98*n*175
Still, William, 13, 15, 16*f*, 17, 18–19, 21,
  30–31, 35, 43, 47, 54, 93*n*57
  "Moses Arrives with Six Passengers,"
  120–21
St. Mark's African Methodist Episcopal
  (AME) Church, Auburn, New York, 78
Stone, Lucy, 81
Stowe, Harriet Beecher, 28, 36, 112, 156, 161
St. Simons Island, 60
sugar cultivation, 3
Sumner, Charles, 42
supernatural powers, 26
Supreme Court, U.S., 33, 49, 70, 78
Sutton, Robert, 62
Swan, Sandy, 122
swindlers, 78–79
Syracuse Herald
  "To End Days in Home She Founded,"
  156–58

Taft, William Howard, 87
Talbert, Mary B., 84–85
Taney, Roger B., 34, 35
"Testimonials" (Douglass and Phillips),
  142–43
Texas, 12, 106
"There Is a White Robe for Thee," 65
Third Rhode Island Battery, 64
Thirteenth Amendment, 71, 162
Thompson, Anthony, 6–7
Thompson, Anthony (Dr., son of Anthony),
  9, 136
Thompson, William, 30
Thoreau, Henry David, 48
Tilghman, Tench, 93*n*57
Tilly (lady's maid), 32
Timbucto, 42
tobacco cultivation, 3
"To End Days in Home She Founded" (*Syra-
  cuse Herald*), 156–58
Toombs, Robert, 73
Townsend, Martin, 50
transcendentalists, 38
Tremont Temple, Boston, 61
Truth, Sojourner, 39, 51, 70, 76, 83, 97*n*151
Tubman, Caroline, 20, 28
Tubman, Harriet, 82*f*
  accomplishments of, 1–3, 24–28, 85–90
  "Affidavit," 149–51
  aid to African Americans, 75, 80, 84, 138
  Auburn, New York, farm, 45
  authority of, 25
  biographies of, 27, 66, 76, 85, 134–39,
    140–42, 145–48, 152–53, 156–58
  biography sales income, 76

books about, 89–90
  in Boston, 29–30, 44, 138, 143, 144
  Brown and, 42, 124–25, 127, 138–39,
    142–43, 158
  in Canada, 21, 44, 56, 145
  care of Katie Stewart by, 81
  Charleston campaign, 67–69
  Cheney biography, 134–39
  childhood, 5, 7–8, 135, 146–47, 157
  children of runaway slaves and, 24–25
  chronology, 161–62
  as Civil War nurse, 60–61, 68–69, 84, 86,
    139, 149, 154, 158
  as Civil War scout and spy, 56–61, 63–67,
    66*f*, 84, 86, 149, 154–55, 158
  clothing, 65
  coded messages, 27, 29–30
  Combahee River raid and, 63–65, 67,
    132–33, 139, 162
  dangers faced by, 32, 36–37, 38–39, 50–51,
    52–53, 54, 55–56, 140–41
  daughter adopted by, 80
  death of, 85, 158
  donations to, 28, 80, 126–27, 141–42
  dreams, 5, 9, 25, 43, 49, 80, 142
  endorsements of, 142–44
  escape from slavery, 5–6, 15, 135–36,
    147–49, 156, 157
  fame of, 1, 99*n*190
  family, 2, 5–7, 17, 19, 21, 29–32, 52, 79–80,
    135, 157
  financial issues, 61, 65, 67, 70–71, 72–73,
    74, 75–76, 78, 80, 139
  fundraising, 37, 38, 44, 75, 112, 133–34
  funeral services, 86
  Harpers Ferry raid and, 43–48, 124–25,
    127
  head injury, 8–9, 135, 153
  health, 8, 27, 83, 84, 135, 141
  hiring out, 8
  honored, 83, 86–89, 159–60
  jobs, 17
  Margaret Stewart (Tubman) and, 57
  marriage to John Tubman, 5, 9, 135, 157
  marriage to Nelson Davis, 76–78, 81, 157
  Maryland trips, 20, 21, 23, 28–33, 36, 52,
    55–57, 136
  as Moses, 20–33, 26, 37, 39, 51, 54, 58, 64,
    86, 120–21, 126, 134–39, 144–45, 146,
    156, 158
  mythology of, 1–2, 76, 89, 120–21, 140,
    158
  Nalle rescue, 50–51, 128–29
  networks, 2, 24, 28, 37–41
  number of people rescued by, 27–28,
    36–37, 141, 156, 158
  obituary, 86, 158
  older years, 80–85
  parents, 6–7, 30, 33, 36, 40, 44, 45, 67, 69,
    75, 78, 79, 80, 135, 136, 138, 139, 157,
    161

Tubman, Harriet (*cont.*)
  pension and back pay claims, 71, 74, 80,
    81, 83, 84, 139, 149–51, 153–55
  personal characteristics, 65, 77–78,
    120–21, 137, 138, 144–45, 152–53, 157–58
  in Philadelphia, 20, 21, 119–21, 136
  physical appearance, 5–6, 26, 147
  physical strength, 8, 26
  popular culture image of, 87, 88, 159–60
  postwar activities, 74–80
  racism and, 74–75
  radical image of, 88–89
  religious faith, 20, 24–28, 32, 58, 72, 80,
    135, 137, 139, 140–41, 157–58
  rescue of brothers by, 29–31
  runaway advertisement for, 6, 116–17
  runaway attempt with brothers, 5
  songs, 38, 53–54, 64–65, 136
  speeches, 38–40, 83, 126–27
  strategies, 26–27, 137
  swindlers and, 78–79
  trances, 8–9, 135, 147
  unequal pay for black soldiers and, 69,
    70–71
  visions, 26, 80, 137
  whippings of, 135
  women's rights and, 2, 22, 24, 39, 51, 75,
    83, 84
Tubman, Harriet, Home for Aged and Infirm
    Negroes, 84, 156
Tubman, John, 5, 9, 38–39, 78–79, 81,
    98*n*176, 135, 136, 151, 156*n*10, 161, 162
Tubman, Margaret (Stewart), 57–58
Tubman, Tom, 19
"Tubman Addresses Fourth of July Meet-
    ing" (*Liberator*), 126–27
Twelfth Baptist Church, 38, 61
Twelve Years a Slave (Northup), 76, 112
Twenty-First U.S. Colored Troops, 69

Uncle Tom's Cabin (Stowe), 28, 36, 112, 161
Underground Railroad
  abolitionists and, 21
  assistance to Harriet Tubman by, 6
  conductors, 13
  history of, 11–14
  Philadelphia, 119–21
  Quakers and, 6, 21–22
  research on, 152
  routes, 23*f*
  Tubman and, 1–2, 6, 19, 26–28, 136–37
  Wilmington station, 140
Underground Railroad, The (Siebert), 152
Underground Rail Road, The (Still), 16, 120
urban areas, 39
U.S Army
  African Americans and, 56–61
  casualties, 56–61, 60
  slaves freed by, 63–65

U.S. Sanitary Commission, 70, 97*n*149
Utah, 106

Victoria, Queen, 83
Vigilance Committee, Boston, 118
Vigilance Committee, Philadelphia, 16, 120
Vincent, Robert, 98*n*176
violence
  antislavery movement and, 14, 15
  Brown and, 42–49
  on Kansas-Missouri border, 44–45
Virginia, western, 42
Vlach, John, 14
voting rights, 84, 97*n*161

Walker, William, 69
Ward, Samuel Ringgold, 10
Washington, Booker T., 87
Washington, D.C.
  aid to fugitive slaves in, 15
  slave trade abolished in, 17, 106, 161
Washington, L. W., 46
Webster, John E., 65
Weld, Theodore Dwight, 81
wheat cultivation, 3
Wheatley, Phillis, 83, 99*n*177
White, Garland H., 73
Whitney, Eli, 3
Wigham, Eliza, 28, 141–42
Wilmington, Delaware, 15, 16, 21, 23, 30, 32,
    33, 35, 54
Wilson, Woodrow, 85, 88
Wise, Henry, 47
women
  abolitionists, 44
  African American, 51
  clothing, 65
  equality of, 14
  gender roles, 39, 77–78
  indentured servants, 11
  religious beliefs, 25–26
  runaway slaves, 13, 18
  slaves, 7–8, 10, 91*n*10
  voting rights, 84, 97*n*161
women's rights
  movement leaders, 24
  speeches about, 51
  Tubman and, 2, 22, 39, 51, 75, 83, 84
Woodbury, Levi, 118
Woodson, Carter G., 88
Woolfley, James, 34
Woolfley, Lavinia, 34
Worden, Lazett, 57
Wright, Courtni C., 89
Wright, David, 22
Wright, Martha Coffin, 22, 80

York, Hank, 129